Best High-Rises

2024/25

31 projects from 13 countries

31 Projekte aus 13 Ländern

The International High-Rise Award

Internationaler Hochhaus Preis

Edited by
Herausgegeben von
Peter Körner
Peter Cachola Schmal

jovis

DAM

Contents

Inhalt

Preface

Vorwort

Dr. Ina Hartwig
Head of the Department of Culture of the City of Frankfurt am Main

Dr. Matthias Danne
Deputy Chairman of the Executive Board of DekaBank

Peter Cachola Schmal
Director of Deutsches Architekturmuseum

Dr. Ina Hartwig
Kulturdezernentin der Stadt Frankfurt am Main

Dr. Matthias Danne
Stellvertretender Vorsitzender des Vorstands der DekaBank

Peter Cachola Schmal
Direktor des Deutschen Architekturmuseums

4/1
Thomas Demand, prize winner's sculpture for The International High-Rise Award, titanium and granite
Statuette für den Internationalen Hochhaus Preis, Titan und Granit

4/2
Peter Cachola Schmal, Deutsches Architekturmuseum, Frankfurt am Main

4/3
2nd from left Zweiter von links
Victor Stoltenburg, Deka Immobilien GmbH, Frankfurt am Main

5/1
Jürgen Heinzel, UNStudio, Amsterdam

5/2
Roland Bechmann, Werner Sobek, Stuttgart; Yasmin Al-Ani Spence, WilkinsonEyre, London

In 2004, construction work began on the tallest human-made building ever created. It was also the year when The International High-Rise Award was presented for the first time. For twenty years now, the exciting development of the fascinating high-rise building typology has been reflected in this award, which is sponsored by the City of Frankfurt am Main, DekaBank, and the Deutsches Architekturmuseum. Unlike the skyscraper in Dubai, the height of a building plays only a minor role in the selection of the best projects. Instead, The International High-Rise Award, with its unique statuette by internationally renowned artist Thomas Demand and a prize money of 50,000 euros, honors high-rises that combine sustainability, external form and internal spatial quality, and social aspects into an exemplary design that points the way to the future.

After the first three buildings to win The International High-Rise Award were purely office towers, the residential high-rise typology also established itself in the following years, as evidenced by the winning projects since 2010. Although all of these projects were still single-use, the trend has steadily been shifting toward mixed-use high-rises in recent years, which have consistently been among the finalists since 2014. Additionally, local preferences and temporary trends have been observed over time. Former peculiarities like extensive greening or the construction of high-rise clusters have long since become standard. Due to the lack of suitable building land and growing environmental awareness, existing buildings have increasingly come into focus in high-rise construction.

Although the COVID-19 pandemic was officially declared over last year, its aftermaths, as well as ongoing wars, continue to have significant economic impacts on the entire real estate sector and, consequently, on international high-rise construction. Thus, the number of completed buildings is significantly lower than pre-2020 levels. Interrupted

2004 begannen die Bauarbeiten für das höchste je von Menschenhand geschaffene Gebäude. Es war auch das Jahr, in dem der Internationale Hochhaus Preis (IHP) zum ersten Mal verliehen wurde. Bereits seit zwanzig Jahren spiegelt sich die spannende Entwicklung der faszinierenden Typologie Hochhaus in dem von der Stadt Frankfurt am Main, der DekaBank und dem Deutschen Architekturmuseum ausgelobten Preis wider. Im Unterschied zum Wolkenkratzer in Dubai spielt die Höhe eines Gebäudes bei der Auswahl der besten Projekte nur eine untergeordnete Rolle. Mit einer einzigartigen Statuette des international renommierten Künstlers Thomas Demand sowie einem Preisgeld von 50.000 Euro prämiert der Internationale Hochhaus Preis vielmehr Hochhäuser, die Nachhaltigkeit, äußere Form und innere Raumqualitäten sowie soziale Aspekte zu einem vorbildlichen Entwurf verbinden und so beispielhaft in die Zukunft weisen.

Nachdem die ersten drei ausgezeichneten Gebäude des Internationalen Hochhaus Preises noch reine Bürotürme waren, etablierte sich in den Folgejahren auch die Typologie Wohnhochhaus gleichermaßen, was sich an den Gewinnerprojekten seit 2010 ablesen lässt. Obwohl all diese Projekte noch Einzelnutzungen waren, geht die Tendenz seit einigen Jahren vermehrt zu gemischt genutzten Hochhäusern, die sich bereits seit 2014 immer wieder unter den Finalisten befinden. Zudem wurden über die Zeit lokale Vorlieben und temporäre Trends beobachtet. Einstige Besonderheiten wie flächendeckende Begrünungen oder der Bau von Hochhausclustern gehören mittlerweile längst zum Standard. Bedingt durch den Mangel an geeigneten Bauflächen sowie wachsendes Umweltbewusstsein rückt der Gebäudebestand beim Hochhausbau vermehrt in den Fokus.

Obwohl die Covid-19-Pandemie bereits im letzten Jahr offiziell für beendet erklärt wurde, haben deren Nachwehen sowie die andauernden Kriege nach wie vor gravierende wirtschaftliche Auswirkungen auf den gesamten Immobiliensektor und

supply chains and increased material prices, coupled with uncertain future prospects, make it difficult to predict when construction activity will return to pre-pandemic levels.

Nevertheless, over 1,000 projects with a height of over 100 meters have been completed since the last jury meeting in 2022. Research identified interesting buildings on all continents. While most high-rises are still being built in China, followed by the USA, Australia and especially Singapore are currently emerging as exciting hotspots for high-rise architecture.

This year, 31 projects from 13 countries were nominated for The International High-Rise Award. According to the regulations, the international jury, chaired by Kim Herforth Nielsen (3XN, winner of The International High-Rise Award 2022/23), selected five finalists, from which the winning project emerged. While two years ago, the innovative transformation of existing, outdated high-rise buildings was particularly decisive, this year, special attention was paid to the added value of the buildings for the general public.

The winner of this year's award, CapitaSpring in Singapore by BIG – Bjarke Ingels Group from Copenhagen/New York and Carlo Ratti Associati from Turin/New York, is not just the new headquarters of the real estate company CapitaLand. Rather, the building offers spaces for open gardens that span several floors and are freely accessible to the public. A market for local street food (hawker centre) and an open living room on the ground floor also serve the public, thus integrating the new tower into Singapore's Central Business District. The project thus exemplifies the ideal of the "good neighbor," benefiting the entire surrounding area.

Among the finalists is another project by BIG: IQON Residences in Quito. The tallest building in Ecuador's capital impresses with particularly striking architecture and extensive greenery, creating a very pleasant indoor climate without elaborate air conditioning systems.

damit auch auf den internationalen Hochhausbau. Somit liegt die Zahl der fertiggestellten Gebäude deutlich unter den Werten vor 2020. Unterbrochene Lieferketten und gestiegene Materialpreise, gepaart mit unsicheren Zukunftsaussichten, erlauben kaum eine Prognose, wann das Baugeschehen wieder das vorpandemische Niveau erreicht.

Dennoch wurden seit der letzten Jurysitzung 2022 wieder über 1.000 Projekte mit einer Höhe von über 100 Metern fertiggestellt. Die Recherche führte dabei auf allen Kontinenten zu interessanten Gebäuden. Während nach wie vor in China, gefolgt von den USA, die meisten Hochhäuser gebaut werden, lassen sich aktuell Australien und insbesondere Singapur als spannende Hotspots für Hochhausarchitektur ausmachen.

In diesem Jahr wurden 31 Projekte aus 13 Ländern für die Auszeichnung mit dem Internationalen Hochhaus Preis nominiert. Gemäß den Regularien wählte die internationale Jury unter dem Vorsitz von Kim Herforth Nielsen (3XN, Gewinner Internationaler Hochhaus Preis 2022/23) fünf Finalisten, aus denen das Preisträgerprojekt hervorging. Nachdem vor zwei Jahren insbesondere die innovative Transformation bestehender, nicht mehr zeitgemäßer Hochhausbauten für die Entscheidung ausschlaggebend war, wurde in diesem Jahr ein besonderes Augenmerk auf den Mehrwert der Gebäude für die Allgemeinheit gerichtet.

So ist der diesjährige Preisträger, CapitaSpring in Singapur von BIG – Bjarke Ingels Group aus Kopenhagen/New York und Carlo Ratti Associati aus Turin/New York, nicht bloß der neue Hauptsitz des Immobilienunternehmens CapitaLand. Vielmehr bietet das Gebäude Raum für offene Gärten, die sich über mehrere Etagen erstrecken und für die Öffentlichkeit kostenfrei zugänglich sind. Ein Markt für lokales Streetfood (*hawker centre*) und eine Art offenes Wohnzimmer im Erdgeschoss bieten darüber hinaus ihre Dienste der Allgemeinheit an und verorten den neuen Turm so in Singapurs Central Business District. Das Projekt verkörpert somit beispielhaft das Idealbild des „guten Nachbarn", von dem die gesamte Umgebung profitiert.

Two other finalists originated from the Dutch office MVRDV. The mixed-use complex Valley revitalizes a district in Amsterdam previously dominated by traditional office buildings. Its three eccentric residential towers, with varying floor plans, emerge from a geometric base in the form of a rocky mountain landscape. This base houses additional uses such as offices, restaurants, and public areas, including a walkway through the "valley."

As an example project of a national program to reduce carbon emissions in China, the architects at MVRDV transformed a high-rise built in the 1990s into the mixed-use and brightly colored Shenzhen Women and Children's Center, thus saving it from demolition – a novelty in China! In addition to various rooms for women and children, the project now includes a hotel, offices, conference rooms, and commercial spaces.

The fifth finalist is the Bunker Tower in Eindhoven, the Netherlands, by Powerhouse Company from Rotterdam. The architects took a low, brutalist student center from the late 1960s as the starting point for a high-rise used primarily for residential purposes, transforming the distinctive architectural language into a vertical format.

Thus, not just height but compelling overall concepts in terms of economic efficiency, integration into the urban context, design, technology, and quality of stay are decisive criteria. Increasing attention is being paid to sustainability aspects.

Mit den IQON Residences in Quito ist ein weiteres Projekt von BIG unter den Finalisten. Das höchste Gebäude der ecuadorianischen Hauptstadt überzeugt mit einer besonders markanten Architektur und viel Begrünung, wodurch ohne aufwendige Klimatechnik ein besonders angenehmes Wohnklima erzeugt wird.

Zwei weitere Finalisten stammen von dem niederländischen Büro MVRDV. Der gemischt genutzte Komplex Valley belebt in Amsterdam ein bisher von klassischen Bürogebäuden dominiertes Quartier. In Form einer felsigen Berglandschaft entwachsen seine drei exzentrischen Wohntürme mit wechselnden Grundrissen einem geometrischen Sockel. In diesem sind weitere Nutzungen wie Büros und Restaurants sowie öffentliche Bereiche wie ein Spazierweg durch das „Tal" untergebracht.

Als Beispielprojekt eines nationalen Programms für die Reduzierung der CO_2-Emissionen in China haben die Architekt:innen von MVRDV ein erst in den 1990er Jahren gebautes Hochhaus in das gemischt genutzte und leuchtend farbige Shenzhen Women and Children's Center umgebaut und so vor dem Abriss bewahrt, in China ein absolutes Novum! Neben diversen Räumlichkeiten für Frauen und Kinder umfasst das Projekt jetzt ein Hotel, Büros und Konferenzräume sowie Gewerbeflächen.

Fünfter Finalist ist der Bunker Tower im niederländischen Eindhoven von Powerhouse Company aus Rotterdam. Die Architekt:innen nahmen ein

7/1
Jurors of The International High-Rise Award 2024/25, from left to right:
Juror:innen des Internationalen Hochhaus Preises 2024/25, von links nach rechts:

Roland Bechmann
Mari Randsborg
Victor Stoltenburg
Kim Herforth Nielsen, Jury chair
Juryvorsitzender
Peter Cachola Schmal
Christopher Lee
Horst R. Muth, Deputy jury member
Stellvertretendes Jurymitglied
Dr. Ina Hartwig
Jürgen Heinzel
Andrea Jürges, Deputy jury member
Stellvertretendes Jurymitglied
Yasmin Al-Ani Spence

The International High-Rise Award is therefore aimed at buildings with a minimum height of 100 meters that make outstanding contributions to the evolution of high-rise architecture worldwide. This commitment is also upheld by the City of Frankfurt am Main through its ongoing support for this award.

High-rise construction enjoys a long tradition in Frankfurt itself. The skyline, which has been evolving since World War II, was singular in Germany and also trend-setting for Europe over decades. Due to limited building land and increasing demand for office space, a level of inner-city density became necessary that could only be achieved with this building type. Today, high-rises shape the cityscape and symbolize the success and self-confidence of this small metropolis, home to the three partners in this competition. Even though no Frankfurt (or German) project is among this year's nominees, the largest high-rise project in the city to date, FOUR Frankfurt by UNStudio from Amsterdam, is nearing completion.

For DekaBank, awarding The International High-Rise Award since it was jointly initiated has been an important part of its social commitment. Through the continuous development of the award and the trusting collaboration among the three partners that has matured in the process, the award has gained international recognition. Deka-

niedriges, brutalistisches Studierendenzentrum aus den späten 1960er Jahren als Ausgangspunkt für ein vorwiegend als Wohnturm genutztes Hochhaus und transformierten die markante Formensprache in die Höhe.

Nicht allein die Höhe, sondern überzeugende Gesamtkonzepte in Bezug auf Wirtschaftlichkeit, Einbindung in den urbanen Kontext, Gestaltung und Technologie sowie Aufenthaltsqualität sind somit maßgebende Kriterien. Ein besonderes Augenmerk liegt in zunehmendem Maße auf Nachhaltigkeitsaspekten. Somit richtet sich der Internationale Hochhaus Preis an Bauten mit einer Mindesthöhe von 100 Metern, die herausragende Beiträge zur Evolution der Gattung Hochhausarchitektur weltweit darstellen. Dafür steht auch die Stadt Frankfurt am Main mit ihrem fortwährenden Engagement für diesen Preis.

In Frankfurt selbst hat der Hochhausbau Tradition. Die seit dem Zweiten Weltkrieg wachsende Skyline war über Jahrzehnte nicht nur singulär in Deutschland, sondern auch richtungsweisend für Europa. Aufgrund der begrenzten Bauflächen und der wachsenden Nachfrage nach Büroräumen wurde eine innerstädtische Dichte erforderlich, die nur mit diesem Gebäudetyp erreicht werden konnte. Heute prägen die Hochhäuser das Stadtbild und symbolisieren den Erfolg und das Selbstbewusstsein dieser kleinen Metropole, der Heimat der drei

8/1
Left Links
Andrea Jürges, Deutsches Architekturmuseum, Frankfurt am Main

Right Rechts
Dr. Ina Hartwig, City of Frankfurt am Main
Stadt Frankfurt am Main

8/2
Left Links
Horst R. Muth, Deka Immobilien GmbH, Frankfurt am Main

Right Rechts
Kim Herforth Nielsen, 3XN, Copenhagen
Kopenhagen

8/3
Left Links
Peter Cachola Schmal, Deutsches Architekturmuseum, Frankfurt am Main

Right Rechts
Christopher Lee, Serie Architects, London

8/4
Mari Randsborg, Cobe, Copenhagen
Kopenhagen

Bank, the securities branch of the Sparkassen (savings banks), together with its subsidiaries forms the Deka Group and is one of the largest securities service providers and real estate asset managers in Germany. With its commitment to The International High-Rise Award, Deka aims to shift the focus to innovative, forward-looking, sustainable, and economical construction. By leveraging its expertise as a real estate investor, Deka contributes its know-how to the award, particularly in the area of economic efficiency, and is part of the jury.

The Deutsches Architekturmuseum (DAM), which researches the projects nominated for the award every two years, contributes to a global long-term analysis of contemporary high-rise development, complete with significant documentation. While the annual DAM Preis deals with projects in and from Germany, The International High-Rise Award is emblematic of DAM's international orientation.

In two decades of The International High-Rise Award, we have been able to observe and accompany many exciting developments. Due to the steadily growing world population and increasingly dense metropolitan areas, the high-rise typology promises to remain relevant in the future – in fact, more high-rises will need to be built to reduce land consumption and land sealing, not only in rapidly growing global regions but also in Europe. The three awarding partners of The International High-Rise Award are convinced that it is important to continue identifying and recognizing pioneering projects. Their goal is to promote the discussion on fundamental criteria such as sustainability, public benefit, as well as urban and social compatibility and to further increase their importance.

Partner der Auslobung. Und auch wenn sich in diesem Jahr kein Frankfurter (und auch kein deutsches) Projekt unter den Nominierten befindet, steht mit FOUR Frankfurt von UNStudio aus Amsterdam das bisher größte Hochhausprojekt der Stadt kurz vor seiner Fertigstellung.

Für die DekaBank ist die Verleihung des Internationalen Hochhaus Preises seit der gemeinsamen Gründung ein wichtiger Teil ihres gesellschaftlichen Engagements. Durch die kontinuierliche Weiterentwicklung des Preises und die dabei gewachsene vertrauensvolle Zusammenarbeit der drei Partner hat sich die Auszeichnung internationale Anerkennung erworben. Die DekaBank, das Wertpapierhaus der Sparkassen, bildet gemeinsam mit ihren Tochtergesellschaften die Deka-Gruppe und ist einer der größten Wertpapierdienstleister und Immobilien-Asset-Manager in Deutschland. Mit ihrem Engagement für den Internationalen Hochhaus Preis möchte die DekaBank den Fokus auf innovatives, zukunftsweisendes, nachhaltiges und wirtschaftliches Bauen richten. Mit ihrem Know-how als Immobilieninvestor lässt die DekaBank ihre Expertise insbesondere zum Punkt Wirtschaftlichkeit in den Preis miteinfließen und ist Teil der Jury.

Das Deutsche Architekturmuseum (DAM), das alle zwei Jahre die zum Preis nominierten Projekte recherchiert, trägt damit zu einer weltweiten Langzeitanalyse der zeitgenössischen Hochhausentwicklung mitsamt einer aussagekräftigen Dokumentation bei. Während sich der jährlich ausgelobte DAM Preis mit Projekten in und aus Deutschland befasst, steht der Internationale Hochhaus Preis also sinnbildlich für die internationale Ausrichtung des DAM.

In zwei Jahrzehnten Internationaler Hochhaus Preis konnten wir viele spannende Entwicklungen verfolgen und begleiten. Durch die stetig wachsende Weltbevölkerung und die immer dichter werdenden Metropolen verspricht die Typologie Hochhaus auch in Zukunft nicht an Relevanz zu verlieren – im Gegenteil werden, um den Flächenverbrauch und die Flächenversieglung zu reduzieren, mehr Hochhäuser gebaut werden müssen, nicht nur in den global stark wachsenden Regionen, sondern auch in Europa. Die drei Auslober des Internationalen Hochhaus Preises sind davon überzeugt, dass es wichtig ist, auch weiterhin richtungsweisende Projekte zu identifizieren und zu würdigen. Ihr Ziel ist es, die Diskussion über grundlegende Kriterien wie Nachhaltigkeit, Öffentlichkeit sowie städtebauliche und soziale Verträglichkeit zu fördern und ihre Bedeutung weiter zu steigern.

31 Projects from 13 Countries

Vancouver

Alberni
Kengo Kuma & Associates
Tokyo, Japan Tokio, Japan

320 Granville
Kohn Pedersen Fox Associates
New York NY, USA

Quito

IQON Residences
BIG – Bjarke Ingels Group
Copenhagen, Denmark/
New York NY, USA
Kopenhagen, Dänemark/
New York NY, USA
Finalist

New York

Central Park Tower
Adrian Smith + Gordon Gill Architecture
Chicago IL, USA

611 West 56th Street
Álvaro Siza
Porto, Portugal

The Spiral
BIG – Bjarke Ingels Group
Copenhagen, Denmark/
New York NY, USA
Kopenhagen, Dänemark/
New York NY, USA

Eagle + West
OMA Office for Metropolitan Architecture
Rotterdam, Netherlands Niederlande

One and Two Manhattan West
Skidmore, Owings & Merrill
Chicago IL, USA

11 Hoyt
Studio Gang
Chicago IL, USA

Gothenburg

Karlatornet
Skidmore, Owings & Merrill
Chicago IL, USA

Amsterdam

Valley
Amsterdam, Netherlands Niederlande
MVRDV
Rotterdam, Netherlands Niederlande
Finalist

Eindhoven

Bunker Tower
Powerhouse Company
Rotterdam, Netherlands Niederlande
Finalist

Paris

Tours Duo
Ateliers Jean Nouvel
Paris, France Frankreich

Vienna

The One
StudioVlayStreeruwitz
Vienna, Austria Wien, Österreich

31 Projekte aus 13 Ländern

Warsaw

Varso Tower
Foster + Partners
London, UK Großbritannien

Dubai

Atlantis The Royal Resort
Kohn Pedersen Fox Associates
New York NY, USA

One Za'abeel Tower
Nikken Sekkei
Tokyo, Japan Tokio, Japan

Nanjing

Nanjing Vertical Forest
Stefano Boeri Architetti
Milan, Italy Mailand, Italien

Hangzhou

Hangzhou Prism
OMA Office for Metropolitan Architecture
Rotterdam, Netherlands Niederlande

Hangzhou Wangchao Center
Skidmore, Owings & Merrill
Chicago IL, USA

Shenzhen

Shenzhen Women & Children's Center
MVRDV
Rotterdam, Netherlands Niederlande
Finalist

Citymark Tower
Kohn Pedersen Fox Associates
New York NY, USA

Qianhai Telecommunication Center
schneider + schumacher
Frankfurt am Main, Germany Deutschland

Hong Kong

Airside
Snøhetta
Oslo, Norway Norwegen

The Henderson
Zaha Hadid Architects
London, UK Großbritannien

Singapore

CapitaSpring
BIG – Bjarke Ingels Group
Copenhagen, Denmark/
New York NY, USA
Kopenhagen, Dänemark/
New York NY, USA;
CRA – Carlo Ratti Associati
Turin, Italy/New York NY, USA
Turin, Italien/New York NY, USA
Prize Winner *Preisträger*

Pan Pacific Orchard
WOHA
Singapore Singapur

Tokyo

Mori JP Tower
Pelli Clarke & Partners
New Haven CT, USA

Tokyu Kabukicho Tower
Yuko Nagayama & Associates
Tokyo, Japan Tokio, Japan

Brisbane

Heritage Lanes, 80 Ann Street
Woods Bagot
Adelaide, Australia Australien

Melbourne

555 Collins Street
COX Architecture
Sydney, Australia Australien;
Gensler
San Francisco CA, USA

1 Prize Winner

Preisträger

CapitaSpring

Singapore, Singapur

Architects Architekt:innen

BIG – Bjarke Ingels Group
Copenhagen, Denmark/New York NY, USA
Kopenhagen, Dänemark/New York NY, USA;
CRA – Carlo Ratti Associati
Turin, Italy/New York NY, USA
Turin, Italien/New York NY, USA

Client Bauherrschaft

CapitaLand;
Mitsubishi Estate

When the jury convened for the 11th International High-Rise Award, it was against the backdrop of the huge global challenges facing the built environment. The jury discussed at length the issue of what should define high-rises going forward, the role they have to play in urban society post-pandemic and in the midst of massive increases in urban populations.

The jury unanimously selected CapitaSpring in Singapore as the winner. Kim Herforth Nielsen succinctly summed up the reasoning in two sentences: "The winning project stands out for its generosity; the public 'sky park' and the street food market at ground level animate the entire area. It's a project that understands itself as part of the city and thus gives something back to the neighborhood and invites the public in."

Als die Jury zu ihrer Sitzung zusammenkam, um die Prämierung für den 11. Internationalen Hochhaus Preis vorzunehmen, geschah dies vor dem Hintergrund der enormen globalen Herausforderungen, denen sich die gebaute Umwelt stellen muss. Die Jury diskutierte die Frage, was das Hochhaus in Zukunft ausmachen soll, welche Rolle es in der urbanen Gesellschaft nach der Pandemie und angesichts des massiven Anstiegs der Stadtbevölkerung spielen soll.

Die Jury wählte CapitaSpring in Singapur einstimmig zum Gewinner. Kim Herforth Nielsen fasste die Begründung in zwei Sätzen prägnant zusammen: „Das Preisträgerprojekt zeichnet sich durch seine Offenheit aus; der öffentliche ‚Sky Park' und der Streetfood-Markt im Erdgeschoss beleben das gesamte Gebiet. Es ist ein Projekt, das sich als Teil der Stadt versteht und somit der Nachbarschaft etwas zurückgibt, die Öffentlichkeit einlädt."

12/1
In Singapore's densely built-up CBD, unobstructed views of CapitaSpring are possible only from the northwest, particularly from Church Street or Pickering Street.
In Singapurs dicht bebautem CBD hat man lediglich aus nordwestlicher Richtung über die Church bzw. Pickering Street freie Sicht auf CapitaSpring.

5 Finalists

Finalisten

	CapitaSpring ***Prize Winner** Preisträger*	IQON Residences	Shenzhen Women & Children's Center	Valley	Bunker Tower
Location Standort	**Singapore** Singapur	**Quito, Ecuador**	**Shenzhen, China**	**Amsterdam, Netherlands** Niederlande	**Eindhoven, Netherlands** Niederlande
Architects Architekt:innen	**BIG – Bjarke Ingels Group Copenhagen, Denmark/ New York NY, USA** Kopenhagen, Dänemark/ New York NY, USA; **CRA – Carlo Ratti Associati Turin, Italy/New York NY, USA** Turin, Italien/New York NY, USA	**BIG – Bjarke Ingels Group Copenhagen, Denmark/ New York NY, USA** Kopenhagen, Dänemark/ New York NY, USA	**MVRDV Rotterdam, Netherlands** Niederlande	**MVRDV Rotterdam, Netherlands** Niederlande	**Powerhouse Company Rotterdam, Netherlands** Niederlande
Client Bauherrschaft	**CapitaLand; Mitsubishi Estate**	**Uribe Schwarzkopf**	**Shum Yip Group**	**EDGE**	**RED Company; Being Development**
Main use Hauptnutzung	**Mixed use comprising offices, residential, hospitality** Mischnutzung aus Büros, Wohnen, Gastronomie	**Residential, offices** Wohnen, Büros	**Mixed use comprising healthcare facilities for women and children, education and learning facilities, hotel, retail** Mischnutzung aus Einrichtungen für das Wohlergehen von Frauen und Kindern, Bildungs- und Lehreinrichtungen, Hotel, Einzelhandel	**Residential, offices** Wohnen, Büros	**Residential, offices, restaurant** Wohnen, Büros, Restaurant
Height Höhe	**280 m**	**130 m**	**108 m**	**100 m**	**100 m**
Completion Fertigstellung	**September 2022**	**December 2022** Dezember 2022	**September 2023**	**September 2022**	**October 2022** Oktober 2022
Detailed information Ausführliche Informationen	**Page 16** Seite 16	**Page 66** Seite 66	**Page 72** Seite 72	**Page 78** Seite 78	**Page 84** Seite 84

Main Jury Statement
Jurystatement

CapitaSpring, Singapore

CapitaSpring, the jury concluded, is "the best high-rise building in the world at the moment." The jurors chose it because it combines the best of two worlds, balancing the city's interests with those of private developers in an ideal architectural solution. Now, the high-rise is symbolizing its strong ability to connect between the public and the private, between the office world up above and the two-story hawker centre down below, where everyone meets for lunch. In-between is a breezy, naturally ventilated green zone that is publicly accessible, as is the Sky Garden on the roof.

All of this is the result of an innovative approach by URA, Singapore's Urban Redevelopment Authority, which demonstrated moral leadership in incentivizing the developer by granting a partial waiver from the regulations (granting additional floor area per unit in exchange for open, public spaces). The outcome: a private office and residential tower that is truly public while adding to the urban resources that had been on site.

The architects have planned a high-rise the way one might draft a village or city, avoiding the "closed-door" syndrome of so many high-rise podiums. As a result, it is a tall building that exudes a sense of cityness, even down to preserving the local identity in the form of the hawker centre.

In the process, by virtue of remaining inclusive, CapitaSpring belongs to the city. The jury agreed that CapitaSpring is essentially successful as it is "co-designed" – because the city has a great planning regime and because the developer had a certain vision to make a private real estate office into a vertical public space. In this way, CapitaSpring moves the tall-building typology a crucial step forward – for the future of the city.

As Kim Herforth Nielsen concluded: "We are honoring the city for giving the developer the right incentives, and the developer for seizing the initiative, and the architects for finding an innovative solution to it all. All of this is reflected in the quality of the architecture. CapitaSpring could simply not have been built elsewhere at present. Other cities can definitely learn from this."

CapitaSpring, Singapur

CapitaSpring ist nach Ansicht der Jury „das derzeit überzeugendste Hochhaus weltweit". Sie entschied sich für das Gebäude, weil es die Interessen der Stadt und der privaten Bauherrschaft in einer idealen Lösung in Einklang bringt. Der Wolkenkratzer symbolisiert die enge Verknüpfung zwischen dem Öffentlichen und dem Privaten, zwischen den Büros oben und dem zweigeschossigen *hawker centre* unten, wo sich alle zum Mittagessen treffen. Dazwischen befindet sich eine natürlich durchlüftete Grünzone, die ebenso wie der Sky Garden öffentlich zugänglich ist.

Ermöglicht wurde dies durch ein innovatives Konzept der URA (Urban Redevelopment Authority), der Stadtentwicklungsbehörde von Singapur, die der Bauherrschaft mit einer teilweisen Ausnahmeregelung (zusätzliche Geschossfläche pro Einheit im Tausch gegen öffentliche Freiflächen) eine verantwortungsvolle Haltung entgegenbrachte. Das Ergebnis: ein privater Büro- und Wohnturm, der im wahrsten Sinne des Wortes öffentlich ist und gleichzeitig die am Standort vorhandenen urbanen Ressourcen erweitert.

Die Architekt:innen haben das Gebäude so geplant, wie man ein Dorf oder eine Stadt entwerfen könnte, und so das Problem „verschlossener Türen", das bei vielen Eingangsbereichen von Hochhäusern vorkommt, vermieden. Das Ergebnis ist ein Wolkenkratzer, der ein Stadtgefühl vermittelt und dabei sogar die lokale Identität in Form des *hawker centre* bewahrt.

CapitaSpring ist Teil der Stadt, weil es inklusiv bleibt. Es ist vor allem deshalb so gut gelungen, weil es „mitgestaltet" wurde. Weil die Stadt ein starkes städtebauliches Konzept hat und weil die Bauherrschaft die Vision hatte, ein privatwirtschaftliches Bürogebäude in einen vertikalen öffentlichen Raum zu verwandeln. Auf diese Weise bringt CapitaSpring die Typologie Hochhaus einen entscheidenden Schritt voran – im Interesse der Zukunft der Stadt.

Kim Herforth Nielsen abschließend: „Wir würdigen die Stadt, die der Bauherrschaft die richtigen Anreize gegeben hat, die Bauherrschaft, die die Initiative ergriffen hat, und die Architekt:innen, die eine innovative Lösung für all das gefunden haben. Dies alles spiegelt sich in der Qualität der Architektur wider. CapitaSpring hätte zum jetzigen Zeitpunkt an keinem anderen Ort gebaut werden können. Andere Städte können zweifellos davon lernen."

14/1
At the height of the Green Oasis, the vertical façade elements open up in a distinctive manner, offering a view of the building's green heart.
Auf Höhe der Green Oasis öffnen sich die vertikalen Lisenen der Fassade charakteristisch und geben den Blick auf das grüne Herz des Gebäudes frei.

BIG – Bjarke Ingels Group; CRA – Carlo Ratti Associati

CapitaSpring

Singapore Singapur

After jointly winning an international competition in 2018, BIG – Bjarke Ingels Group and CRA – Carlo Ratti Associati have completed Singapore's second tallest high-rise in the heart of the densely built-up CBD (Central Business District). The building, constructed on the site of an obsolete parking garage, is accessed via covered walkways that lead to the 18-meter-high, open lobby, known as the City Room. From there, people reach the actual entrance halls leading to the various uses, as well as the Market Street Hawker Centre located in the base of the building, a type of public food court that was also previously located here. At 56 stalls, typical Singaporean street food is offered to both the building's users and visitors.

Nachdem BIG – Bjarke Ingels Group und CRA – Carlo Ratti Associati im Jahr 2018 gemeinsam einen internationalen Wettbewerb für sich entscheiden konnten, haben sie inmitten von Singapurs dicht bebautem CBD (Central Business District) das zweithöchste Hochhaus des Stadtstaats realisiert. Das auf dem Gelände eines obsolet gewordenen Parkhauses errichtete Gebäude lässt sich über geschützte Fußwege erreichen, die in die 18 Meter hohe, offene Lobby, den sogenannten City Room, münden. Dort befindet sich der Zugang zu den eigentlichen Eingangshallen der unterschiedlichen Nutzungen sowie zu dem im Sockelgebäude befindlichen Market Street Hawker Centre, einer Art öffentlichem *food court*, der sich ebenfalls an diesem Ort befunden hatte. Hier bieten 56 Stände das für Singapur typische Streetfood sowohl Nutzer:innen des Gebäudes als auch Besucher:innen an.

Project team Projektteam
Gorka Calzada Medina, Martino Hutz, Song He, Eric Li, Günther Weber, Tore Banke, Anders Holden Deleuran, Dina Brændstrup, Kirsty Badenoch, Ulla Hornsyld, Aime Desert, Aleksander Wadas, Aleksandra Domian, Alessandro Zanini, Anke Kristina Schramm, Augusto Lavieri Zamperlini, Dalma Ujvari, David Schwarzman, David Vega y Rojo, Davide Tarditi, Dimitrie Grigorescu, Dominika Trybe, Elise Cauchard, Eriko Maekawa, Espen Vik, Ewa Szajda, Federica Locati, Filippo Lorenzi, Francisco Castellanos, Frederik Skou Jensen, Gabrielé Ubareviciute, Guoyu Liu, Helen Chen, Jacek Baczkowski, Jakub Wlodarczyk, Jonas Käckenmester, Julieta Muzzillo, Luca Pileri, Luis Torsten Wagenführer, Lukas Kerner, Malgorzata Mutkowska, Maria Teresa Fernandez Rojo, Matilde Tavanti, Moa Carlsson, Nataly Timotheou, Niu Jing, Orges Guga, Patrycja Lyszczyk, Pedro Savio Jobim Pinheiro, Philip Rufus Knauf, Praewa Samachai, Qamelliah Nassir, Rahul Girish, Ramon Julio Muros Cortes, Rebecca Carrai, Roberto Fabbri, Samuel Rubio Sanchez, Shuhei Kamiya, Sofiia Rokmaniko, Sorcha Burke, Steen Kortbæk Svendsen, Szymon Kolecki, Teodor Fratila Cristian, Viktoria Millentrup, Vilius Linge, Vinish Sethi, Weijia Lu, Xin Su, Xinying Zhang, Zari van de Merwe, Zhen Ton (all alle **BIG),**
Monika Löve, Antonio Atripaldi, Gary di Silvio, Gianluca Zimbardi, Saverio Panata, Alberto Bottero, Chiara de Grandi, Giovanni de Niederhausern, Andrea Giordano, Damiano Gui, Mariachiara Mondini, Andrea Pedrina, Andrea Riva (all alle **CRA)**

Architects Architekt:innen	**BIG – Bjarke Ingels Group Copenhagen, Denmark/ New York NY, USA** Kopenhagen, Dänemark/ New York NY, USA; **CRA – Carlo Ratti Associati Turin, Italy/ New York NY, USA** Turin, Italien/ New York NY, USA
Project architects Projektarchitekt:innen	**Bjarke Ingels, Brian Yang, Carlo Ratti**
Architects of record Lokale Architekt:innen	**RSP Architects Planners & Engineers**
Client Bauherrschaft	**CapitaLand; Mitsubishi Estate**
Digital technologies/ New media Digitale Technologien/ Neue Medien	**Dotdotdot**
Structural engineers Tragwerksplanung	**Arup; Meinhardt**
MEP Haustechnik	**Beca Carter Hollings & Ferner (S.E.Asia)**
Landscape architects Landschaftsarchitekt:innen	**Coen Design International; BIG – Bjarke Ingels Group**
Height Höhe	**280 m**
Stories Geschosse	**51**
Site area Grundstücksfläche	**6104 m²**
Building footprint Bebaute Fläche	**5468 m²**
Gross floor area Bruttogeschossfläche	**93 350 m²**
Structure Konstruktion	**Composite construction** Verbundbauweise
Completion Fertigstellung	**September 2022**
Main use Hauptnutzung	**Mixed use comprising offices, residential, hospitality** Mischnutzung aus Büros, Wohnen, Gastronomie

17/1
The elongated shape of the site was one reason why it had not been redeveloped earlier.
Die langgestreckte Form des Grundstücks war ein Grund dafür, dass es nicht früher neu bebaut wurde.

18/1
The high, open lobby, known as the City Room, extends the public space in Singapore's densely built-up CBD.
Die hohe, offene Lobby, der sogenannte City Room, erweitert den öffentlichen Raum in Singapurs dicht bebautem CBD.

19/1
Section
Schnitt

19/2
Façade concept
Konzept Fassade

On the lower floors of CapitaSpring, above the parking garage, there are partly two-story serviced residences available primarily for business guests from the upper office floors but also for tourists. This offer is complemented by a wide range of amenities such as a swimming pool, running track, fitness rooms, communal kitchen, and barbecue areas, as well as the restaurants located in the building.

In den unteren Etagen von CapitaSpring befinden sich über der Parkgarage teils zweigeschossige *serviced residences*, die vorrangig Firmengäst:innen aus den oberen Büroetagen, aber auch Tourist:innen zur Verfügung stehen. Dieses Angebot wird durch umfassende Serviceeinrichtungen wie Swimmingpool, Laufstrecke, Fitnessräume, Gemeinschaftsküche und Grillplätze sowie die im Gebäude befindlichen Restaurants komplettiert.

Sustainability certification:
Green Mark Platinum,
Universal Design Gold
Sustainability:
abundant greenery, including the Sky Garden; renaturation of formerly sealed areas; bicycle lots and connection to the city's cycling path network

Nachhaltigkeitszerifizierung:
Green Mark Platinum,
Universal Design Gold
Nachhaltigkeit:
üppige Begrünung, einschließlich des Sky Gardens; Renaturierung von ehemals versiegelten Flächen; Fahrradstellplätze und Anbindung an das städtische Radwegenetzwerk

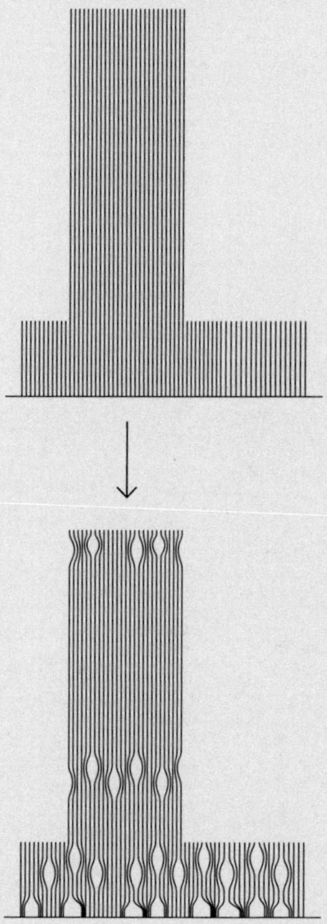

Above the residential floors is the green heart of the building, the so-called Green Oasis. Here, the vertical façade elements are pulled apart like light curtains, offering glimpses of a green landscape spanning four floors that invites people to linger, take a walk, and even do sports. Together with the also public green space on the rooftop, a total of 80,000 plants create a pleasant microclimate in the midst of the densely built-up environment.

Über den Wohnetagen liegt das grüne Herz des Gebäudes, die sogenannte Green Oasis. An dieser Stelle sind die vertikalen Lisenen der Fassade wie leichte Gardinen auseinandergezogen. So wird der Blick frei auf eine grüne, sich über vier Etagen erstreckende Landschaft, die zum Verweilen oder zu Spaziergängen und sogar zu Sport einlädt. Gemeinsam mit der ebenfalls öffentlichen Grünfläche auf dem Dach des Gebäudes sorgen insgesamt 80.000 Pflanzen für ein angenehmes Mikroklima inmitten der dicht bebauten Umgebung.

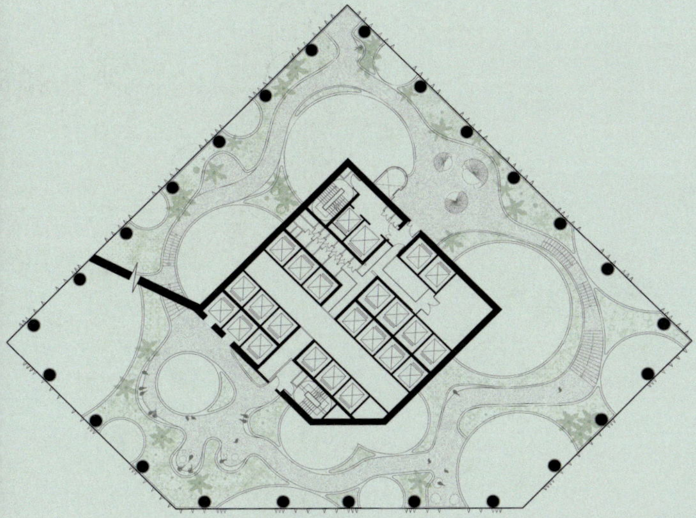

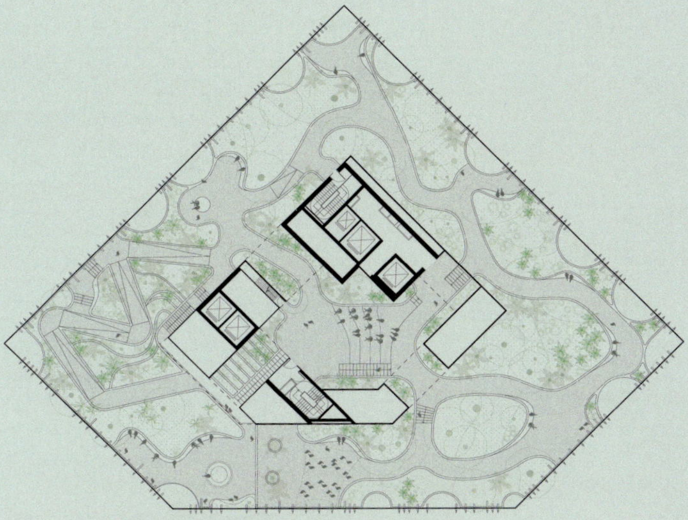

20/1, 21/3–5
Views through the publicly accessible Green Oasis
Blicke durch die öffentlich zugängliche Green Oasis

21/1
19th floor plan, Green Oasis
Grundriss 19. Obergeschoss, Green Oasis

21/2
51st floor plan, rooftop garden
Grundriss 51. Obergeschoss, Dachgarten

twp

39
O
P
R
S

The floors accommodating the building's actual main use, the offices for the headquarters of CapitaLand, an international real estate company that is also the project's developer, extend above the serviced residences.

At the top of the high-rise, the façade opens up again, similar as it does at the height of the Green Oasis. The roof garden located there offers its visitors unique views over the city and the harbor out to the sea. In addition, well over 100 types of fruits, vegetables, herbs, and flowers are grown here to supply the building's restaurants.

In total, 8,300 square meters of green spaces have been integrated into CapitaSpring, which corresponds to 140 percent of the actual site area. Thus, the high-rise, with its offices, apartments featuring extensive amenities, restaurants, food court, and green spaces including recreational facilities, incorporates almost all the functions of a complete neighborhood.

Erst darüber beginnt die eigentliche Hauptnutzung des Gebäudes, die Büroetagen des Firmensitzes von CapitaLand, eines internationalen Immobilienunternehmens, das zugleich die Bauherrschaft des Projekts innehat.

An der Spitze des Hochhauses öffnet sich ähnlich wie bei der Green Oasis die Fassade abermals. Der dortige Dachgarten bietet seinen Besucher:innen einzigartige Ausblicke über die Stadt und den Hafen bis hinaus aufs Meer. Außerdem werden hier weit über 100 Arten Obst, Gemüse, Kräuter und Blumen angebaut, die in den Restaurants im Gebäude verarbeitet werden.

Insgesamt besitzt CapitaSpring 8.300 Quadratmeter Grünfläche, was 140 Prozent der eigentlichen Grundstücksfläche entspricht. Somit beinhaltet das Hochhaus mit seinen Büros, Wohnungen mit breitem Serviceangebot, Restaurants, dem *food court* sowie den Grünflächen mit Freizeitanlagen nahezu alle Funktionen eines kompletten Stadtviertels.

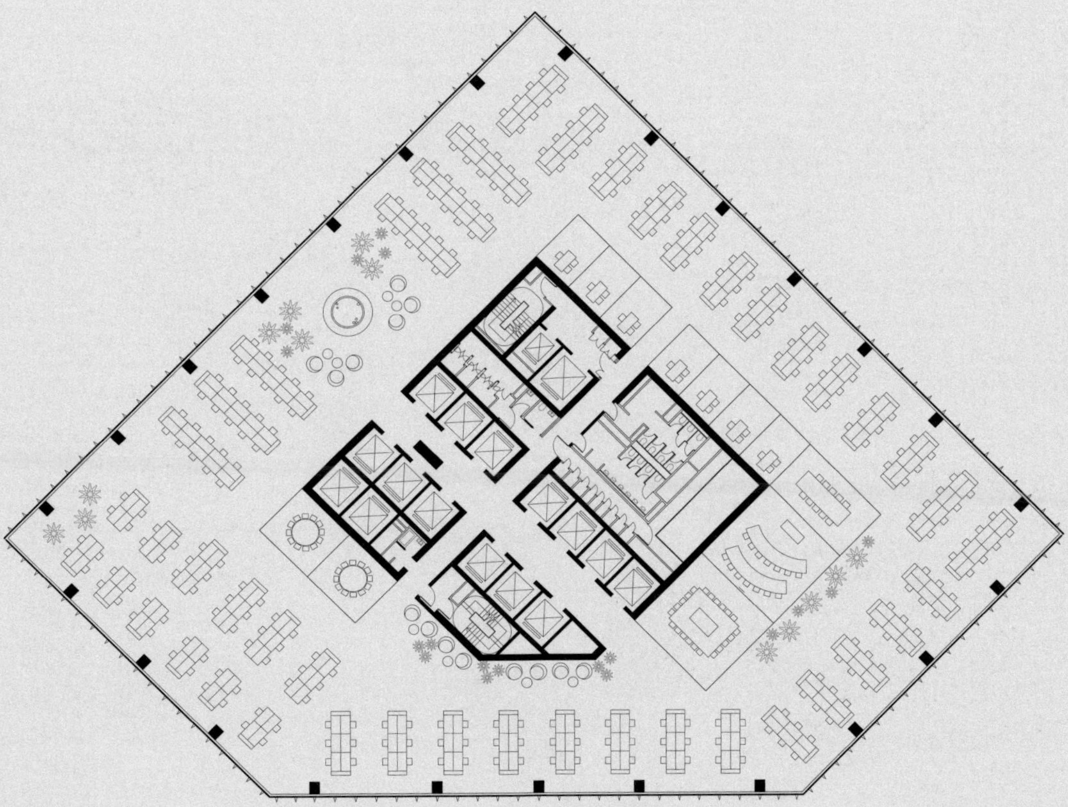

22/1
View of the famous Marina Bay from the office floors
Blick aus den Büroetagen auf die bekannte Marina Bay

22/2
Elevator lobby on the office floors
Aufzugsvorraum in den Büroetagen

23/1
Standard office floor
Büroetagen Regelgeschoss

24/1+25/1
CapitaSpring in the Singapore skyline at night amidst high-rise buildings by Kenzo Tange, I. M. Pei, Kisho Kurokawa, and Toyo Ito, among others
CapitaSpring in der nächtlichen Skyline Singapurs inmitten von Hochhäusern, u. a. von Kenzo Tange, I. M. Pei, Kisho Kurokawa und Toyo Ito

CapitaSpring

Prize Winner 2024/25 Preisträger 2024/25

Jury statements

Yasmin Al-Ani Spence: ***"Apart from being an elegant structure, what stuck out was the approach to urban greening and the building's ability to integrate local culture, while responding to the Singapore climate."***

Roland Bechmann: ***"I found the concept of taking a downtown brownfield site, which had been used wastefully to park cars, and 'returning it' to the public as greenery very convincing. The underlying idea was truly re-engineering, as the car park is now situated on floors 4–8 of the high-rise, along with the coolers, M&E, and chillers. The idea could and should be applied elsewhere, along with the way the architects revisited the timeworn idea of cross-ventilation for the gardens and meetings areas on Floors 18–19."***

Jürgen Heinzel: ***"This year, we chose a winner that stands out for its seamless integration of sustainability and vibrant community spaces, establishing new benchmarks for urban high-rise projects.***

I'm inspired by this year's winner and the exemplary model it sets for future high-rise developments."

Ina Hartwig: ***"CapitaSpring is the result of a negotiation between the public (as represented by the municipal authorities) and the developers. The City was agile enough to grant the developers the license to deviate from the norms set for high-rises in Singapore, and in return, the developers created new and in part lushly greened spaces for the public. I think this sort of flexibility on the part of the authorities can be taken as a pioneering way to solve some of the issues our cities face in partnership with the private sector."***

Christopher Lee: ***"This project is truly a mixed-use tower. In most cities, high-rises tend to be monoprogrammatic, trading diversity and vitality for efficiency. Instead of following developer instincts for a prime site, packing the ground floor, for example, with high-yield F&B rentals, the modest hawker centre that once stood on the site has instead been retained and proudly installed on the second and third floors."***

Jurystatements

Yasmin Al-Ani Spence: *„Bemerkenswert ist nicht nur die Eleganz des Gebäudes, sondern auch der Aspekt der Stadtbegrünung und die Einbindung der lokalen Kultur bei gleichzeitiger Anpassung an das Klima in Singapur."*

Roland Bechmann: *„Ich fand die Entscheidung, eine Industriebrache mitten in der Stadt, die bisher einfach nur als Parkhaus vergeudet wurde, der Öffentlichkeit als Grünfläche ‚zurückzugeben', sehr überzeugend. Die dem Projekt zugrunde liegende Idee ist ein echtes Reengineering, denn die Parkplätze befinden sich jetzt auf den Etagen 4 bis 8 des Hochhauses, zusammen mit den Kühlsystemen und der Gebäudetechnik. Diese Idee könnte und sollte auch andernorts umgesetzt werden, ebenso wie das von den Architekt:innen wieder aufgegriffene Konzept der Querlüftung für die Gärten und Begegnungsräume auf den Etagen 18 und 19."*

Jürgen Heinzel: *„In diesem Jahr haben wir einen Preisträger ausgewählt, der sich durch die nahtlose Integration von Nachhaltigkeit und belebten Gemeinschaftsbereichen auszeichnet und neue Maßstäbe für urbane Hochhausprojekte setzt.*

Der diesjährige Preisträger begeistert mich durch seine Vorbildfunktion für künftige Hochhausprojekte."

Ina Hartwig: *„CapitaSpring ist das Ergebnis einer Einigung zwischen der Öffentlichkeit (vertreten durch die städtischen Behörden) und den Bauherr:innen. Die Stadt war flexibel genug, der Bauherrschaft Abweichungen von den in Singapur geltenden Normen für Hochhäuser zu gestatten, und die Bauherr:innen schufen im Gegenzug neue, zum Teil üppig begrünte Flächen für die Öffentlichkeit. Ich denke, mit dieser Art von Flexibilität nehmen die Behörden eine Vorreiterrolle ein, die dazu beiträgt, einige der Probleme, mit denen unsere Städte konfrontiert sind, in Partnerschaft mit dem privaten Sektor zu lösen."*

Christopher Lee: *„Dieses Projekt ist im wahrsten Sinne des Wortes ein gemischt genutztes Hochhaus. In den meisten Städten tendieren Hochhäuser zu einer monoprogrammatischen Nutzung, bei der Vielfalt und Lebendigkeit gegen Effizienz eingetauscht werden. Anstatt den Instinkten der Bauherr:innen zu folgen und beispielsweise das Erdgeschoss mit renditeträchtigen gastronomischen Betrieben zu füllen, wurde das bescheidene* hawker centre, *das sich früher an diesem Ort befand, erhalten und mit Stolz im zweiten und dritten Stock untergebracht."*

27/1
At different levels, the project brings much-needed greenery to Singapore's architectural density.
Auf verschiedenen Höhenniveaus bringt das Projekt dringend benötigtes Grün in die architektonische Dichte Singapurs.

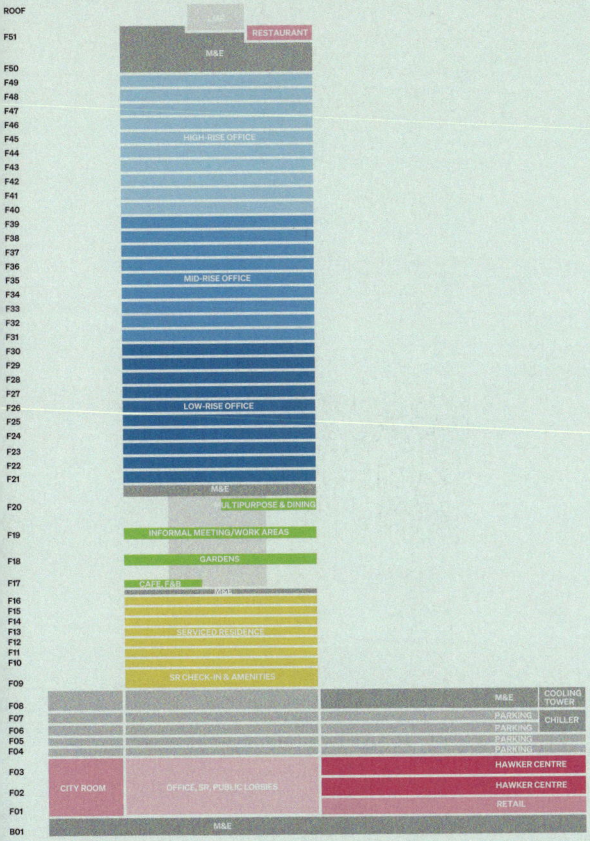

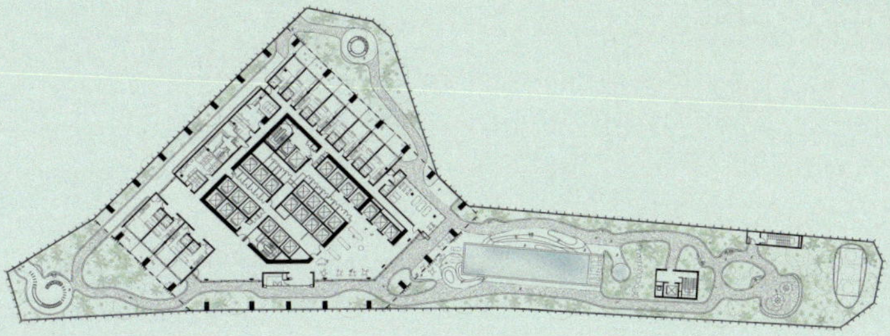

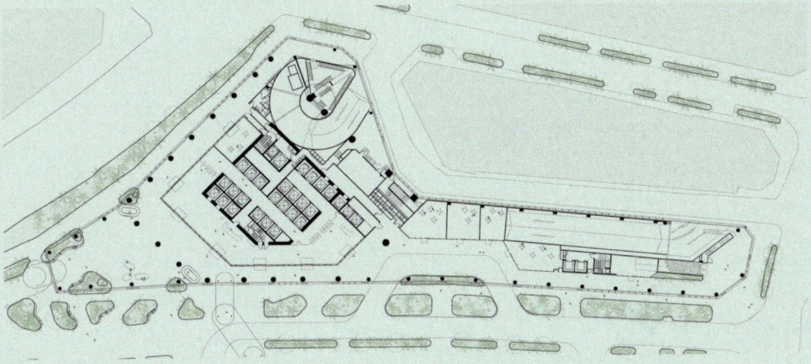

28/1
View of the building from the south
Blick von Süden auf das Gebäude

29/1
Distribution of uses
Nutzungsverteilung

29/2+3
9th floor plan and ground floor plan
Grundriss 9. Obergeschoss und Grundriss Erdgeschoss

Mari Randsborg: ***"CapitaSpring is a celebration of life in public spaces. It's an inclusive and inviting livability engine that invites everyone in and gives the best square meters to the many – not the few."***

Peter Cachola Schmal: ***"This high-rise could not have been built anywhere else on the planet than in Singapore at this moment. Other cities should learn from this example, because this is the way to get good projects: to incentivize developers who want to invest money, and the architects to find a good solution, and to give them something in return."***

Victor Stoltenburg & Horst R. Muth: ***"The skyscraper is a classic example of a property that combines being a place to work with simultaneously being a place to live, contributing strongly to improving the quality of urban life."***

Mari Randsborg: *„CapitaSpring zelebriert das Leben im öffentlichen Raum. Es ist ein integrativer und einladender Impulsgeber für die Lebensqualität, der alle Menschen einbezieht und die besten Quadratmeter vielen – und nicht nur wenigen – zugutekommen lässt."*

Peter Cachola Schmal: *„Dieses Hochhaus hätte zum jetzigen Zeitpunkt nirgendwo anders auf der Welt gebaut werden können als in Singapur, und andere Städte sollten davon lernen. Denn das ist die beste Methode, um gute Projekte zu realisieren: Anreize für Bauherr:innen zu schaffen, die Geld investieren wollen, und eine gute Lösung für die Architekt:innen zu finden, die dann auch eine adäquate Gegenleistung bieten werden."*

Victor Stoltenburg & Horst R. Muth: *„Der Wolkenkratzer ist ein Musterbeispiel für eine Immobilie, die Arbeits- und Lebensort zugleich ist und damit einen wichtigen Beitrag zur Verbesserung der urbanen Lebensqualität leistet."*

In Conversation with the Architects

Im Gespräch mit den Architekten

Bjarke Ingels, Brian Yang (both BIG) & Carlo Ratti (CRA)

Bjarke Ingels, Brian Yang (beide BIG) & Carlo Ratti (CRA)

In Copenhagen, the team from the City of Frankfurt and the DAM (Stefan Jäger, Kulturamt Stadt Frankfurt; Peter Cachola Schmal and Peter Körner, both DAM) talked to Bjarke Ingels and Brian Yang, followed by an online interview with Carlo Ratti. The entire conversation was compiled in this text.

In Kopenhagen führte das Team der Stadt und des DAM (Stefan Jäger, Kulturamt Stadt Frankfurt; Peter Cachola Schmal und Peter Körner, beide DAM) Gespräche mit Bjarke Ingels und Brian Yang; danach folgte ein Online-Interview mit Carlo Ratti.

DAM: ***BIG has won The International High-Rise Award for the second time now. Do you remember when you first won it in 2016?***

Bjarke Ingels (BI): Via 57 in New York was our first real high-rise. This kind of hybrid between the European courtyard and the American skyscraper. It had verticality and identity and became a striking silhouette. It was a great honor and privilege to be awarded the Thomas Demand trophy for Via 57. Many awards you can only win once, so we consider it a great compliment and a great honor that CapitaSpring was awarded The International High-Rise Award this year.

DAM: ***It's been eight years since you first received The International High-Rise Award. What has changed since then for BIG, and for your approach to architecture?***

BI: The big change is that architecture is governed by this catch-22, that no one will ever hire you to do a skyscraper, unless you've already done a skyscraper. In the wake of the success of Via 57, we've done a handful of high-rises. CapitaSpring is one of the most recent, and we we've had many opportunities to examine the typology of this kind of dense, vertical building.

Brian Yang (BY): The way we work as architects is to try to take the forces that shape society, the opportunities, the constraints, and to discover how we can create something new that might not have been expected. To discover hidden values, things that might emerge from resolving seeming contradictions.

DAM: *BIG bekommt den Internationalen Hochhaus Preis nun schon zum zweiten Mal. Erinnern Sie sich an 2016, als Sie ihn das erste Mal gewonnen haben?*

Bjarke Ingels (BI): Ja, Via 57 in New York war unser erstes echtes Hochhaus. Eine Art Hybrid aus europäischem Innenhof und amerikanischem Wolkenkratzer. Es besitzt Vertikalität und Identität und besticht durch seine markante Silhouette. Es war eine große Ehre und ein Privileg, die von Thomas Demand gestaltete Trophäe für Via 57 entgegenzunehmen. Viele Auszeichnungen kann man nur einmal bekommen, und so empfinden wir es als riesiges Kompliment und enorme Anerkennung, dass CapitaSpring in diesem Jahr mit dem Internationalen Hochhaus Preis ausgezeichnet wird.

DAM: *Es sind acht Jahre vergangen, seitdem Sie den Internationalen Hochhaus Preis zum ersten Mal erhielten. Was hat sich seither für BIG verändert? Für Ihre Herangehensweise an die Architektur?*

BI: Er half uns aus dem Teufelskreis, von dem die Architektur beherrscht wird, dass man nie einen Auftrag für einen Wolkenkratzer erhält, wenn man nicht bereits einen gebaut hat. Nach dem Erfolg von Via 57 haben wir eine Handvoll Hochhäuser gebaut, CapitaSpring ist eines der jüngsten, und es gab viele Gelegenheiten, die Typologie des kompakten vertikalen Gebäudes zu untersuchen.

Brian Yang (BY): Die Art und Weise, wie wir als Architekt:innen arbeiten, besteht darin, dass wir versuchen, die Kräfte, die die Gesellschaft formen, die Möglichkeiten und die Zwänge zu nutzen und zu entdecken, wie wir etwas Neues schaffen können, das vielleicht nicht erwartet wurde. Es geht darum, versteckte Werte zu entdecken, Dinge, die aus der Lösung scheinbarer Widersprüche entstehen können.

30/1
From the rooftop garden, the highest viewing platform in Singapore, one has a unique view over the city and the harbor, extending out to the sea.
Vom Dachgarten, der höchsten Aussichtsplattform Singapurs, hat man einen einzigartigen Blick über die Stadt und den Hafen bis hinaus aufs Meer.

DAM: ***Can you please explain how you went about working on CapitaSpring in all those years? How did you divide your work between BIG and Carlo Ratti Associati?***

Carlo Ratti (CR): At the very beginning, we were invited by CapitaLand to participate in the competition. We had been working with them for several years and had held several discussions. The first thing you do in a competition, you put together a great team. I thought, this would be a very interesting way to start collaborating with BIG. We had often had dealings with each other over the years. And that's how things started. Then we added all the other specialist planners to the team, related to engineering, to local architects and so on. But what really started it all was the contacts with CapitaLand.

DAM: ***What other firms were taking part in the initial design competition?***

BI: The initial competition was between Heatherwick Studios, MVRDV, WOHA, and us, a very daunting competition.

DAM: ***How can we recognize BIG's approach in the CapitaSpring building?***

BI: In the case of CapitaSpring, it's a dialog with the typology of the midtown high-rise. One of the basic ideas is that the envelope of the building or the building form is determined by the eccentric existing footprint and the concerns of various neighbors regarding the volume of the high-rise itself. It's a slightly odd polygon, and we came up with the idea to dress the entire volume in a typical pinstripe suit of a high-rise with the vertical articulation of the mullions, and the result is this hermetic corporate, maybe beautiful and well-proportioned, but Miesian tower of glass with expressive mullions. A gift toward the city and the people working and living there is to open the pinstripe suit and create these invitations by turning one of the streets into a park and a promenade opening underneath the building into a covered square in the middle of the building.

BY: Inside, there are a lot of very unexpected experiences and spaces, such as a 10-story-high atrium or the incredible 30-meter-wide tropical garden – a great pleasure to discover.

DAM: *Bitte beschreiben Sie, wie Sie bei den Arbeiten an CapitaSpring in all den Jahren vorgegangen sind. Wie haben Sie die Arbeit zwischen BIG und Carlo Ratti Associati aufgeteilt?*

Carlo Ratti (CR): Ganz am Anfang wurden wir von CapitaLand eingeladen, an dem Wettbewerb teilzunehmen. Wir arbeiteten schon seit einigen Jahren mit ihnen zusammen und hatten viele Gespräche geführt. Das Erste, was man bei einem Wettbewerb macht, ist, ein gutes Team zusammenzustellen. Ich hielt dies für eine sehr interessante Möglichkeit, eine Zusammenarbeit mit BIG anzubahnen. Wir hatten im Laufe der Jahre schon oft miteinander zu tun gehabt. Und so kam nun alles in Gang. Dann haben wir all die anderen Fachplaner:innen ins Team geholt, die mit dem Ingenieurwesen, den örtlichen Architekt:innen und so weiter zu tun hatten. Aber der eigentliche Startschuss war der Kontakt zu CapitaLand.

DAM: *Welche anderen Firmen nahmen an dem ursprünglichen Wettbewerb teil?*

BI: An dem ursprünglichen Wettbewerb nahmen Heatherwick Studios, MVRDV, WOHA und wir teil, ein sehr anspruchsvolles Feld.

DAM: *Woran kann man den Ansatz von BIG bei CapitaSpring erkennen?*

BI: Im Fall von CapitaSpring geht es um die Auseinandersetzung mit der Typologie des Midtown-Hochhauses, und eine der wesentlichen Überlegungen war, dass die Gebäudehülle bzw. die Gebäudeform bereits durch die vorhandene exzentrische Grundfläche und das Volumen des Hochhauses durch die Belange der zahlreichen Nachbarn vorgegeben waren. Es handelt sich um ein etwas merkwürdiges Vieleck, und wir kamen auf die Idee, das gesamte Volumen in den für Hochhäuser typischen Nadelstreifenanzug mit vertikaler Gliederung durch Profile zu kleiden. Das Ergebnis ist ein hermetischer, recht schöner und wohlproportionierter Glasturm mit ausgeprägten Profilen im Mies'schen Stil. Als Geschenk an die Stadt und die Menschen, die dort arbeiten und leben, öffnen wir den Nadelstreifenanzug und laden sie alle ein: durch die Umwandlung einer der Straßen in einen Park und eine Promenade, die sich innerhalb des Gebäudes als überdachter Platz in der Mitte des Gebäudes öffnet.

BY: Im Inneren gibt es viele unerwartete Erlebnisse und Räume, wie zum Beispiel ein 10 Stockwerke hohes Atrium oder den unglaublichen, 30 Meter breiten tropischen Garten – ein großes Vergnügen für Entdecker:innen.

33/1
Openings in the façade at the parking levels
Die Öffnungen der Fassade auf Höhe der Parkgarage

DAM: ***What were your initial thoughts when you heard of the CapitaSpring project?***

BY: My father is Singaporean. He moved to the US for college. I was born there, and I grew up in Singapore, studied in the US, and have been living in Denmark for a long time. There's my personal affinity for Singapore, but there is also the feeling of the great weight of responsibility to build in the historical CBD and to do something great given the opportunity. But there were other challenges at play because the historical CBD had become a place that was only active from nine to five. And we were challenged not only by the client, CapitaLand, but also by the Urban Redevelopment Authority (URA) to imagine how the building could be a catalyst for the reinvigoration of the CBD over a 24-hour period.

DAM: *Was waren Ihre ersten Gedanken, als Sie von dem Projekt CapitaSpring hörten?*

BY: Mein Vater stammt aus Singapur. Er zog zum Studium in die USA. Ich bin dort geboren und in Singapur aufgewachsen, habe in den USA studiert und lebe seit Langem in Dänemark. Da ist also meine persönliche Nähe zu Singapur, aber auch das Gefühl der großen Verantwortung, in der historischen Innenstadt zu bauen und etwas Großes zu schaffen, wenn sich die Gelegenheit bietet. Aber es gab auch andere Herausforderungen, denn das historische Stadtzentrum hatte sich zu einem Ort entwickelt, der nur noch von 9 bis 17 Uhr belebt war. Nicht nur die Bauherrschaft CapitaLand, sondern auch die Stadtentwicklungsbehörde (URA) stellte uns vor die Aufgabe, uns vorzustellen, wie das Gebäude als Katalysator für die Wiederbelebung des CBD über einen Zeitraum von 24 Stunden dienen könnte.

34/1
Arrival situation by car
Ankunftssituation mit dem Pkw

34/2
Entrance to the parking garage
Einfahrt in die Parkgarage

34/3
Parking level, which can be converted for other uses if required
Parkebene, die sich bei Bedarf für andere Nutzungen umwandeln lässt

DAM: ***Which part of this unique project CapitaSpring were you particularly interested in developing?***

CR: At the very beginning, we set up a joint team. Part of the time we worked in Turin, part of the time in Copenhagen. We used some of the research we've been doing at MIT (Massachusetts Institute of Technology) to inform the design. I'll give you one example. At the very beginning, the Urban Redevelopment Authority (URA) of Singapore wanted all the parking to go underground. We had been doing a lot of research at our Senseable City Lab at MIT with Singapore as part of our "Unparking" initiative, to look at what happens when a city moves more and more toward new mobility systems. Singapore was very interested in autonomous cars, which need much less parking space. The car can give you a lift to your office in the morning, and then the car can give a lift to anybody else in the city. You need less parking space, and the car is used more often. What impact would this have on a building? If you build underground parking, you will never be able to use that space differently in the future. If you build it above ground, you have a possibility in the future to turn it into something else. This is becoming more common in many other developments around the world. But it was probably the first time that this thinking was inspired by research done in Singapore with MIT. This informed part of the design. There's another interesting component about the design of the building and how it ties into the research at MIT. We have been using big data to measure the importance of creating common spaces where people can come together, where you can create what in sociology is called weak ties. Not strong ties with people you work with every day, but random, serendipitous connections with other people. Weak ties are important for creativity and for developing new ideas. The physical space of the office is important for creating these weak ties. The whole building was built around a number of those weak ties. The spring in the middle, the garden space, is like a vertical European plaza full of greenery. People from different communities and workplaces can come together here. It is a way to create new connections, a place where people can meet other people and where people can meet nature.

DAM: *Was hat Sie an diesem einmaligen Projekt CapitaSpring besonders gereizt?*

CR: Gleich zu Beginn haben wir ein gemeinsames Team zusammengestellt. Zum Teil arbeiteten wir in Turin, zum Teil in Kopenhagen. Bei der Entwicklung des Entwurfs stützten wir uns auf einige Forschungsarbeiten, die wir am MIT (Massachusetts Institute of Technology) durchgeführt hatten. Ich nenne Ihnen ein Beispiel: Ganz am Anfang wollte die Stadtentwicklungsbehörde (URA) von Singapur, dass alle Parkplätze unterirdisch angelegt werden. Wir haben in unserem Senseable City Lab am MIT im Rahmen unserer „Unparking"-Initiative intensiv am Beispiel von Singapur geforscht, um herauszufinden, was passiert, wenn eine Stadt zunehmend auf neue Mobilitätssysteme umsteigt. Singapur war sehr an autonomen Fahrzeugen interessiert, die viel weniger Parkraum benötigen. Das Auto kann Sie morgens ins Büro fahren und danach noch jemand anderen in der Stadt abholen. Man braucht weniger Parkplätze, und Autos werden häufiger genutzt. Wie würde sich das auf ein Gebäude auswirken? Wenn Sie eine Tiefgarage bauen, können Sie diesen Raum in Zukunft nie mehr anders nutzen. Baut man oberirdisch, hat man die Möglichkeit, die Fläche später anderweitig nutzbar zu machen. Das wird bei vielen anderen Bauprojekten überall auf der Welt immer häufiger der Fall sein. Aber es war wahrscheinlich das erste Mal, dass solche Überlegungen durch die Forschungen des MIT in Singapur angestoßen wurden. Dies hat einen Teil des Entwurfs beeinflusst. Es gibt noch eine weitere interessante Komponente bei der Gebäudegestaltung, die mit der Forschung am MIT zusammenhängt. Wir haben Big Data verwendet, um zu messen, wie wichtig es ist, gemeinsame Räume zu entwickeln, in denen Menschen zusammenkommen können, in denen man das aufbauen kann, was man in der Soziologie schwache Bindungen (*weak ties*) nennt. Dabei handelt es sich nicht um starke Bindungen (*strong ties*) zu Menschen, mit denen man täglich zusammenarbeitet, sondern um Verbindungen zu anderen Menschen, die sich zufällig und unerwartet ergeben. Schwache Bindungen sind wichtig für Kreativität und die Entwicklung neuer Ideen. Der physische Raum des Büros ist wichtig für die Schaffung dieser schwachen Bindungen. Das gesamte Gebäude wurde um eine Reihe dieser schwachen Bindungen herum gebaut. Die Oase in der Mitte, der Gartenbereich, ist wie ein vertikaler europäischer Platz voller Grün. Hier können Menschen aus verschiedenen Communitys und von verschiedenen Arbeitsplätzen zusammenkommen. Auf diese Weise werden neue Verbindungen geschaffen, ein Ort, an dem Menschen andere Menschen treffen und der Natur begegnen können.

DAM: ***How can future projects benefit from this experience of CapitaSpring?***

BY: There's been a lot of conversations about the biophilic skyscraper, all the advantages of sitting and working next to greenery, having views both in and out. The CapitaSpring building is evidence that greenery and landscaping are not only aesthetic but also functional at multiple scales throughout the building, beginning with the scale of the urban farms on the top that grow 70 to 90 kilograms of produce a month for the three restaurants in the building. It's been so successful that the restaurants have asked to take over a much larger area of the rooftop. So, the greenery is in a way part of an economic unit within the life of the building. It also creates amenity spaces people can go to from the residences, from the office spaces – places to sit and enjoy working in an outdoor environment and stay connected to all the amenities and the support of the office. It's one of the reasons why, when the building was completed toward the very end of the pandemic, it opened with almost 100 percent occupancy in the office spaces, which I think is a testament to the value of this planning. At the scale of the city, we've pedestrianized the ground floor, the public realm, to facilitate more connectivity. CapitaSpring is now one of the most popular tourist spots because it is the highest free lookout point in Singapore, where you can enjoy a 360-degree view of the city. And that means that introducing all this greenery into the building has allowed it to perform at the scale of individual business units, of the large program components of the office, of the residences, but also in the context of the city and even the country as a driver for tourism. This wasn't our original plan, but that's one kind of unexpected outcomes we're really looking for as architects.

DAM: *Wie können künftige Projekte von dieser Erfahrung von CapitaSpring profitieren?*

BY: Es wird viel über biophile Wolkenkratzer gesprochen, über all die Vorteile, die es mit sich bringt, in der Nähe von Grünflächen zu sitzen und zu arbeiten und den Blick nach draußen und drinnen zu haben. CapitaSpring ist der Beweis dafür, dass Begrünung und Landschaftsgestaltung nicht nur ästhetisch, sondern auch funktional sind, und zwar auf verschiedenen Ebenen des Gebäudes, angefangen bei den urbanen Farmen auf dem Dach, die monatlich 70 bis 90 Kilogramm Obst und Gemüse für die drei Restaurants im Gebäude produzieren. Der Erfolg war so groß, dass die Restaurants darum gebeten haben, einen größeren Teil des Daches zu übernehmen. Die Begrünung ist also in gewisser Weise Teil einer wirtschaftlichen Einheit im Leben des Gebäudes. Sie schafft auch Annehmlichkeiten für die Menschen, die von den Wohnungen und Büros aus nach draußen gehen können, einen Ort, an dem sie sich hinsetzen und die Arbeit im Freien genießen können, während sie gleichzeitig mit allen Annehmlichkeiten und der Infrastruktur des Büros in Verbindung bleiben. Das ist einer der Gründe, warum das Gebäude bei seiner Fertigstellung gegen Ende der Pandemie mit einer fast hundertprozentigen Belegung der Büroräume eröffnet wurde, was meiner Meinung nach den Wert dieser Planung unterstreicht. Im Maßstab der Stadt haben wir das Erdgeschoss, den öffentlichen Raum, zur Fußgängerzone gemacht, um mehr Konnektivität zu schaffen. CapitaSpring ist jetzt einer der beliebtesten Touristenorte, weil es der höchste freie Aussichtspunkt in Singapur ist, von dem aus man einen 360-Grad-Blick auf die Stadt hat. Und das bedeutet, dass die Einführung dieser ganzen Begrünung des Gebäudes es ermöglicht hat, auf der Ebene der einzelnen Geschäftseinheiten, der großen Programmkomponenten der Büros, der Wohnungen, aber auch im Kontext der Stadt und sogar des Landes als Motor für den Tourismus zu wirken. Das war nicht unser ursprünglicher Plan, aber das ist eines der unerwarteten Ergebnisse, nach denen wir als Architekt:innen wirklich suchen.

37/1
Chef of one of the restaurants harvesting herbs in the rooftop garden
Koch aus einem der Restaurants bei der Ernte von Kräutern im Dachgarten

37/2
Outdoor area of the restaurant on the top floor
Außenbereich des Restaurants im Dachgeschoss

37/3
Entrance and outdoor area of the restaurants in the Green Oasis on the 17th floor
Eingang und Außenbereich zur Gastronomie in der Green Oasis im 17. Obergeschoss

DAM: ***We have noticed that this three-story garden you're referring to, is now a tourist hotspot. Do the guests of the Citadines Raffles Place Hotel, located inside the building, and the office workers use the garden space? What is your experience?***

CR: Le Corbusier said, "Architecture is wrong, life is right." Life will always surprise you with something you didn't expect. The space is used differently now. We thought it would be just a place for different communities to meet inside the building. But the data has been appropriated, it has become a place where lots of tourists go. This is a surprise, but a good surprise. Every project develops with different input. You start with a concept, and it evolves. CapitaSpring was enriched by different inputs. Some of the images show features from the very beginning. The green had not yet fully developed. If you go there now, you see how all the greenery inside the building, in the façade, in the spring space, and at the top has taken over. This is what we wanted to achieve from the beginning.

DAM: *Uns ist aufgefallen, dass der dreistöckige Garten, den Sie erwähnten, jetzt ein Hotspot für Tourist:innen ist. Nutzen die Gäst:innen des Citadines Raffles Place Hotels, das sich im Gebäude befindet, und die Büroangestellten ebenfalls den Gartenbereich? Wie sind Ihre Erfahrungen?*

CR: Le Corbusier sagte: „Die Architektur hat Unrecht, das Leben hat Recht." Das Leben steckt voller Überraschungen. Der Bereich wird jetzt anders genutzt. Wir dachten, dass sich hier nur die verschiedenen Communitys innerhalb des Gebäudes treffen würden. Aber das ist nicht der Fall, das Gebäude ist zu einem Ort geworden, den viele Tourist:innen besuchen. Das ist eine Überraschung, aber eine positive. Jedes Projekt nimmt einen anderen Verlauf. Man fängt mit einem Konzept an, und es entwickelt sich weiter. CapitaSpring ist durch unterschiedliche Einflüsse bereichert worden. Einige der Bilder zeigen Details aus der Anfangszeit. Das Grün war noch nicht voll entwickelt. Wenn Sie jetzt hingehen, sehen Sie, wie sich das Grün im Inneren des Gebäudes, an der Fassade, in der Oase und auf dem Dach ausgebreitet hat. Genau das war von Anfang an unser Ziel.

38/1
Stefan Jäger in conversation with Brian Yang
Stefan Jäger im Gespräch mit Brian Yang

38/2
Peter Körner, Silke Schuster-Müller (DekaBank), Kim Herforth Nielsen (jury chair), and Peter Cachola Schmal in Copenhagen
Peter Körner, Silke Schuster-Müller (DekaBank), Kim Herforth Nielsen (Juryvorsitz) und Peter Cachola Schmal in Kopenhagen

38/3
Carlo Ratti in an online interview
Carlo Ratti im Online-Interview

38/4
Peter Cachola Schmal and Brian Yang looking at a model of CapitaSpring
Peter Cachola Schmal und Brian Yang am Modell von CapitaSpring

39/1
Office of Bjarke Ingels Group in Copenhagen
Büro der Bjarke Ingels Group in Kopenhagen

39/2
Bjarke Ingels in an interview
Bjarke Ingels im interview

DAM: *To what extent was BIG's landscape department involved in this project?*

BY: We basically defined the initial concept for all the landscape, the idea of a kind of spiral of green spaces, the lush landscaping. We worked closely with a Singapore firm, Coen, who were the landscape architects of record, to look at the availability of photosynthetically active radiation (PAR) and to understand what that meant for the planting range, how you could place different plants in different areas. We learned a lot of very interesting things, like what they call the leaf architecture, how the scale and size of a plant's leaves relates to how high up you can place it in the building because it has an impact on how the plants interact with the wind at different levels.

DAM: *What was your experience with the URA in Singapore?*

CR: I think the URA in Singapore is doing a great job. They're looking at the research on cities and translating it into real projects. Our Senseable City Lab at MIT has been working with the URA a lot before CapitaSpring. They take the city as a place to experiment with, from digital twins to the future of traffic, to different scenarios about the future and how these can be implemented. We already started implementing them today.

DAM: *Inwieweit war die Landschaftsplanungsabteilung von BIG an diesem Projekt beteiligt?*

BY: Wir haben im Grunde das ursprüngliche Konzept für die gesamte Landschaft, die Idee einer Spirale von Grünflächen und die üppige Landschaftsgestaltung festgelegt. Wir arbeiteten eng mit einem Büro in Singapur, Coen, zusammen, das für die landschaftsarchitektonische Gestaltung des Projekts verantwortlich war. Um die Verfügbarkeit von fotosynthetisch aktiver Strahlung (PAR) zu prüfen und zu verstehen, was das für die Bepflanzungspalette bedeutet, wie man verschiedene Pflanzen in verschiedenen Bereichen platzieren kann, lernten wir eine Menge interessanter Dinge. Wir erfuhren zum Beispiel, wie die sogenannte Blattarchitektur, d. h. der Maßstab und die Größe des Blattes einer Pflanze, damit zusammenhängen, wie hoch man sie im Gebäude platzieren kann, weil es einen Einfluss darauf hat, wie die Pflanzen auf verschiedenen Ebenen mit dem Wind interagieren.

DAM: *Welche Erfahrungen haben Sie mit der URA in Singapur gemacht?*

CR: Ich bin der Meinung, dass die URA in Singapur hervorragende Arbeit leistet. Die URA-Mitarbeitenden beschäftigen sich mit der wissenschaftlichen Erforschung von Städten und setzen die Erkenntnisse in konkrete Projekte um. Unser Senseable City Lab am MIT hat schon vor CapitaSpring viel mit der URA zusammengearbeitet. Die URA nutzt die Stadt als Experimentierfeld, vom digitalen Zwilling über die Zukunft des Verkehrs bis hin zu verschiedenen Zukunftsszenarien und wie diese umgesetzt werden können. Wir haben bereits heute mit der Umsetzung begonnen.

DAM: ***Do you think that CapitaSpring represents a new typology or a major trend of high-rise buildings?***

CR: In the 20th century, we tried to expand high-rise buildings but also cities into nature. Think of Broadacre City by Frank Lloyd Wright and the Cité Radieuse by Le Corbusier. These were towers extending into nature. Today's challenge is the opposite. It is about bringing nature closer to us in the center of our cities. There are different ways. Lots of experiments are underway. CapitaSpring is one of these experiments to blend nature and the built environment in our cities. It's about how people live and work, and how they connect with infrastructure, with the city, in particular, with the parking infrastructure. We are learning how to close the feedback loop. We're learning how people use things versus what we thought at the beginning. This kind of living interaction helps us to learn from the building and make it even better in the future.

DAM: ***In your opinion, what could European and American city planning authorities learn from Singapore?***

CR: Cities across the planet are experimenting with different dimensions. Singapore is experimenting a lot with the digital component. The city's digital twin started from the beginning. Other European cities are experimenting with other dimensions. Copenhagen is looking at sustainability and bringing nature back to the city. Boston is looking at cities and participation. Today there is a lot of innovation at the urban scale. Every city can contribute to this kind of overall innovation ecosystem by adding to and enriching the debate.

DAM: *Meinen Sie, dass CapitaSpring eine neue Typologie oder einen wesentlichen Trend bei Hochhäusern darstellt?*

CR: Im 20. Jahrhundert wurde versucht, Hochhäuser, aber auch Städte in die Natur zu erweitern. Denken Sie an Broadacre City von Frank Lloyd Wright und die Cité Radieuse von Le Corbusier. Das waren Türme, die sich in die Natur erstreckten. Heute besteht die Herausforderung darin, das Gegenteil zu erreichen. Es geht darum, die Natur ins Zentrum unserer Städte zu holen. Hier gibt es verschiedene Möglichkeiten. Es wird viel experimentiert. CapitaSpring ist eines dieser Experimente, um die Natur und die gebaute Umwelt in unseren Städten zu vereinen. Es geht darum, wie Menschen leben und arbeiten, wie sie mit der Infrastruktur, mit der Stadt und insbesondere mit der Parkplatzinfrastruktur verbunden sind. Wir lernen, wie wir die Feedbackschleife schließen können. Wir erfahren, wie die Menschen die Dinge nutzen, und zwar anders, als wir ursprünglich dachten. Diese Art der lebendigen Interaktion hilft uns, aus dem Gebäude zu lernen und es in Zukunft noch besser zu machen.

DAM: *Was könnten europäische und amerikanische Stadtentwicklungsbehörden Ihrer Meinung nach von Singapur lernen?*

CR: Städte auf der ganzen Welt experimentieren mit verschiedenen Kategorien. Singapur experimentiert viel mit der digitalen Komponente. Der digitale Zwilling der Stadt war von Anfang an dabei. Andere europäische Städte experimentieren mit anderen Aspekten. Kopenhagen setzt auf Nachhaltigkeit und holt die Natur zurück in die Stadt. Boston beschäftigt sich mit dem Thema Kommunen und Partizipation. Es gibt heute viele Innovationen auf städtischer Ebene. Jede Stadt kann zu dieser Art von übergreifendem Innovationsökosystem beitragen, indem sie die Debatte ergänzt und bereichert.

41/1
View of CapitaSpring from the Singapore River, framed by skyscraper classics by Kenzo Tange (UOB Plaza, on the left) and I. M. Pei (OCBC Centre, on the right)
Blick vom Singapore River auf CapitaSpring, eingerahmt von Hochhausklassikern von Kenzo Tange (UOB Plaza, links) und I. M. Pei (OCBC Centre, rechts)

CapitaLand
OCBC Bank

GNC

In Conversation with the City of Singapore

Im Gespräch mit der Stadt Singapur

Urban Redevelopment Authority of Singapore (URA)
FUN Siew Leng (Chief Urban Designer) &
Andrew Fassam (Senior Director)

Urban Redevelopment Authority of Singapore (URA)
FUN Siew Leng (Chef-Stadtplanerin) &
Andrew Fassam (Leitender Direktor)

FUN Siew Leng (FSL): The Urban Redevelopment Authority (URA) as a planning authority oversees all developments in Singapore. They all have to come through us. This site originally was a public parking garage for the surrounding area, right in the heart of our CBD, called the Raffles Place. It has one of the highest real estate values in the whole of Singapore. CapitaLand owned this parking garage with a hawker centre, which is like a food court, selling affordable food to the office workers in the area. This building was constructed in the 1970s. Over time, all the high-rise developments around it had come up. The garage was obviously a suboptimal use of the land on which it sat. CapitaLand approached us in 2007 and told us that they would like to redevelop this site and inquired about a lot of upsides to be granted in terms of the gross floor area (GFA) for transforming the infrastructure building into a mixed-use development comprising grade-A offices, serviced residences, and retail.

FUN Siew Leng (FSL): Die Urban Redevelopment Authority (URA) hat als Planungsbehörde die Aufsicht über alle Entwicklungen in Singapur. Sie müssen alle über uns abgewickelt werden. Auf diesem Gelände befand sich ursprünglich ein öffentliches Parkhaus für die Umgebung, direkt im Herzen unseres Central Business Districts (CBD), dem Raffles Place. Es besitzt einen der höchsten Immobilienwerte in ganz Singapur. Der Eigentümer CapitaLand betrieb dort neben dem Parkhaus ein *hawker centre*, das so etwas wie ein *food court* ist und den Büroangestellten in der Umgebung erschwingliche Mahlzeiten anbietet. Dieses Gebäude wurde in den 1970er Jahren gebaut. Im Laufe der Zeit wurden alle Hochhäuser in der Umgebung darum herum errichtet. Dadurch konnte das Grundstück, auf dem es steht, offensichtlich nicht mehr optimal genutzt werden. CapitaLand kam 2007 auf uns zu und teilte uns mit, dass sie das Grundstück gerne entwickeln würden und wir ihnen zahlreiche Vorteile in Bezug auf die Bruttogrundfläche (BGF) des Infrastrukturgebäudes für eine Mischnutzung mit erstklassigen Büros, *serviced residences* und Einzelhandel einräumen sollten.

42/1
Singapore's tropical climate not only presents specific challenges for architecture but also offers special opportunities.
Das tropische Klima Singapurs stellt nicht nur spezifische Anforderungen an die Architektur, sondern bietet zugleich auch besondere Möglichkeiten.

43/1+2
As part of the new development, the public spaces around the building have been redesigned and enhanced, not least through lush greenery.
Im Zuge des Neubaus wurden die öffentlichen Räume um das Gebäude neu gestaltet und nicht zuletzt durch üppige Begrünung aufgewertet.

44/1
Over 100 different types of fruit, vegetables, herbs, and flowers that grow in the rooftop garden are used by the restaurants in the building.
Über 100 verschiedene Arten Obst, Gemüse, Kräuter und Blumen, die im Dachgarten wachsen, werden von den Restaurants im Gebäude verwertet.

This sounded like a good opportunity to work with the owner and the architects to bring about a lot of good for the city and the area surrounding the site. With Singapore being a very small city-state where land is very scarce, we advocate optimization of land use. We were prepared to allow the gross floor area (GFA), or what we call the gross plot ratio (GPR), to increase significantly to match the surrounding office buildings. But in so doing, we wanted to make sure that this new development would provide a lot of public good. For example, CapitaLand and the architects had to provide an updated hawker centre within their development. Then we looked at the surrounding roads and felt that they should pedestrianize part of Market Street, which the building sits on, and reclaim that road as a park for people to enjoy because this is a very high-density environment. In addition, along Market Street itself, they had to do road dieting of the whole street outside of the site boundary, provide a cycle lane and a wider sidewalk, and plant more trees to enhance the public environment. And they also would have to design a very sustainable building to achieve the Green Mark Platinum, our green building rating system.

Das klang nach einer guten Gelegenheit, mit dem Eigentümer und dem Architekturbüro zusammenzuarbeiten und der Stadt und ihrer Umgebung etwas Gutes zu tun. Da Singapur ein sehr kleiner Stadtstaat ist, in dem Land knapp ist, befürworteten wir eine Optimierung der Flächennutzung. Wir waren bereit einzuwilligen, dass die Bruttogrundflächenzahl (BGF), die von uns so genannte Bruttogrundstücksverhältniszahl (*gross-plot ratio*, GPR), deutlich ansteigt und an die der umliegenden Bürogebäude angepasst wird. Dabei wollten wir jedoch sicherstellen, dass dieses neue Bauvorhaben einen bedeutenden Beitrag zum Gemeinwohl leistet. So musste zum Beispiel ein modernes *hawker centre* in dem Projekt untergebracht werden. Außerdem haben wir uns die umliegenden Straßen angesehen und waren der Meinung, dass ein Teil der Market Street, an der das Gebäude steht, als Fußgängerzone gestaltet und dass diese Straße in einen Park umgewandelt werden sollte. Die Menschen sollen sich an der Begrünung erfreuen, da es sich hier um eine sehr dicht bebaute Umgebung handelt. Darüber hinaus mussten die gesamte Market Street außerhalb der Grundstücksgrenzen verkehrsberuhigt, ein Fahrradweg und ein breiterer Gehweg angelegt und viele Bäume gepflanzt werden, um das öffentliche Umfeld aufzuwerten. Außerdem war zu berücksichtigen, dass die Errichtung eines nachhaltigen Gebäudes erforderlich war, um die höchste Stufe unseres Zertifizierungssystems für umweltfreundliche Gebäude, Green Mark Platinum, zu erreichen.

<u>DAM:</u> *How do you work with project developers to create such a high-quality building to contribute to the skyline of Singapore?*

<u>FSL:</u> We set up a Design Advisory Panel (DAP), overseen by me and comprising very established architects with relevant experience, to have a peer review with the client CapitaLand and the architects from BIG and CRA. The aim was to see how through their development they can realize a much better-quality public realm and elevate the whole area. We must all remember that every high-rise building touches the ground and the people around it. The street level is very important. We asked them to provide a privately owned public space called POPs, we call it a "city living room," a loungeroom, where people can just go, sit down, take a break, enjoy activities, and that could become a new covered, sheltered public space. Our weather is always hot and humid, with a lot of rain. Therefore, such a public space would be a very valuable contribution to the city and to the people. We wanted them to make Market Street a much better street with lots of active users so that when you walk, it's a very pleasant experience. We want to encourage people to walk, cycle, and use public transport. Also, Singapore prides itself on being a very green city with lots of trees, lots of plants, lots of landscaping. We required the developer to have a 100 percent landscape replacement within the building, meaning for every square meter of greenery or landscape on the ground that is taken away, they have to replace it within their development, such as on the Sky Terraces and the rooftop garden. You will have seen that CapitaSpring exhibits all this fantastic provisions and the top quality it brings to the CBD.

<u>DAM:</u> *Wie arbeiten Sie genau mit den Projektentwickler:innen zusammen, um solch ein hochwertiges Gebäude zu schaffen, das zur Skyline von Singapur beiträgt?*

<u>FSL:</u> Wir haben ein Design Advisory Panel (DAP) eingerichtet, das mir unterstellt ist. Das aus etablierten Architekt:innen mit einschlägiger Erfahrung bestehende Gremium führte mit der Bauherrschaft CapitaLand und den Architekt:innen von BIG und CRA ein Peer-Review durch, dessen Ziel es war herauszufinden, wie sich durch diese Entwicklung ein sehr viel hochwertiger öffentlicher Raum schaffen und so das gesamte Gebiet aufwerten lässt. Wir müssen immer bedenken, dass jedes Hochhaus den Boden und die Menschen in seiner Umgebung beeinflusst. Die Straßenebene ist sehr wichtig. Wir forderten BIG und CRA auf, einen öffentlichen Raum in Privatbesitz zu schaffen, den wir POPS (*privately owned public space*) nennen. Ein „Wohnzimmer der Stadt", ein Raum, wo die Menschen einfach hingehen, sich hinsetzen, eine Pause einlegen und Aktivitäten genießen können und der zu einem neuen überdachten, geschützten öffentlichen Raum werden kann. Unser Wetter ist immer heiß, feucht und niederschlagsreich. Daher ist ein solcher öffentlicher Raum ein richtig guter Beitrag für die Stadt und die Menschen. So sollte die Market Street zu einer attraktiveren Straße mit vielen aktiven Nutzer:innen werden und zu einem angenehmen Spaziergang einladen. Wir wollen die Menschen dazu ermutigen, zu Fuß zu gehen, das Fahrrad und die öffentlichen Verkehrsmittel zu nutzen. Außerdem ist Singapur stolz darauf, eine Stadt mit sehr viel Grün zu sein, mit vielen Bäumen, vielen Pflanzen und viel Landschaftsgestaltung. Unsere Vorgabe beinhaltete einen hundertprozentigen Landschaftsersatz innerhalb des Gebäudes, das heißt jeder Quadratmeter Grün oder Landschaft auf dem Boden, der weggenommen wurde, musste innerhalb des Projekts ersetzt werden, zum Beispiel in den Sky Terraces und auf dem Dachgarten. CapitaSpring erfüllt all diese besonderen Anforderungen und überzeugt mit höchster Qualität in Singapurs CBD, das haben Sie sicher gesehen.

DAM: ***Yes, it's very impressive. Of course, the architects are happy to go along with this astonishing way of mixing uses and the way the high-rise touches the ground, but what seems a bit more complicated is the role of the client. CapitaLand now has this fantastic place. The gardens, however, need a lot of maintenance, which they have to pay for, but they don't get revenue from the gardens because admission is free of charge. Where are the advantages for CapitaLand in the long run?***

FSL: Well, the garden that they provided, the Green Oasis right in the middle of the building, is exempted from the GFA computation, so they don't lose any leasable area. That is a very big incentive that we give as part of our policy to encourage such provisions. Over time, our clients have seen the value of creating such kind of products with a lot of greenery, a lot of public spaces for the larger community, including the office community, and they use it to brand their developments. I think it will all pay off for them in the end. The rooftop garden is even a kitchen garden, not an ornamental garden. There are several restaurants in the building that work with the gardener and the chefs to understand what is needed for their cuisine and grow these edible plants. That is a good story for the restaurants as well, because they all have a certain brand and a certain approach to their cuisine. This is like a farm-to-table kind of approach right here on site.

DAM: ***How do you cope with the point that this has now become a major tourist hotspot? This wasn't planned. It is practically impossible to be in the city for three days as a tourist and get a ticket for the two gardens because all the places are already booked up.***

FSL: Oh, I didn't know that. We didn't plan for it to become a major attraction. We just wanted to do something for the city. So, it's a good problem, I'll call it.

DAM: *Ja, das ist sehr beeindruckend. Natürlich sind die Architekt:innen mit dieser erstaunlichen Art der Nutzungsmischung und der Art, wie Gebäude und Boden aufeinandertreffen, einverstanden, aber was etwas komplizierter zu sein scheint, ist die Rolle der Bauherrschaft. Sie haben jetzt diesen fantastischen Ort, die Gärten brauchen viel Pflege, für die sie bezahlen müssen, aber sie bekommen keine Einnahmen aus den Gärten, weil der Eintritt kostenlos ist. Wo liegen die Vorteile für CapitaLand auf lange Sicht?*

FSL: Nun, der Garten, den sie zur Verfügung gestellt haben, die Green Oasis in der Mitte des Gebäudes, ist von der Berechnung der BGF ausgenommen, sodass sie keine vermietbare Fläche verlieren. Das ist ein sehr großer Anreiz, den wir im Rahmen unserer Politik zur Förderung dieser Art der Bereitstellung geben. Im Laufe der Zeit haben unsere Kund:innen den Wert solcher Projekte mit viel Grün und öffentlichen Räumen für die Allgemeinheit, auch für die Büroangestellten, erkannt und nutzen dies als Markenzeichen für ihr Projekt. Ich glaube, dass sich das am Ende auszahlt. Der Garten auf dem Dach ist sogar ein Nutzgarten, kein Ziergarten. Es gibt dort mehrere Restaurants, und es besteht eine Zusammenarbeit zwischen Gärtner und Chefkoch, sodass die für die Küche benötigten essbaren Pflanzen angebaut werden. Dies ist ein wichtiger Bestandteil des Brandings und des Konzepts der Küche. Die Restaurants verfolgen ein Farm-to-Table-Konzept.

DAM: *Wie gehen Sie damit um, dass dies nun ein wichtiger touristischer Hotspot geworden ist? Das war so nicht geplant. Es ist jetzt praktisch unmöglich, als Tourist:in drei Tage in der Stadt zu sein und eine Eintrittskarte für die beiden Gärten zu bekommen, weil alle Plätze bereits ausgebucht sind.*

FSL: Oh, das wusste ich nicht. Wir hatten nicht geplant, dass es zu solch einer großen Attraktion wird. Wir wollten einfach etwas für die Stadt tun. Es ist also ein erfreuliches Problem, ich nenne es mal so.

DAM: ***Yes, it is. Other clients are also looking at the building, evaluating it, and talking to you about their upcoming projects. What insights did you gain from this experience? And where is the future of Singapore's town planning heading?***

FSL: One of the things is that we must keep trying. We must be ambitious. Singapore started with the claim "Garden City," mainly greening a lot of streetscapes, planting a lot of trees. We have moved on. The next stage was the claim "City in a Garden." Not just "Garden City" but "City in a Garden." Now we are aiming to be the "City in Nature." The ambition is evolving. At each stage we learn what we can do, what we cannot do, how to do it in an efficient way, in a cost-effective way, and how to carry people along. You must educate people. How do you treat nature? We are now learning that sometimes there is a conflict between humans and wildlife. How do we deal with that? We find solutions, but such conflicts should not stop us from being ambitious. That's my message. We must keep at it, be ambitious, and strive for an even higher level of excellence all the time.

DAM: *Ja, das ist es. Auch andere Kund:innen schauen sich dieses Projekt an, bewerten es und sprechen mit Ihnen über ihre kommenden Projekte. Welche Erkenntnisse haben Sie aus dieser Erfahrung gewonnen? Und wohin geht die Zukunft der Stadtplanung in Singapur?*

FSL: Eine Erkenntnis ist, dass wir diesen Weg fortsetzen müssen. Wir müssen ehrgeizig sein. Singapur hatte zunächst den Anspruch, eine „Gartenstadt" (*garden city*) zu werden. Hauptsächlich wurden viele Straßenlandschaften bepflanzt, viele Bäume gepflanzt. Wir haben uns weiterentwickelt. Die nächste Stufe war der Anspruch „Stadt im Garten" (*city in a garden*). Nicht nur „Gartenstadt", sondern „Stadt im Garten". Jetzt wollen wir die „Stadt in der Natur" (*city in nature*) sein. Der Anspruch entwickelt sich weiter. In jeder Phase lernen wir, was möglich ist, was nicht möglich ist, wie wir es auf effiziente und kostengünstige Weise umsetzen und wir die Menschen mitnehmen können. Man muss die Menschen anleiten. Wie geht man mit der Natur um? Wir lernen jetzt, dass es manchmal zu Konflikten zwischen Menschen und Wildtieren kommt. Wie gehen wir damit um? Wir finden Lösungen, aber das sollte uns nicht davon abhalten, ehrgeizig zu bleiben. Das ist meine Botschaft. Wir müssen dranbleiben, ehrgeizig sein und immer wieder nach neuen Höchstleistungen streben.

47/1
The rooftop garden and the Green Oasis have already become so popular that visitors have to book free slots online in advance.
Der Dachgarten und die Green Oasis sind bereits so beliebt, dass Besucher:innen freie Slots vorab online buchen müssen.

Andrew Fassam (AF): We always see to it that the development is really a collaboration with the client and the design team. We can provide the overall vision, guide the urban environment, the development of the city, provide the necessary policies to encourage and facilitate the redevelopment of sites, and then work with the client who brings in the business side of things, what works in terms of the mix of uses. And with the design team bringing in the creative vision, the architectural design expertise. It's a long process. This one goes back to 2007. When we understand that there's an opportunity for redevelopment, we first do a lot of our own internal studies to investigate the site, to understand what can be realized. Before we assign a GFA to a site, we need to examine exactly and simulate what that outcome is. We look at guidelines to determine where the high-rise components should be located and where the vehicular access routes. The CapitaSpring site is quite a large site for the CBD. It provided an opportunity to look at introducing things like the city living room, which you couldn't have introduced on a smaller site. But it was also a very difficult configuration in terms of the shape of the site, like a water drop, with a large contiguous area and a tail that leads toward Singapore River. Once the design team is on board, we try to work out solutions to many of the identified conflicts. All the buildings within the main built-up areas will have a covered walkway that provides a sheltered connection. But then you must organize the public drop-off zone, the taxi points. How are these located and interface with pedestrians? One of the key things we worked on together, which is very successful, is the city living room. The main public space in this part of the CBD is Raffles Place itself, which has a certain character because of the open area around which you have the high-rise office buildings. Most of the sites are very small, very narrow, but built-up with high-rise buildings. The CapitaSpring site is also a very strategic site, because it's located just off the main Raffles Place area. It had a lot of heritage to it, a lot of positive association with office workers and people working in the CBD when it was a major parking garage and a popular hawker centre. It was a hub that we wanted to continue.

Andrew Fassam (AF): Wir sehen die Entwicklung immer als eine Zusammenarbeit mit der Bauherrschaft und dem Planungsteam. Wir können die Gesamtvision liefern, um das städtische Umfeld, die Entwicklung der Stadt und eine Reihe von Maßnahmen zur Förderung und Erleichterung der Neuentwicklung von Standorten zu steuern. Bei der Zusammenarbeit mit der Bauherrschaft, die die geschäftliche Sicht einbringt, geht es darum, was im Hinblick auf die Nutzungsmischung funktioniert. Dann kommt das Planungsteam mit seiner kreativen Vision und dem architektonischen Fachwissen hinzu. Das ist ein langwieriger Prozess, der in diesem Fall bis ins Jahr 2007 zurückreicht. Wenn wir merken, dass es eine Möglichkeit zur Umgestaltung gibt, führen wir zunächst intensive interne Studien durch, um den Standort zu untersuchen und herauszufinden, was realisiert werden kann. Bevor wir einem Standort eine BGF zuweisen, müssen wir genau prüfen und simulieren, wie das Ergebnis aussieht. Wir schauen uns Leitlinien an, um zu ermitteln, wo die Hochhauskomponenten hinkommen und wo die Zufahrtswege enden sollen. Das CapitaSpring-Gelände ist für den CBD ein recht großes Grundstück. Es bot die Möglichkeit, Dinge wie den City Room einzuführen, die man auf einem kleineren Grundstück nicht hätte einführen können. Die Konfiguration des Geländes stellte aber auch eine Herausforderung dar, da es die Form eines Wassertropfens mit einer großen zusammenhängenden Fläche und einem Ende, das zum Singapore River führt, besitzt. Als das Planungsteam an Bord kam, versuchten wir, Lösungen für viele der wahrgenommenen Konflikte zu finden. Alle Gebäude innerhalb der Hauptbebauung sollten über einen überdachten Gehweg verfügen, der eine geschützte Verbindung ermöglicht. Aber dann müssen die öffentlichen Haltestellen und die Taxistände organisiert werden. Wie sind diese anzuordnen und wie sieht die Schnittstelle zu den Fußgänger:innen aus? Eines der wichtigsten Dinge, an denen wir gemeinsam gearbeitet haben, war der City Room, der zu einem Erfolg wurde. Der wichtigste öffentliche Raum in diesem Teil des Stadtzentrums ist der Raffles Place selbst, der einen gewissen Charakter hat, weil es sich um einen offenen Bereich handelt, um den herum sich die Bürohochhäuser gruppieren. Die meisten Grundstücke sind sehr klein, sehr schmal, aber mit Hochhäusern bebaut. Es ist auch ein strategisch wichtiger Standort, weil er direkt am Raffles Place liegt. Der Ort hat eine lange Tradition und ist bei Büroangestellten und Menschen, die im Stadtzentrum arbeiten, mit positiven Erinnerungen an die Zeit besetzt, als er noch ein wichtiges Parkhaus und ein beliebtes *hawker centre* war. Diese Funktion als Knotenpunkt wollten wir erhalten.

49/1
Canopies provide covered walkways, sheltered from tropical sun and rain, to the surrounding buildings.
Überdachungen ermöglichen vor tropischer Sonne und Regen geschützte Fußwege zu den umliegenden Gebäuden.

<u>DAM:</u> *I especially like the roofed paths extending from the city living room across Market Street and in the direction of Church Street, under which you are sheltered from the rain as you walk to the buildings on the other side of the street.*

<u>AF:</u> Indeed. Within the city, there's a great emphasis on pedestrian connectivity. We look at a very dense area and at the efficient movement of people around the MRT (Mass Rapid Transit) stations. Several buildings are directly connected to the Raffles Place MRT station at basement level. People stream up and into the covered walkway network. All the buildings have a covered walkway around their perimeter, along the main frontages. Where the buildings have service roads in between them, we link up the covered walkways with what we call covered linkways to provide more continuous shelters. We studied the opportunity of whether we could integrate CapitaSpring into the underground pedestrian network and link it to Raffles Place MRT directly. As we couldn't realize that connection, we looked at how we could provide enhanced connectivity at street level. We really wanted to make sure that it's not just a connection on a block-by-block basis between buildings but a block-to-block connection that would then link back to the pedestrian network system around the MRT station.

<u>DAM:</u> *Besonders gut gefallen mir die überdachten Wege vom City Room über die Market Street und Church Street, unter denen man regengeschützt zu den nächsten Gebäuden auf der anderen Straßenseite gehen kann.*

<u>AF:</u> Ja, das stimmt. In der Stadt wird großer Wert auf Fußgängerverbindungen gelegt. Es geht hier um ein sehr dicht bebautes Gebiet und die effiziente Bewegung von Menschen rund um die MRT-Bahnhöfe (Mass Rapid Transit). Mehrere Gebäude sind direkt im Untergeschoss mit der MRT-Station Raffles Place verbunden. Die Menschen strömen nach oben und in das überdachte Fußgängernetz. Alle Gebäude verfügen über einen überdachten Gehweg entlang der Hauptfassaden. Dort, wo zwischen den Gebäuden Anliegerstraßen verlaufen, verbinden wir die überdachten Gehwege mit ebenfalls überdachten Straßenquerungen, um einen durchgängigen Schutz zu bieten. Wir hatten geprüft, ob wir CapitaSpring in das unterirdische Fußgängernetz integrieren und direkt mit der MRT-Station Raffles Place verbinden könnten. Da sich dies nicht realisieren ließ, haben wir uns überlegt, wie wir eine bessere Anbindung auf Straßenebene schaffen können. Damit soll sichergestellt werden, dass es sich nicht nur um eine blockweise Verbindung zwischen den Gebäuden handelt, sondern um eine Verbindung von Block zu Block, die dann wieder in das Fußgängernetz rund um die MRT-Station einfließt.

50/1+51/1
CapitaSpring in the evening sun
Abendsonne auf CapitaSpring

In Conversation with the Clients

Im Gespräch mit der Bauherrschaft

CapitaLand, Singapore
Gregory Chua (Project Director) &
LEE Yi Zhuan (Development Management)

CapitaLand, Singapur
Gregory Chua (Projektleiter) &
LEE Yi Zhuan (Entwicklungsmanagement)

DAM: ***How did the incentivizing of the URA work for CapitaLand?***

LEE Yi Zhuan (LYZ): If you take a look back at the existing program, there was originally a 10-story public car park with a hawker centre and some auxiliary retail. Over time, as new buildings got built around the area, resulting in intensified land use, there was a very good opportunity to intensify the land use on Market Street. A few years earlier, we had completed a similar project just across the road, known as CapitaGreen, which was previously also a public hub building. That was definitely not the best use of the prime property given its proximity to central Mass Rapid Transit (MRT) stations in Singapore. We had the opportunity to increase the plot ratio and build up to the maximum height of around 280 meters. The URA will provide you with additional incentives, such as additional GFA, for achieving certain Green Mark ratings in Singapore or having proximity to MRT stations. From our perspective, we do have other buildings within the Raffles Place area that we want to rejuvenate. The area was originally a straightforward office business district, a traditional CBD with a lot of office buildings built at a certain point in time.

Gregory Chua (GC): CapitaSpring is situated within Singapore's original Central Business District (CBD), with easy access to two MRT stations. And it is well connected to the major expressway, which provides a good link for drivers traveling back to the suburbs. We believe there is an opportunity to enhance the area by connecting a cycling path to the existing cycling network. This is a goal that Singapore agencies are actively pursuing.

DAM: *Wie haben die Anreize der URA für CapitaLand funktioniert?*

LEE Yi Zhuan (LYZ): Wenn man sich das bestehende Programm anschaut, gab es ursprünglich ein zehnstöckiges öffentliches Parkhaus mit einem *hawker centre* und einigen zusätzlichen Einzelhandelsgeschäften darin. Im Laufe der Zeit wurden in der Gegend neue Gebäude gebaut, und es bot sich daher eine sehr gute Gelegenheit, die Nutzung des Grundstücks an der Market Street zu intensivieren. Einige Jahre zuvor hatten wir ein ähnliches Projekt auf der gegenüberliegenden Straßenseite fertiggestellt, das unter dem Namen CapitaGreen bekannt ist und zuvor ebenfalls ein öffentliches Zentrum war. Angesichts der Nähe zu den zentralen MRT-Bahnhöfen (Mass Rapid Transit) in Singapur war das bestimmt nicht die beste Nutzung für ein erstklassiges Grundstück. Wir hatten die Möglichkeit, das Grundstücksverhältnis zu erhöhen, um bis zu einer maximalen Höhe von etwa 280 Metern bauen zu können. Und die URA bot uns zusätzliche Anreize. Wenn man zum Beispiel bestimmte Green-Mark-Ratings in Singapur erreicht oder sich in der Nähe von MRT-Bahnhöfen befindet, gibt es zusätzliche Bruttogrundfläche. Wir besitzen noch weitere Gebäude in der Gegend um den Raffles Place, die wir gerne verjüngen möchten. Es handelt sich um einen einfachen traditionellen Central Business District (CBD) mit vielen Bürogebäuden, die alle etwa zum gleichen Zeitpunkt gebaut wurden.

Gregory Chua (GC): CapitaSpring liegt im ursprünglichen CBD von Singapur, mit einfachem Zugang zu zwei MRT-Bahnhöfen. Außerdem ist es gut an die Hauptverkehrsstraßen angebunden, wovon die in den Vororten lebenden Pendler:innen, die das eigene Auto nutzen, profitieren. Wir sind der Meinung, dass das Gebiet durch den Anschluss eines Radwegs an das bestehende Radwegenetz aufgewertet werden kann. Dies ist ein Ziel, das die Behörden in Singapur aktiv verfolgen.

53/1
When lit up in the evening, the levels of the Green Oasis stand out even more clearly from the office and residential floors.
Bei abendlicher Beleuchtung heben sich die Etagen der Green Oasis noch deutlicher von den Büro- und Wohnetagen ab.

CapitaLand
citibank
Securities

DAM: ***You held a short competition with four firms for this project, from which the team of BIG and Carlo Ratti emerged as the winner. What was their advantage?***

GC: Our objective was to make CapitaSpring a vibrant vertical community. Our objective was to create flexible, sustainable, and technologically advanced workspaces. Our objective was to facilitate integration of commercial experts within the CBD, while also providing social spaces that foster a sense of community. Prior to the design pitching process, we engaged in brainstorming. Our objective was to establish a place-making initiative with the goal of fostering a vibrant, work-focused community. To attract a new generation of office workers and employees. It was essential that the project be unique. The CBD was lacking in green and naturally ventilated spaces. It was for this reason that we wanted to create natural indoor spaces and enhance the greenery. We realized that the majority of existing sky terraces within the CBD were simply landscaped spaces with no active use.

DAM: *Sie haben für dieses Projekt einen kurzen Wettbewerb mit vier Firmen durchgeführt, den das Team von BIG und Carlo Ratti gewonnen hat. Was war ihr Vorteil?*

GC: Unser Ziel war es, CapitaSpring zu einer lebendigen vertikalen Community zu machen. Es ging uns darum, flexible, nachhaltige und technologisch fortschrittliche Arbeitsräume zu schaffen. Ein weiteres Ziel bestand darin, die Integration von Fachleuten aus der Wirtschaft in den CBD zu erleichtern und gleichzeitig soziale Räume zu schaffen, die das Gemeinschaftsgefühl fördern. Vor dem Wettbewerbsverfahren haben wir ein Brainstorming durchgeführt. Dabei ging es darum, eine Placemaking-Initiative zu entwickeln und so eine lebendige, arbeitsorientierte Gemeinschaft zu fördern. Wir wollten eine neue Generation von Büroangestellten und Mitarbeitenden für den Standort begeistern. Daher musste das Projekt einzigartig sein. Im CBD fehlte es an grünen und natürlich belüfteten Räumen. Aus diesem Grund wollten wir natürliche Innenräume schaffen und die Grünflächen aufwerten. Wir stellten fest, dass die meisten bestehenden Dachterrassen im CBD einfach nur begrünte Flächen waren, die nicht aktiv genutzt wurden.

54/1
Entrance area to the residential floors
Eingangsbereich zu den Wohnetagen

54/2
Atrium extending through the serviced residences floors
Atrium durch die Etagen der *serviced residences*

55/1
Fitness trail and ...
Fitnessparcours und ...

55/2
... swimming pool for residents on the rooftop of the base section
... Schwimmbecken für die Bewohner:innen auf dem Dach des Sockelgebäudes

Furthermore, our objective was to create a tower that is forward-thinking and timeless. From a sustainability perspective, it was essential that the project contributes to the environment. In addition, we aim to adopt new technologies and a new way of working. All of these specific elements were included in the design brief. It was also necessary to maximize the building height. On top of that, we sought to create an original shape for the space. The design from BIG in collaboration with Carlo Ratti was very close to our initial design vision. So the hardware was there.

In terms of the software, there were ongoing reviews and discussions about how this Green Oasis can create user-friendly spaces for office users, guests of the serviced residences, and nearby workers. This would allow us to provide additional spaces for them within the densely populated CBD. That is why we have incorporated facilities such as yoga spaces and a Jungle Gym, among others. In terms of plant selection, we planted approximately 80,000 plants representing 130 different species with the aim of creating an additional space that will help to mitigate and reduce urban heat. Furthermore, it will enhance the wellness of the building users.

Darüber hinaus war es unser Ziel, einen zukunftsorientierten und zeitlosen Turm zu schaffen. Unter dem Gesichtspunkt der Nachhaltigkeit sollte das Projekt einen Beitrag zur Umwelt leisten. Des Weiteren wollten wir neue Technologien und eine neue Arbeitsweise einführen. All diese spezifischen Elemente wurden in die Entwurfsvorgaben aufgenommen. Es war auch notwendig, die Gebäudehöhe zu maximieren. Nicht zuletzt wollten wir eine originelle Form für den Raum schaffen. Der Entwurf von BIG in Zusammenarbeit mit Carlo Ratti kam unserer ursprünglichen Designvision sehr nahe. Die Hardware war also vorhanden.

In Bezug auf die Software gab es ständige Überprüfungen und Diskussionen darüber, wie diese Green Oasis benutzerfreundliche Räume für Büronutzende, Gäst:innen der *serviced residences* und in der näheren Umgebung Arbeitende schaffen kann. Dies würde es uns ermöglichen, ihnen in dem dicht besiedelten CBD zusätzliche Räume zur Verfügung zu stellen. Aus diesem Grund haben wir unter anderem Einrichtungen wie Yogaräume und ein Jungle Gym integriert. Was die Auswahl der Pflanzen betrifft, so haben wir etwa 80.000 Pflanzen aus 130 verschiedenen Arten gepflanzt, um einen zusätzlichen Raum zu schaffen, der zur Abmilderung und Reduktion der städtischen Hitze beiträgt. Außerdem wird er das Wohlbefinden der das Gebäude Nutzenden verbessern.

During the development process, the developers and the URA collaborated. We aligned our objectives with theirs. The URA was also working to fulfill their own planning and development guidelines. We are aware that BIG has a strong track record in place-making. They design environmentally friendly buildings that serve as unique public spaces. They have been supportive of including green spaces and renewable energy sources in the design. Carlo Ratti is renowned for his contributions to innovation, sustainability, and the future of design. The collaboration between the two was an excellent choice for constructing an office building that will serve as a model for the future city.

DAM: ***The gardens in the middle, referred to as the Green Oasis, and the gardens at the top are open to the public free of charge. As the owner, you are responsible for covering the costs of maintaining the gardens, including the operation of the lifts and the provision of additional personnel. Please describe your business model and the methods you use to offset these costs.***

LYZ: It is important to be aware that the distinction between the various asset classes and the different users within a building is becoming blurred. Newer buildings will no longer be designed for a single use. They will not be pure office buildings. We have to accommodate multiple needs in a seamless manner. Previously, the space was accessible only to occupants, and it was not open to the public. Naturally, we anticipated increased costs, which would have been inevitable regardless. The maintenance of the landscape is a requisite regardless of whether the space is open to the public or not. The time required for watering the plants would be the same.

Während des Entwicklungsprozesses arbeiteten die Entwickler:innen mit der URA zusammen. Wir stimmten unsere jeweiligen Ziele miteinander ab. Sie hatten schließlich auch ihre eigenen Planungs- und Entwicklungsrichtlinien zu erfüllen. Wir sind uns bewusst, dass BIG eine großartige Erfolgsbilanz im Placemaking haben. Sie entwerfen umweltfreundliche Gebäude, die als einzigartige öffentliche Räume fungieren. Sie setzten sich bei der Gestaltung für die Berücksichtigung von Grünflächen und erneuerbaren Energiequellen ein. Carlo Ratti ist bekannt für seine Beiträge zu Innovation, Nachhaltigkeit und der Zukunft des Designs. Die Zusammenarbeit zwischen den beiden war eine ausgezeichnete Wahl für den Bau eines Bürogebäudes, das als Modell für die Stadt der Zukunft dienen wird.

DAM: *Die Gärten in der Mitte, die sogenannte Green Oasis, und die Gärten im oberen Bereich stehen der Öffentlichkeit kostenlos zur Verfügung. Als Eigentümer sind Sie dafür verantwortlich, die Kosten für die Pflege der Gärten zu decken. Dies gilt auch für den Betrieb der Aufzüge und die Bereitstellung von zusätzlichem Personal. Bitte beschreiben Sie Ihr Geschäftsmodell und die Methoden, mit denen Sie diese Kosten ausgleichen.*

LYZ: Man muss sich darüber im Klaren sein, dass die Unterscheidung zwischen den verschiedenen Vermögensklassen und den verschiedenen Nutzergruppen innerhalb der Baurechte immer mehr verschwimmt. Neuere Gebäude werden nicht mehr für eine einzige Nutzung ausgelegt sein. Es wird keine reinen Bürogebäude mehr geben. Wir müssen eine Vielzahl von Bedürfnissen nahtlos unter einem Dach unterbringen. Bisher war der Raum nur für die Nutzer:innen zugänglich, nicht aber für die Öffentlichkeit. Natürlich haben wir mit höheren Kosten gerechnet, die aber in jedem Fall unvermeidlich gewesen wären. Die Pflege der Grünflächen ist ein Erfordernis, das unabhängig davon besteht, ob der Raum öffentlich zugänglich ist oder nicht, da die Pflege der Landschaftsrechte erforderlich ist. Der Zeitaufwand für die Bewässerung der Pflanzen wäre derselbe.

There are a few aspects we have considered. As previously stated, one of the initial design objectives was to have the capability to reach a maximum height of 280 meters. Once the massing of the various properties within the development had been completed, we proceeded to the next stage. The strategic placement of the Green Oasis in the middle of the development enabled us to lift the office section. The lowest office floor is located on Level 21, allowing the majority of office floors to rise above the height of the surrounding properties. This strategy has increased the value of the property and the potential to achieve higher rents. While opening the rooftop to the public comes at a cost, the office product is now more attractive. It is rare to find an observation deck with such impressive views. This is the highest observation deck in Singapore, and it is accessible to the public at no cost. It has become a destination in itself and also draws people to the restaurants. This, too, has a positive impact on the sales of our tenants in the building. It benefits them, and it's not a win-lose situation. By opening to the public, we provided people with the opportunity to experience our brand. Our tenants are also pleased to see that the building is well-known. We believe this is a win-win situation. The value created exceeds the additional costs incurred.

Wir haben einige Überlegungen angestellt. Wie bereits erwähnt, bestand eines der ersten Planungsziele darin, eine maximale Höhe von 280 Metern zu erreichen. Sobald die Massierung der verschiedenen Nutzungen innerhalb der Entwicklung abgeschlossen war, sind wir zur nächsten Phase übergegangen. Die strategische Platzierung der Green Oasis in der Mitte der Anlage ermöglichte es uns, den Büroanteil anzuheben. Die unterste Büroetage befindet sich auf Ebene 21, sodass die meisten Büroetagen die Höhe der umliegenden Grundstücke überragen. Diese Strategie steigerte den Wert der Immobilie und erhöhte das Potenzial für höhere Mieten. Auch wenn die Öffnung der Dachterrassen für die Öffentlichkeit mit Kosten verbunden ist, ist das Büroangebot nun attraktiver. Eine Aussichtsplattform mit einer derart beeindruckenden Aussicht findet man selten. Dies ist die höchste Aussichtsplattform in Singapur, die für die Öffentlichkeit kostenfrei zugänglich ist. CapitaSpring ist zu einem Ausflugsziel geworden und lockt die Menschen zugleich in die Restaurants. Das wirkt sich auch positiv auf den Umsatz unserer Mietparteien im Gebäude aus. Sie profitieren also alle davon. Als wir für die Öffentlichkeit geöffnet haben, haben wir den Menschen die Möglichkeit gegeben, unsere Marke zu erleben. Auch unsere Mieter:innen freuen sich, dass das Gebäude bekannt ist. Wir glauben, dass dies eine Win-win-Situation ist. Der geschaffene Wert übersteigt die Kosten.

57/1
Peter Cachola Schmal, Gregory Chua, and Brian Yang on site at CapitaSpring
Peter Cachola Schmal, Gregory Chua und Brian Yang vor Ort in CapitaSpring

DAM: ***How does your user management work? Do you know how many people use this building every day? Broken down by the different user groups, such as office workers, staff and visitors, tourists in the hotel, and the people visiting the garden areas.***

LYZ: Over the past twelve months, the average number of office tenants and visitors per day has been approximately 4,000 to 4,500. Regarding the Green Oasis and the rooftop, the number of visitors per month ranges from 15,000 to 20,000. This figure includes local residents, visitors to the restaurants, and tourists. With regard to the Citadines Raffles Place, we have almost 300 serviced residences of various sizes. The occupancy rate has been consistently high, with almost full occupancy on a regular basis.

GC: During the design phase, this issue was also identified. As a vertical city, it was essential to identify the types of user groups that would be present. From office tenants to visitors, maintenance staff, CBD workers going to the hawker centre, guests in the serviced residences, and tourists, our building will cater to a diverse range of users. We are pleased to see that our building attracts a large number of tourists, which is an unexpected outcome. The small site area is approximately 6,000 square meters. It is crucial to plan for all these user flows. We have implemented a seamless flow for regular office users using facial recognition technology. For visitors, we have implemented a QR code and app system to facilitate access to the office spaces. Given the limited site area, the space on Level 1 is of great value. Accordingly, we direct guests of the serviced residences to Level 9, where they are greeted by a spacious and welcoming lobby. Furthermore, we anticipate that the hawker centre will experience high traffic during lunch hours. One of the primary reasons for this design is to separate the flows to the offices and the hawker centre at opposite ends of the floor plan, thus reducing congestion. The specifics are based on the programming requirements of the various user groups. The green voids can be easily accessed by all relevant parties. In total, we have identified 36 different user groups that require separate programming in this vertical city.

DAM: *Wie funktioniert Ihre Benutzerverwaltung? Wissen Sie, wie viele Personen dieses Gebäude täglich nutzen? Aufgeschlüsselt nach den verschiedenen Nutzergruppen, wie Büroangestellte, Mitarbeiter:innen und Besucher:innen, Tourist:innen im Hotel sowie Besucher:innen der Gartenbereiche.*

LYZ: In den letzten zwölf Monaten lag die durchschnittliche Zahl der Büromieter:innen und Besucher:innen bei etwa 4.000 bis 4.500. Was die Green Oasis und die Dachterrasse betrifft, so liegt die Zahl der Besucher:innen pro Monat zwischen 15.000 und 20.000. Diese Zahl umfasst die Anwohner:innen, die Besucher:innen der Restaurants und die Tourist:innen. Das Citadines Raffles Place verfügt über fast 300 *serviced residences* unterschiedlicher Größe. Die Belegungsrate ist konstant hoch, es ist regelmäßig nahezu voll ausgelastet.

GC: In der Entwurfsphase wurde auch dieses Problem erkannt. Da es sich um eine vertikale Stadt handelt, war es von entscheidender Bedeutung zu ermitteln, welche unterschiedlichen Nutzergruppen sich dort aufhalten würden. Von Büromieter:innen über Besucher:innen, Wartungspersonal, im CBD Tätige, die das *hawker centre* besuchen, bis hin zu Anwohner:innen und Tourist:innen – unser Gebäude spricht eine Vielzahl von Nutzer:innen an. Wir freuen uns, dass unser Bauwerk auch bei Tourist:innen beliebt ist. Damit hatten wir nicht gerechnet. Die kleine Grundstücksfläche beträgt etwa 6.000 Quadratmeter. Die Planungen müssen all diese Nutzerströme einbeziehen. Wir nutzen Gesichtserkennungstechnologien, um einen nahtlosen Ablauf für normale Büronutzer:innen zu schaffen. Für Besucher:innen gibt es ein QR-Code- und App-System, das die Anmeldung für die Büroräume erleichtert. Angesichts der begrenzten Fläche des Grundstücks ist die Nutzung des Erdgeschosses von großem Wert. Dementsprechend leiten wir die Gäst:innen der *serviced residences* auf Ebene 9, wo sie von einer geräumigen und einladenden Lobby empfangen werden. Außerdem gehen wir davon aus, dass das *hawker centre* während der Mittagszeit stark frequentiert sein wird. Einer der Hauptgründe für diesen Entwurf ist die Trennung der Ströme zu den Büros und zum *hawker centre* an den gegenüberliegenden Enden des Grundstücks, um so Staus zu vermeiden. Die Einzelheiten beruhen auf den Programmierungsanforderungen der verschiedenen Nutzergruppen. Die grünen Zwischenräume sind für alle Beteiligten leicht zugänglich. Insgesamt haben wir 36 verschiedene Nutzergruppen identifiziert, die in dieser vertikalen Stadt eine separate Programmierung benötigen.

DAM: ***Given the complexity of this hybrid, mixed-use tower, I would like to inquire whether you are still developing pure office towers or if your focus has shifted to hybrid towers.***

LYZ: A review of CapitaLand's operations reveals a diversified portfolio across multiple sectors. Our focus extends to real estate and investment, as well as management and real estate development. We offer a comprehensive range of real estate expertise, encompassing the full spectrum of services. The development of any project must align with the specific location, ownership parameters, urban planning and design parameters set forth by the relevant authorities. It is not simply a hybrid mixed development. Additionally, we engage in the development of pure residential properties. We undertake integrated developments that incorporate shopping malls as well as residences. CapitaSpring also encompasses hospitality, office, and public spaces. The specific type of development depends on the nature of the land, the location, the characteristics of the surrounding community, and the characteristics of the precinct in which it is situated.

It is essential that we identify the best and most appropriate use for the entire area. Integrated developments are one of the areas that we can make a difference in. It requires a different level of proficiency and knowledge to integrate the various functions in the most seamless manner. Our company offers a comprehensive range of services, including investment, operations, growth and improvement, asset management, design management, and project management. We have a dedicated team of experts who oversee the entire product life cycle. This is a unique capability that other developers are unlikely to be able to replicate. We believe these projects will be more resilient. There was considerable debate about the CBD in Singapore and in many other cities. The presence of singular office uses results in a high daytime population, with a ghost town at night. Furthermore, they are susceptible to the same challenges and volatility in space utilization that many office developers face. Hybrid mixed developments offer a certain degree of resilience.

DAM: *Angesichts der Komplexität dieses hybriden, gemischt genutzten Turms möchte ich Sie fragen, ob Sie immer noch reine Bürotürme entwickeln oder ob sich Ihr Schwerpunkt auf hybride Türme verlagert hat.*

LYZ: Ein Blick auf die Aktivitäten von CapitaLand zeigt ein diversifiziertes Portfolio über mehrere Sektoren hinweg. Unser Schwerpunkt liegt auf Immobilien und Investitionen sowie auf der Verwaltung und Entwicklung von Immobilien. Wir bieten eine umfassende Palette von Immobilienkompetenzen, die das gesamte Spektrum an Dienstleistungen umfasst. Die Entwicklung eines jeden Projekts muss mit den spezifischen Standort-, Eigentums-, städtebaulichen und gestalterischen Vorgaben der zuständigen Behörden in Einklang gebracht werden. Es handelt sich nicht einfach um eine Hybrid- oder Mischentwicklung. Darüber hinaus beschäftigen wir uns auch mit der Entwicklung von reinen Wohnimmobilien. Wir führen integrierte Entwicklungen durch, die sowohl Einkaufszentren als auch Wohngebäude umfassen. CapitaSpring bietet auch Gastgewerbe, Büronutzung und öffentliche Räume an. Die spezifische Art der Entwicklung hängt von der Beschaffenheit des Grundstücks, dem Standort, den Merkmalen der unmittelbaren Umgebung und den Merkmalen des Viertels ab, in dem es sich befindet.

Es geht darum, dass wir die beste und angemessenste Nutzung für das gesamte Gebiet finden. Integrierte Projektentwicklungen sind einer der Bereiche, in denen wir etwas bewirken können. Es erfordert ein anderes Maß an Fähigkeiten und Wissen, um die verschiedenen Funktionen so nahtlos wie möglich zu integrieren. Unser Unternehmen bietet eine umfassende Palette von Dienstleistungen an, darunter Investitionen, Betrieb, Wachstum und Verbesserung, Asset-Management, Design-Management und Projektmanagement. Wir verfügen über ein engagiertes Team von Expert:innen, die den gesamten Produktlebenszyklus überwachen. Dies ist eine einzigartige Fähigkeit, über die andere Entwickler wahrscheinlich nicht so leicht verfügen. Wir glauben, dass diese Projekte widerstandsfähiger sein werden. In Singapur und in vielen anderen Städten gab es erhebliche Diskussionen über den CBD. Das Vorhandensein einzelner Büronutzungen führt dazu, dass sich tagsüber viele Menschen dort aufhalten, während der CBD nachts eine Geisterstadt ist. Außerdem ist die reine Büronutzung anfällig für die Herausforderungen und Schwankungen bei der Flächennutzung, mit denen viele Büroentwickler konfrontiert sind. Hybride, gemischt genutzte Entwicklungen bieten ein gewisses Maß an Widerstandsfähigkeit.

60/1+61/1
Escalators to the Market Street Hawker Centre
Aufgang zum Market Street Hawker Centre

Market Street
Hawker Centre Levels 2 & 3
Market Street
Hawker Centre

DAM: ***What key insights did you gain from the CapitaSpring project that will inform the future of your developments?***

GC: I was directly involved in this particular development from the initial design phase through to completion, spanning a seven-year period. The column-free office concept proved highly popular, with 100 percent occupancy achieved just a few months after the project's completion. Furthermore, the project achieved a 93 percent occupancy rate for commuters' office space upon completion. This provided us with confidence and a deeper insight into market requirements. From a development standpoint, it would be beneficial to engage some of the occupants as well as the stakeholders from the outset. This would ensure that we are aware of their requirements from the beginning. We engaged a diverse range of stakeholders, including architects, urban planners, maintenance and operations personnel, and leasing professionals, to ensure their voices were heard throughout the design and development process. This allowed us to create a solution that will already address many of the issues that the next team will face when taking over management and operations. This approach helps to avoid mistakes and time losses, and it minimizes the need for subsequent changes. The COVID-19 pandemic has demonstrated how rapidly the ways in which people use and perceive buildings can evolve. It is more important to embed as much flexibility as possible into the building form, rather than presetting a lot of things in the design that leave little room for maneuver. In considering the carbon footprint of demolishing existing skyscrapers and rebuilding them, it is essential to plan for the impact in order to ensure the property has the flexibility to have a meaningful and extended life cycle.

DAM: *Welche wichtigen Erkenntnisse haben Sie aus diesem Projekt CapitaSpring gewonnen, die Sie für Ihre zukünftigen Projekte nutzen werden?*

GC: An diesem Projekt war ich von der ersten Entwurfsphase bis zur Fertigstellung über einen Zeitraum von sieben Jahren direkt beteiligt. Das stützenfreie Bürokonzept erwies sich als äußerst populär, und bereits wenige Monate nach Fertigstellung des Projekts war es zu 100 Prozent ausgelastet. Darüber hinaus erreichte das Projekt bei Fertigstellung eine Belegungsrate von 93 Prozent bei Büroflächen für Pendler:innen. Dies gab uns Zuversicht und einen tieferen Einblick in die Marktanforderungen. Vom Entwicklungsstandpunkt aus gesehen war es von Vorteil, einige der Nutzer:innen sowie die Interessengruppen von Anfang an einzubeziehen. So konnten wir sicherstellen, dass wir über ihre Anforderungen von Anfang an Bescheid wussten. Wir haben ein breites Spektrum von Interessengruppen einbezogen, darunter Architekt:innen, Stadtplaner:innen, Wartungs- und Betriebspersonal und Vermietungsexpert:innen, um zu gewährleisten, dass ihre Stimmen während des gesamten Entwurfs- und Entwicklungsprozesses gehört wurden. Auf diese Weise konnten wir eine Lösung finden, die bereits viele der Probleme berücksichtigt, mit denen das nächste Team konfrontiert sein wird, wenn es die Verwaltung und den Betrieb übernimmt. Dieser Ansatz hilft, Fehler und Zeitverluste zu vermeiden, und er minimiert die Notwendigkeit späterer Änderungen. Die Covid-19-Pandemie hat gezeigt, wie schnell sich die Art und Weise, wie Menschen Gebäude nutzen und wahrnehmen, verändern kann. Es ist wichtiger, so viel Flexibilität wie möglich in die Gebäudeform zu integrieren, als viele Dinge im Entwurf vorzugeben, die später wenig Spielraum lassen. In Bezug auf den CO_2-Fußabdruck, den der Abriss und Wiederaufbau bestehender Wolkenkratzer hinterlassen, ist es von entscheidender Bedeutung, die potenziellen Auswirkungen im Voraus zu berücksichtigen, um sicherzustellen, dass das Gebäude die Flexibilität für einen sinnvollen und verlängerten Lebenszyklus besitzt.

63/1–3
Market Street Hawker Centre in the base of the building
Market Street Hawker Centre im Sockelgebäude

5

CapitaSpring ***Prize Winner*** *Preisträger*	**IQON Residences**	**Shenzhen Women & Children's Center**	**Valley**	**Bunker Tower**	
Singapore Singapur	**Quito, Ecuador**	**Shenzhen, China**	**Amsterdam, Netherlands** Niederlande	**Eindhoven, Netherlands** Niederlande	**Location** Standort
BIG – Bjarke Ingels Group Copenhagen, Denmark/ New York NY, USA Kopenhagen, Dänemark/ New York NY, USA; **CRA – Carlo Ratti Associati Turin, Italy/New York NY, USA** Turin, Italien/New York NY, USA	**BIG – Bjarke Ingels Group Copenhagen, Denmark/ New York NY, USA** Kopenhagen, Dänemark/ New York NY, USA	**MVRDV Rotterdam, Netherlands** Niederlande	**MVRDV Rotterdam, Netherlands** Niederlande	**Powerhouse Company Rotterdam, Netherlands** Niederlande	**Architects** Architekt:innen
CapitaLand; Mitsubishi Estate	**Uribe Schwarzkopf**	**Shum Yip Group**	**EDGE**	**RED Company; Being Development**	**Client** Bauherrschaft
Mixed use comprising offices, residential, hospitality Mischnutzung aus Büros, Wohnen, Gastronomie	**Residential, offices** Wohnen, Büros	**Mixed use comprising healthcare facilities for women and children, education and learning facilities, hotel, retail** Mischnutzung aus Einrichtungen für das Wohlergehen von Frauen und Kindern, Bildungs- und Lehreinrichtungen, Hotel, Einzelhandel	**Residential, offices** Wohnen, Büros	**Residential, offices, restaurant** Wohnen, Büros, Restaurant	**Main use** Hauptnutzung
280 m	**130 m**	**108 m**	**100 m**	**100 m**	**Height** Höhe
September 2022	**December 2022** Dezember 2022	**September 2023**	**September 2022**	**October 2022** Oktober 2022	**Completion** Fertigstellung
Page 16 Seite 16	**Page 66** Seite 66	**Page 72** Seite 72	**Page 78** Seite 78	**Page 84** Seite 84	**Detailed information** Ausführliche Informationen

Finalists
Finalisten

Criteria:
- good neighbor (urban integration, enriching its surroundings)
- technological and engineering excellence
- sustainability (in all aspects)
- pioneering design / architecture
- cost efficiency and affordability (social impact)
- ESG

They jury members agreed that the challenges in high-rise construction can be summed up as the need to greenify, the need to densify, and the need to use what's already in place to the greatest possible extent.

Combining all three needs is the task facing architects and urban planners alike from now on, and it was in light of this that jury chair Kim Herforth Nielsen set out the main criteria the jury would apply when assessing the total of 31 projects. Over and above beauty and technical ingenuity, the jury's assessment was thus based specifically on the social value of each project as a "good neighbor," its sustainable character, how innovative it is in solving local issues, and whether it offered a good, future-proof design. Against this backdrop, the jury process required three rounds, whittling the 31 buildings first down to six towers, then down to five, before finally choosing the winning high-rise.

Kriterien:
- Gute Nachbarschaft (städtebauliche Integration, bereichernde Ergänzung für die Umgebung)
- Technologische und konstruktive Spitzen-leistungen
- Nachhaltigkeit (in jeder Hinsicht)
- Wegweisende(s) Design / Architektur
- Kosteneffizienz und Bezahlbarkeit (soziale Auswirkungen)
- ESG

Die Jurymitglieder vertraten übereinstimmend die Auffassung, dass sich die Herausforderungen im Hochhausbau als die Notwendigkeit zur Begrünung, Verdichtung und maximalen Nutzung des Vorhandenen zusammenfassen lassen.

Alle drei Aspekte miteinander zu verbinden, ist die Aufgabe, der sich Architekt:innen und Stadtplaner:innen in Zukunft stellen müssen. Vor diesem Hintergrund legte der Juryvorsitzende Kim Herforth Nielsen die Hauptkriterien fest, nach denen die Jury die insgesamt 31 Projekte bewertete. Neben dem ästhetischen und technischen Einfallsreichtum ging es der Jury demnach vor allem um den sozialen Wert des jeweiligen Projekts als „guter Nachbar", um seinen nachhaltigen Charakter, um die innovative Lösung lokaler Probleme und um eine gute, zukunftsfähige Gestaltung. Unter Berücksichtigung dieser Kriterien wählte die Jury in drei Runden aus den 31 Gebäuden zunächst sechs und dann fünf Hochhäuser aus, bevor sie schließlich den Preisträger kürte.

BIG – Bjarke Ingels Group

IQON Residences

Quito, Ecuador

Since the relocation of the international airport to an outlying district a good ten years ago, Quito, which was originally characterized by low-rise and sprawling buildings, has been growing upwards. With the brutalist-looking IQON Residences, the skyline of the burgeoning Ecuadorian capital gains a residential and office high-rise full of character set against the spectacular backdrop of the surrounding Andes. Situated on the edge of La Carolina Park, a city forest with expansive parklands in Quito's business district, the city's tallest high-rise offers unobstructed views of the park and the Pichincha volcano.

Seit der Verlegung des internationalen Flughafens in einen Außenbezirk vor gut zehn Jahren wächst das ursprünglich eher niedrig und ausufernd bebaute Quito in die Höhe. Mit den brutalistisch anmutenden IQON Residences gewinnt die Skyline der aufstrebenden ecuadorianischen Hauptstadt ein charaktervolles Wohn- und Bürohochhaus vor der spektakulären Kulisse der die Stadt umgebenden Anden. Am Rande des Parks La Carolina gelegen, einem Stadtwäldchen mit großzügigen Parkanlagen im Geschäftsviertel Quitos, bietet das höchste Hochhaus der Stadt einen unverbaubaren Blick auf den Park und den Vulkan Pichincha.

Architects Architekt:innen	**BIG – Bjarke Ingels Group Copenhagen, Denmark/ New York NY, USA** Kopenhagen, Dänemark/ New York NY, USA
Project architects Projektarchitekt:innen	**Bjarke Ingels, Thomas Christoffersen, Lucia Sanchez Ramirez, Stephanie Choi**
Project team Projektteam	**Francesca Portesine, Amir Mikhaeil, Andrea Di Pompeo, Angel Barreno Gutierrez, Beat Schenk, Bell Cai, Benjamin Caldwell, Benjamin Novacinski, Chengjie Jacob Li, Claire Djang, Clara Sanfeliu, Deb Campbell, Douglass Alligood, Jan Leenknegt, Jason Wu, Josiah Poland, Juan David Ramirez, Ma Ning, Magdalena Narkiewicz, Margaret Tyrpa, Maria Sole Bravo, Megan Ng, Peter Sepassi, Rune Wriedt, Sebastian Grogaard, Sijia Zhou, Stephanie Mauer, Stephen Kwok, Terrence Chew, Tracy Sodder, Ziad Shehab**
Architects of record Lokale Architekt:innen	**Uribe Schwarzkopf**
Client Bauherrschaft	**Uribe Schwarzkopf**
Structural engineers Tragwerksplanung	**René Lagos Engineers; Fernando Romo Consultores**
MEP Haustechnik	**Consel; Incoayam; Trialmech**
Landscape architects Landschaftsarchitekt:innen	**BIG – Bjarke Ingels Group; Uribe Schwarzkopf**
Height Höhe	**130 m**
Stories Geschosse	**32**
Site area Grundstücksfläche	**2200 m²**
Building footprint Bebaute Fläche	**1300 m²**
Gross floor area Bruttogeschossfläche	**55 000 m²**
Structure Konstruktion	**Reinforced concrete** Stahlbeton
Completion Fertigstellung	**December 2022** Dezember 2022
Main use Hauptnutzung	**Residential, offices** Wohnen, Büros

67/1
View from La Carolina Park to the residential tower
Blick aus dem Park La Carolina auf den Wohnturm

The building's form follows the geometric contours of the site, which is shaped like a mirror-inverted "L." At the corner, the façade fans out on both sides, creating a curve from which the individual stacked apartments with their terraces protrude like pixels. Each terrace is planted with greenery and a tree, whose planter extends into the apartment below as a funnel-shaped sculpture. Once the native trees and plants outgrow their planters, they can be relocated to green spaces throughout the city and replaced with new greenery cultivated on site. Ideally, IQON Residences will thus become not only a vertical extension of La Carolina Park but also part of a city-wide green cycle.

Der Baukörper folgt dabei den geometrischen Vorgaben des Grundstücks in Form eines spiegelverkehrten „L". An der Ecke fächert sich die Fassade zu beiden Seiten auf – es entsteht eine Rundung, aus der sich die einzelnen übereinandergestapelten Wohnungen mit ihren Terrassen wie Pixel herausschieben. Jede Terrasse ist begrünt und mit einem Baum bepflanzt, dessen Pflanzgefäß als trichterförmige Wohnskulptur in die jeweils darunterliegende Wohnung ragt. Sobald die einheimischen Bäume und Pflanzen aus ihren Pflanzgefäßen herausgewachsen sind, können sie in Grünflächen in der ganzen Stadt umgesetzt und durch neue, ebenfalls vor Ort kultivierte Pflanzen ersetzt werden. Im Idealfall werden die IQON Residences so nicht nur zu einer vertikalen Fortsetzung des Parks La Carolina, sondern zu einem stadtweiten Bindeglied in einem grünen Kreislauf.

68/1
Access to the building
Zugang zum Gebäude

68/2
From the balconies of Quito's tallest high-rise building, one can overlook the entire capital of Ecuador.
Von den Balkonen des höchsten Hochhauses Quitos kann man die gesamte Hauptstadt Ecuadors überblicken.

69/1
Each residential unit has at least one balcony.
Jede der Wohneinheiten verfügt über mindestens einen Balkon.

69/2
The floor-to-ceiling glazing of the living rooms additionally creates a strong connection to the outdoors.
Die raumhohe Verglasung der Wohnräume schafft zusätzlich einen starken Außenbezug.

Quito's temperate, perpetually spring-like climate – the city is located around 20 kilometers south of the equator – makes it possible to operate the high-rise building without insulation, air conditioning or heating systems. The raw exposed concrete characterizes the building's lively look, while serving as a structural framework. In addition, the concrete provides thermal regulation by retaining heat at night and cooling during the day. Each floor is made up of apartments extending across the entire depth of the building, thus featuring terraces on both the north and south façades – naturally facilitating cross-ventilation. The 215 residential units are composed of three contemporary apartment types of varying sizes, complemented by communal leisure facilities such as a spa and squash court. The ground floor, which includes a public plaza, retail spaces, and artworks, connects the park to the rest of the neighborhood via a new pathway. Inside, marble, green shades, and blackened steel set subtle accents in combination with the dominant exposed concrete.

Das gemäßigte, stets frühlingshafte Klima von Quito – die Stadt liegt rund 20 Kilometer südlich des Äquators – macht es möglich, dass das Hochhaus ohne Isolierung, Klimaanlage oder Heizung auskommt. Der rohe Sichtbeton prägt den lebendigen Look des Gebäudes und verleiht ihm zugleich Struktur. Zudem sorgt der Beton für thermischen Ausgleich, indem er nachts die Wärme hält und tagsüber kühlt. Jedes Stockwerk besteht aus durchgesteckten Wohneinheiten, die sowohl an der Nord- als auch an der Südfassade über Terrassen verfügen – Querlüftung natürlich inklusive. Die 215 Wohnungen setzen sich aus drei unterschiedlich großen, zeitgemäßen Wohnungstypen zusammen, die durch gemeinschaftliche Freizeitflächen wie Spa oder *squash court* ergänzt werden. Das Erdgeschoss umfasst eine öffentliche Plaza, Einzelhandelsflächen und Kunst – und verbindet über eine neue Durchwegung den Park mit dem Rest des Viertels. Im Inneren setzen Marmor, grüne Farbtöne und geschwärzter Stahl im Zusammenspiel mit dem dominierenden Sichtbeton feine Akzente.

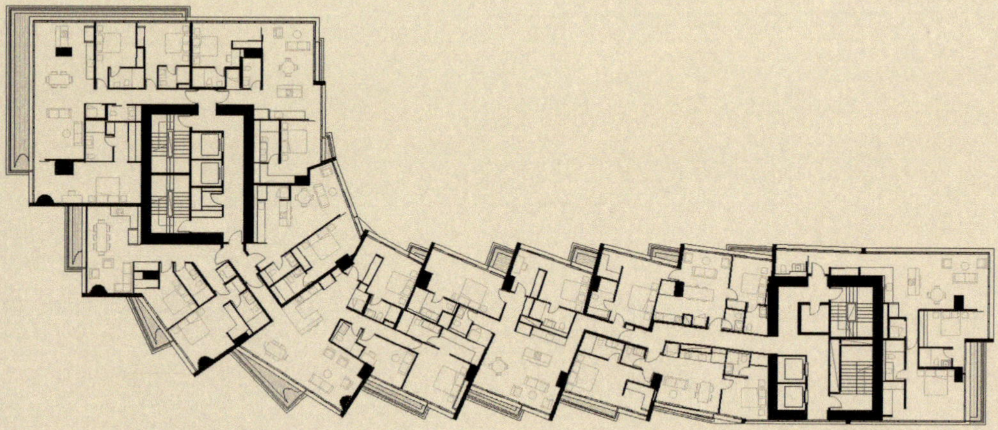

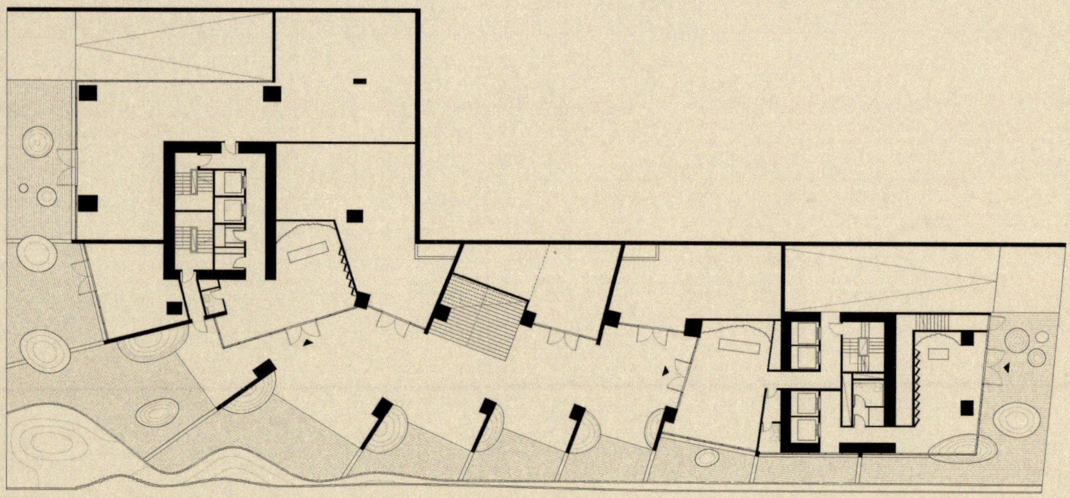

70/1
Detail of façade section
Detail Fassadenschnitt

70/2
Standard floor plan
Grundriss Regelgeschoss

70/3
Ground floor plan
Grundriss Erdgeschoss

71/1
Entrance hall
Eingangshalle

71/2
Rooftop terrace with swimming pool
Dachterrasse mit Swimmingpool

Sustainability certifications:
EDGE
Sustainability:
cross-ventilated apartments; no heating or cooling required due to heat equalization through structured concrete façade; greenery with native trees and plants serves as an urban tree farm

Nachhaltigkeitszertifizierung:
EDGE
Nachhaltigkeit:
Wohnungen mit Querlüftung; kein Heiz- oder Kühlbedarf aufgrund des Wärmeausgleichs durch strukturierte Betonfassade; Begrünung mit standortgerechten Bäumen und Pflanzen dient als städtische Baumschule

Jury statement

The jury was impressed by this residential tower in many ways. Its configuration adds surprising spatial qualities to such buildings through the use of an elegant, curved shape, meaning that form enhances function. The floor plans of the individual apartments are optimally aligned to the outside world thanks to the curvature, with each and every unit enjoying optimal views on the two main sides of the structure. This alignment of layouts has a second benefit: it allows for cross ventilation, leading to a significant reduction in heating/cooling requirements and thus emissions and costs. As the tallest apartment building in Quito, it sets an example for urban densification, while insisting on simplicity, doffing its hat to early Brutalism in the process.

Jurystatement

Dieser Wohnturm hat die Jury in mehrfacher Hinsicht überzeugt. Die elegante, geschwungene Form verleiht dem Gebäude überraschende räumliche Qualitäten, sodass die Form die Funktion verstärkt. Durch die Rundung sind die Grundrisse der einzelnen Wohnungen bestmöglich zur Außenwelt ausgerichtet: Jede Einheit an den beiden Hauptseiten des Gebäudes bietet optimale Ausblicke. Diese Grundrissorientierung hat aber noch einen zweiten Vorteil: Sie ermöglicht eine Querlüftung, die den Heiz- und Kühlbedarf und damit die Emissionen und Kosten deutlich reduziert. Als höchstes Wohngebäude von Quito ist es ein Beispiel für urbane Verdichtung; dabei setzt es auf Schlichtheit und orientiert sich am frühen Brutalismus.

Shenzhen Women & Children's Center

Shenzhen, China

To achieve China's self-imposed commitment to be carbon-neutral by 2060, the National Development and Reform Commission has launched a revitalization model program comprising 24 projects. As part of this, MVRDV transformed a 1994 office tower into a colorful skyscraper hosting a hotel and a wide range of facilities for the well-being of women and children. Due to fire safety issues and poor energy performance, the building had previously stood empty for a long time.

Um Chinas selbst auferlegte Verpflichtung, bis 2060 CO_2-neutral zu sein, realisieren zu können, wurde durch die National Development and Reform Commission ein 24 Projekte umfassendes Modellprogramm für Revitalisierung gestartet. Im Zuge dessen haben MVRDV einen 1994 errichteten Büroturm in einen farbenfrohen Wolkenkratzer mit Hotelnutzung sowie einem breiten Angebot für das Wohl von Frauen und Kindern transformiert. Probleme beim Brandschutz und schlechte energetische Werte ließen das Projekt zuvor lange leer stehen.

72/1
Existing building from the 1990s
Bestandsgebäude aus den 1990er Jahren

73/1
Due to the new façade, the building is hardly recognizable after its revitalization.
Aufgrund der neuen Fassade ist das Gebäude nach der Revitalisierung kaum wiederzuerkennen.

Architects Architekt:innen	**MVRDV** **Rotterdam, Netherlands** Niederlande
Project architects Projektarchitekt:innen	**Jacob van Rijs, Wenchian Shi**
Project team Projektteam	**Lorenzo Mattozzi, Marco Gazzola, Giuseppe Mazzaglia, Fokke, Moerel, Pim Bangert, Giovanni Nardi, Daehee Suk, Chi Zhang, Siyi Pan, Bertrand Tan, Albert Parfonov, Andrius Ribikauskas, Enrica Perrot, Martina Franco, Peter Chang, Luca Xu, Apsara Flury, Fredy Fortich, Jiameng Li, Agnieszka Dabek, Paula Vargas Torres, Elisa Paneni, Yang Hong, Leo Zhang, Huang Cai, Echo Zhai, Ruochen Zhang**
Architects of record Lokale Architekt:innen	**Shenzhen General Institute of Architectural Design and Research**
Client Bauherrschaft	**Shum Yip Group**
Structural engineers Tragwerksplanung	**Yuanlizhu Engineering Consultants**
MEP Haustechnik	**Shenzhen General Institute of Architectural Design and Research**
Landscape architects Landschaftsarchitekt:innen	**MVRDV; Shenzhen General Institute of Architectural Design and Research**
Height Höhe	**108 m**
Stories Geschosse	**28**
Site area Grundstücksfläche	**12 527 m²**
Gross floor area Bruttogeschossfläche	**57 900 m²**
Structure Konstruktion	**Reinforced concrete** Stahlbeton
Completion Fertigstellung	**September 2023**
Main use Hauptnutzung	**Mixed use comprising healthcare facilities for women and children, education and learning facilities, hotel, retail** Mischnutzung aus Einrichtungen für das Wohlergehen von Frauen und Kindern, Bildungs- und Lehreinrichtungen, Hotel, Einzelhandel

MVRDV's sustainable and economical concept aimed to redesign the existing structure without major structural interventions, allowing only small necessary additions. The focus was particularly on the new façade and some spatial adjustments. The one-meter-deep aluminum frames placed in front of the façade not only protect against views from outside but also provide extra shading to reduce heat gain inside the building. At the same time, the interior of the building is still provided with sufficient natural light and fresh air.

The bright colors on the façade are also used inside. Yellow, orange, pink, and green guide visitors through the building, creating a welcoming atmosphere. The location of various functional units such as a library, children's theater, or "discovery hall" is also communicated to the outside through color. In the multicolored plinth, the facilities for women and children stand out visually from the hotel use above.

In front of the building, physical and visual barriers were removed, and the former parking lot in the courtyard was transformed into a lively public space with a playground, cafés, and restaurants. Featuring barrier-free access and a multi-faceted spatial program, the project quickly became a social center in the business-dominated environment.

The revitalization of the building preserved and reused 80 percent of the original concrete structure. The thus achieved carbon saving equates to the amount produced by nearly 12,000 flights from Amsterdam to Shenzhen. It is expected that in the economically flourishing and rapidly growing metropolis, numerous adaptive repurposing projects for buildings from the same era will soon follow this project's example.

Das nachhaltige und wirtschaftliche Konzept von MVRDV sah vor, den Bestand ohne größere strukturelle Eingriffe umzugestalten und nur möglichst kleine Ergänzungen vorzunehmen. Der Fokus lag dabei insbesondere auf der neuen Fassade und einigen räumlichen Anpassungen. Die einen Meter tiefen, vorgelagerten Aluminiumrahmen der Fassade schützen nicht nur vor Blicken von außen, sondern reduzieren auch die Sonneneinstrahlung und die damit verbundene Aufheizung des Gebäudes. Gleichzeitig können noch immer ausreichend natürliches Licht und frische Luft in das Gebäudeinnere gelangen.

Dort finden sich auch die bunten Farben der Fassade wieder. Gelb, Orange, Rosa und Grün leiten die Besucher:innen durch das Gebäude und schaffen eine freundliche Atmosphäre. Die Verortung der verschiedenen Nutzungseinheiten wie unter anderem Bibliothek, Kindertheater oder Erlebnishalle wird durch die Farbe auch nach außen kommuniziert. Die Einrichtungen für Frauen und Kinder heben sich im farbenfrohen Sockel optisch deutlich von der darüberliegenden Hotelnutzung ab.

Vor dem Gebäude wurden physische und visuelle Barrieren beseitigt, der frühere Parkplatz im Innenhof wurde in einen belebten, öffentlichen Raum mit Spielplatz, Cafés und Restaurants umgewandelt. Durch den schwellenlosen Zugang und das vielschichtige Raumprogramm fungiert das Projekt bereits nach kurzer Zeit als soziales Zentrum in der geschäftlich geprägten Umgebung.

Durch die Revitalisierung des Gebäudes konnten 80 Prozent der ursprünglichen Betonstruktur erhalten und wiederverwendet werden. Das dadurch eingesparte CO_2 entspricht ungefähr der Menge, die bei knapp 12.000 Flügen zwischen Amsterdam und Shenzhen entsteht. Es ist davon auszugehen, dass in der wirtschaftlich florierenden und dadurch schnell wachsenden Metropole bereits in nächster Zeit analog zu diesem Projekt eine Vielzahl an adaptiven Umnutzungen von Gebäuden derselben Ära erfolgen wird.

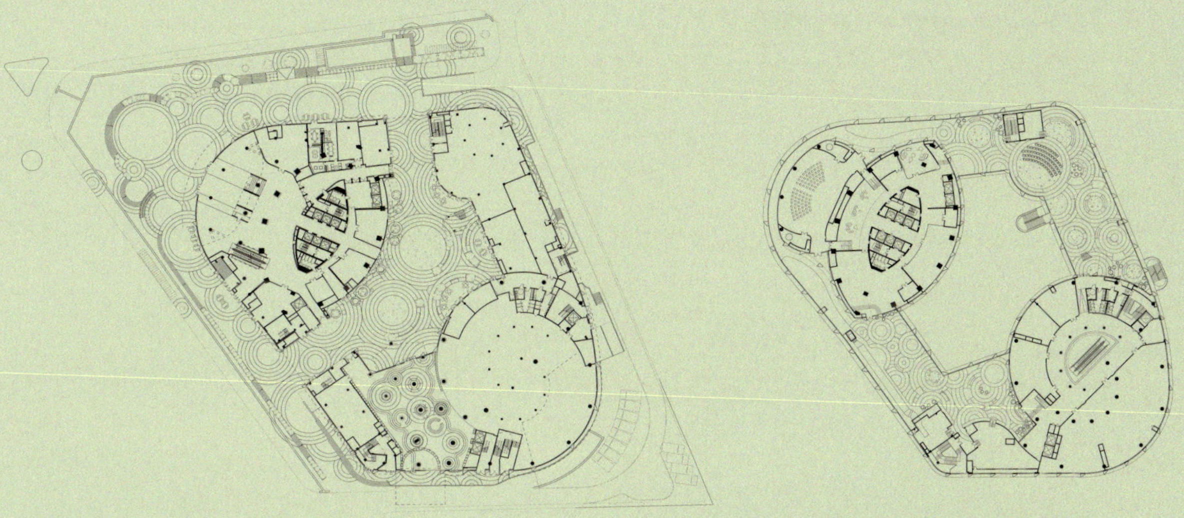

Sustainability:
carbon savings through the reuse of 24,000 m³ of concrete; grid of multi-colored exterior frames providing extra shading to reduce thermal heat gain; extensive natural ventilation

Nachhaltigkeit:
Einsparung an CO_2 durch die Wiederverwendung von 24.000 m³ Beton; Raster aus verschiedenfarbigen Außenrahmen bietet zusätzlichen Sonnenschutz zur Reduzierung des Wärmeeintrags; großflächige natürliche Belüftung

75/1
Ground floor and 5th floor plans
Grundrisse Erdgeschoss und 5. Obergeschoss

75/2
The new façade brings color to the rather drab surroundings.
Die neue Fassade bringt Farbe in die eher triste Umgebung.

75/3
The color concept not only extends across the façade but also consistently across the roof areas of the base and the courtyard.
Dabei zieht sich das Farbkonzept nicht nur über die Fassade, sondern auch konsequent über die Dachflächen des Sockels und den Innenhof.

Jury statement

The project is, the jury felt, a strong indication that the People's Republic of China is progressing rapidly in its efforts to address the issue of an ageing first generation of high-rises while paying attention to preserving the gray energy of existing structures. The jury was taken by the eye-catching colorful and cheerful appearance given to the new old build. It brings a breath of fresh air to the neighborhood, creating an urban space for all, and is very well integrated into the urban fabric. It's made for connecting people. Overall, the revitalization has resulted in a beautiful building.

Jurystatement

Nach Ansicht der Jury ist das Projekt ein deutliches Zeichen dafür, dass die Volksrepublik China in ihren Bemühungen, das Problem der in die Jahre gekommenen ersten Generation von Hochhäusern anzugehen und gleichzeitig dafür zu sorgen, dass die graue Energie der bestehenden Bausubstanz erhalten bleibt, rasch vorankommt. Die Jury war von der auffallend farbenfrohen und heiteren Gestaltung des neuen Altbaus angetan. Der Wolkenkratzer bringt frischen Wind in das Viertel, schafft einen urbanen Raum für alle und ist städtebaulich sehr gut integriert. Er verbindet die Menschen. Insgesamt ist durch die Revitalisierung ein attraktives Gebäude entstanden.

76/1+4
Although there were few changes to the internal building structure, the elaborate interior design lends the high-rise a completely new appearance.
Obwohl wenig in die innere Gebäudestruktur eingegriffen wurde, lässt die aufwendige Innenarchitektur das Gebäude gänzlich neu erscheinen.

76/2+3
Publicly accessible courtyard
Innenhof mit öffentlichem Zugang

77/1
Section
Schnitt

77/2
The colorful concept was also applied in the hotel rooms.
Das bunte Farbkonzept setzt sich auch in den Hotelzimmern fort.

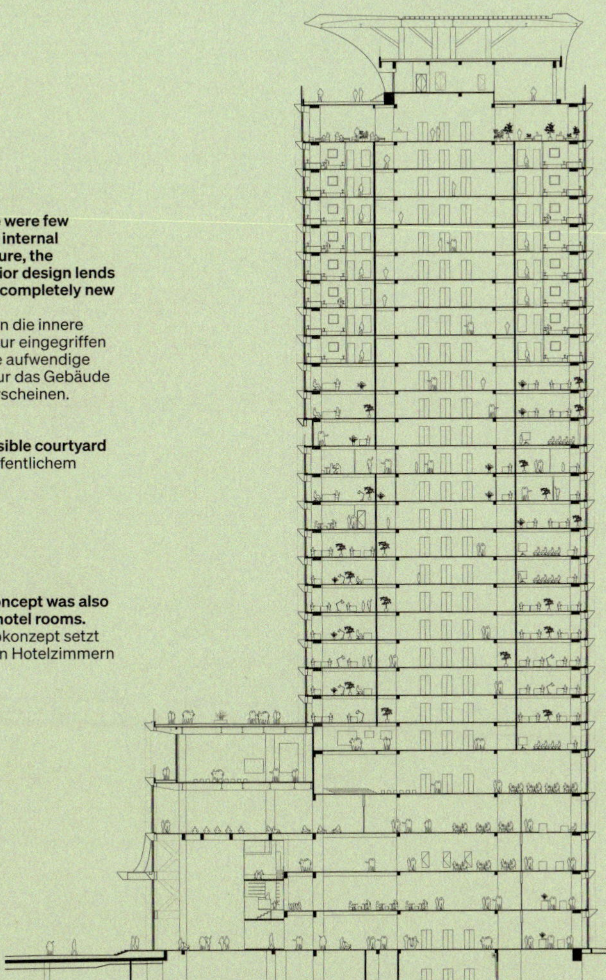

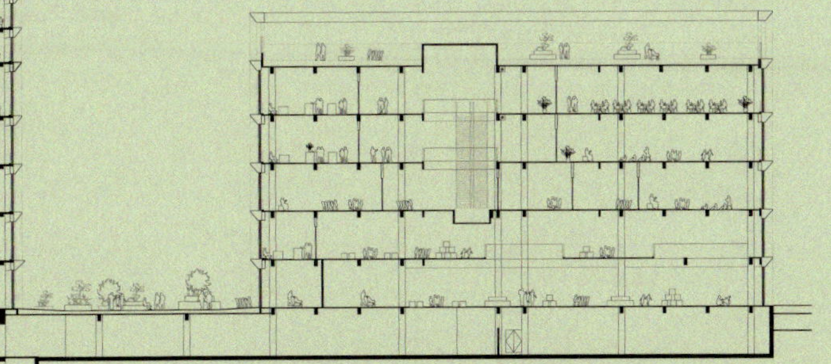

MVRDV

Valley

Amsterdam, Netherlands Niederlande

Architects Architekt:innen	**MVRDV, Rotterdam, Netherlands** Niederlande
Project architects Projektarchitekt:innen	**Winy Maas**
Project team Projektteam	**Competition** Wettbewerb: **Jeroen Zuidgeest, Anton Wubben, Luca Moscelli, Sanne van Manen, Elien Deceuninck, Marco Gazzola, Jack Penford Baker, Brygida Zawadzka, Francis Liesting, Annette Lam, Hanna Knudsen** **Design team** Planungsteam: **Gideon Maasland, Gijs Rikken, Guido Boeters, Wietse Elswijk, Saimon Gomez Idiakez, Rik Lambers, Javier Lopez Menchero, Sanne van Manen, Stephanie McNamara, Thijs van Oostrum, Frank Smit, Boudewijn Thomas, Maria Vasiloglu, Laurens Veth, Cas Esbach, Mark van Wasbeek, Olesya Vodenicharska, Leo Stuckardt, Arnd van Waart**
Architects of record Lokale Architekt:innen	**Inbo**
Client Bauherrschaft	**EDGE**
Structural engineers Tragwerksplanung	**Van Rossum Raadgevende Ingenieurs**
MEP Haustechnik	**Deerns**
Landscape architects Landschaftsarchitekt:innen	**Piet Oudolf; Deltavormgroep**
Height Höhe	**100 m**
Stories Geschosse	**26**
Site area Grundstücksfläche	**5840 m²**
Building footprint Bebaute Fläche	**5336 m²**
Gross floor area Bruttogeschossfläche	**75 000 m²**
Structure Konstruktion	**Reinforced concrete** Stahlbeton
Completion Fertigstellung	**September 2022**
Main use Hauptnutzung	**Residential, offices** Wohnen, Büros

Amsterdam's Zuidas neighborhood is to be transformed from a pure office environment into a mixed-use district. Surrounded by highways and previously developed in an architecturally rather stereotypical manner, Valley stands out as a solitaire, impressively embodying the desired transformation. Externally, the building blends unobtrusively into the office environment with its mirrored glass façade. Internally, the mixed-use high-rise reveals its namesake appearance: rising from a common base are three rock-like towers with a deep valley winding between them. The contrast to the smooth exterior façade could not be greater – warm natural stone, abundant greenery, and spectacular projections and recesses characterize the interior view.

Das Amsterdamer Stadtviertel Zuidas soll von einer reinen Bürostadt in ein gemischtes Quartier umgewandelt werden. Autobahnumtost und bislang eher stereotyp bebaut, verkörpert das Valley als Solitär die erwünschte Transformation auf eindrucksvolle Weise. Nach außen fügt sich das Gebäude mit seiner verspiegelten Glasfassade unauffällig und kühl in die Büroumgebung ein. Nach innen zeigt das mischgenutzte Hochhaus sein namensgebendes Antlitz: Über einem gemeinsamen Sockel erheben sich drei felsenartige Türme, die von einem tiefen Tal zerschnitten sind. Der Kontrast zur glatten Außenfassade könnte größer nicht sein – warmer Naturstein, viel Grün und spektakuläre Vor- und Rücksprünge charakterisieren die Innenansicht.

78/1
Accessible to all, the footpaths wind their way up to the actual valley between the three towers.
Für alle zugänglich schlängeln sich die Fußwege hinauf ins eigentliche Valley zwischen den drei Türmen.

Two external stone staircases make the valley accessible to everyone directly from the street level up to the 5th and 6th floors. Like a hiking trail, the public path meanders through the rugged "landscape" of the Valley. At its bottom are two small water pools that – doubling as skylights – allow daylight to enter the lobby below, the so-called Grotto. It is also clad in natural stone and connects restaurants, shops, cultural areas, and the offices located on the floors above.

Around 200 apartments, all differing in size, layout, and view, are distributed from the 8th floor upwards. Almost all of them feature a balcony or terrace, while in the remaining flats, floor-to-ceiling folding glass walls create a connection to the outside. On the top two floors, a panoramic bar affords a sweeping view over Amsterdam.

Parametric design tools were used to optimize factors such as privacy, thermal insulation, structure, daylighting, and wind protection for the complex building. These tools also enabled the determination of the seemingly random pattern of over 40,000 stone tiles of different dimensions. Furthermore, a matrix was used to select the right plants for each location in the building, taking into account criteria such as wind, sunlight, temperature, and maintenance. The trees and plants on the terraces are maintained by an automatic irrigation system and by "façade gardeners." Nesting boxes for birds and bats as well as bee and insect hotels promote biodiversity all year round. The landscaping developed specifically for the high-rise is intended to have a positive impact on the well-being of the people living and working in the Valley.

Zwei steinerne Außentreppen machen das Tal direkt von der Straße aus bis zum 5. bzw. 6. Obergeschoss für alle zugänglich. Wie ein Wanderweg schlängelt sich der öffentliche Weg durch die zerklüftete „Landschaft" des Valley. An dessen Boden befinden sich zwei kleine Seen, die als Oberlicht die darunter befindliche Lobby, die sogenannte Grotte, mit Tageslicht versorgen. Sie ist ebenfalls mit Naturstein verkleidet und verbindet Restaurants, Geschäfte, Kulturflächen und die in den Stockwerken darüberliegenden Büros miteinander.

Ab dem 8. Obergeschoss verteilen sich die rund 200 Wohnungen, die sich alle in Größe, Zuschnitt und Ausblick unterscheiden. Fast alle verfügen über einen Balkon oder eine Terrasse, in den übrigen Wohnungen lässt sich der Außenbezug über raumhohe Glasfaltwände herstellen. In den beiden obersten Geschossen bietet eine Panoramabar einen weiten Blick über Amsterdam.

Um für das komplexe Gebäude Faktoren wie Privatsphäre, Wärmeschutz, Struktur, Tageslicht sowie Windschutz zu optimieren, wurden parametrische Entwurfswerkzeuge verwendet. Sie ermöglichten es auch, das scheinbar zufällige Muster von über 40.000 Steinfliesen unterschiedlicher Dimension zu erstellen. Weiterhin kam eine Matrix zur Auswahl der richtigen Pflanzen für jeden Standort im Gebäude zum Einsatz; dabei wurden Kriterien wie Wind, Sonnenlicht, Temperatur und Pflege berücksichtigt. Die Bäume und Pflanzen auf den Terrassen werden von einem automatischen Bewässerungssystem und von „Fassadengärtner:innen" gepflegt. Brutkästen für Vögel und Fledermäuse sowie Bienen- und Insektenhotels fördern die ganzjährige Artenvielfalt. Die eigens für das Hochhaus entwickelte Landschaftsgestaltung soll eine positive Wirkung auf das Wohlbefinden der Menschen haben, die im Valley leben und arbeiten.

The public valley
Das öffentliche Valley

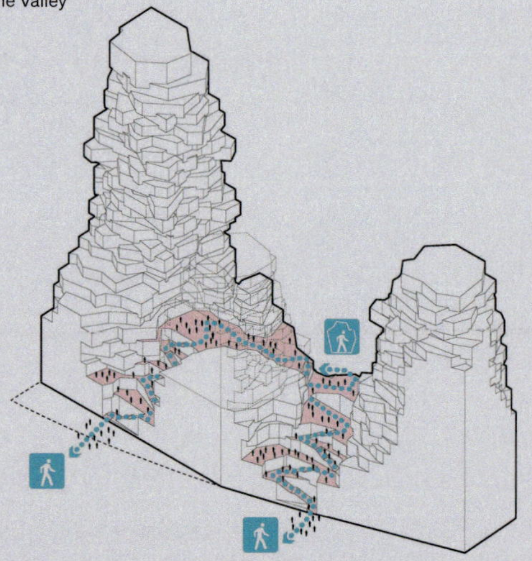

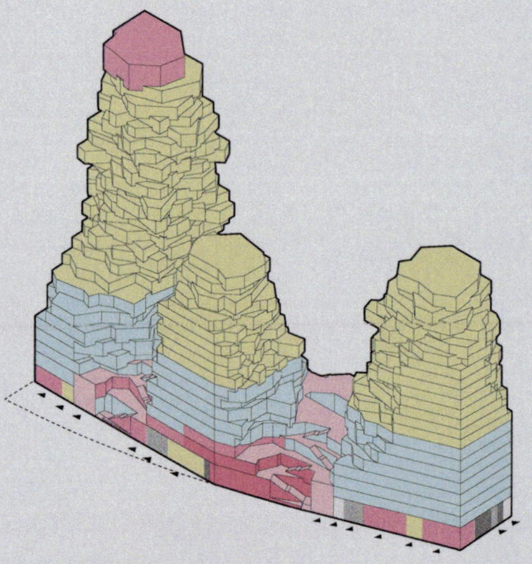

Utilization program
Nutzungsprogramm

- **Housing** Wohnen
- **Offices** Büros
- **Valley**
- **F & B / retail** Gastronomie und Geschäfte
- **Culture** Kultur
- **Parking** Parken
- **Bike parking** Fahrradgarage
- **Technical spaces** Technikräume

80/1
The public valley
Das öffentliche Valley

80/2
Utilization program
Nutzungsprogramm

81/1
The smooth exterior façade mediates between the jagged interior façade and the surrounding office buildings.
Die glatte Außenfassade vermittelt zwischen der zerklüfteten Innenfassade und den umliegenden Bürogebäuden.

81/2
Section
Schnitt

Sustainability certifications: BREEAM Excellent; 8 out of 10 rating on the GPR Building Scale
Sustainability: IP-based building automation systems and various sensors to monitor usage; façade material made from recycled stone; landscaping and vegetation concept based on ecological and biodiversity criteria; offices designed for potential conversion into residential units; photovoltaic system

Nachhaltigkeitszertifizierung: BREEAM Excellent; 8 von 10 Punkten im GPR-Bewertungssystem
Nachhaltigkeit: IP-basierte Gebäudeautomationssysteme und verschiedene Sensoren zur Überwachung der Nutzung; Fassadenmaterial aus recyceltem Stein; Landschaftsgestaltung und Vegetationskonzept basierend auf ökologischen und biodiversitätsrelevanten Kriterien; Büroräume sind für eine mögliche Umwandlung in Wohneinheiten konzipiert; Photovoltaikanlage

82/1
The stacking of the varying floor plans creates a heterogeneous mountain landscape.
Durch die Stapelung der variierenden Grundrisse entsteht eine heterogene Gebirgslandschaft.

82/2
The Grotto
Die Grotte

82/3 As diverse as the floor plans are, so are the resulting terraces with their respective views.
So unterschiedlich wie die Grundrisse sind die daraus resultierenden Terrassen mit den jeweiligen Blickbeziehungen.

83/1
The water areas illuminate the Grotto below.
Über die Wasserflächen wird die darunterliegende Grotte beleuchtet.

83/2
5th floor plan
Grundriss 5. Obergeschoss

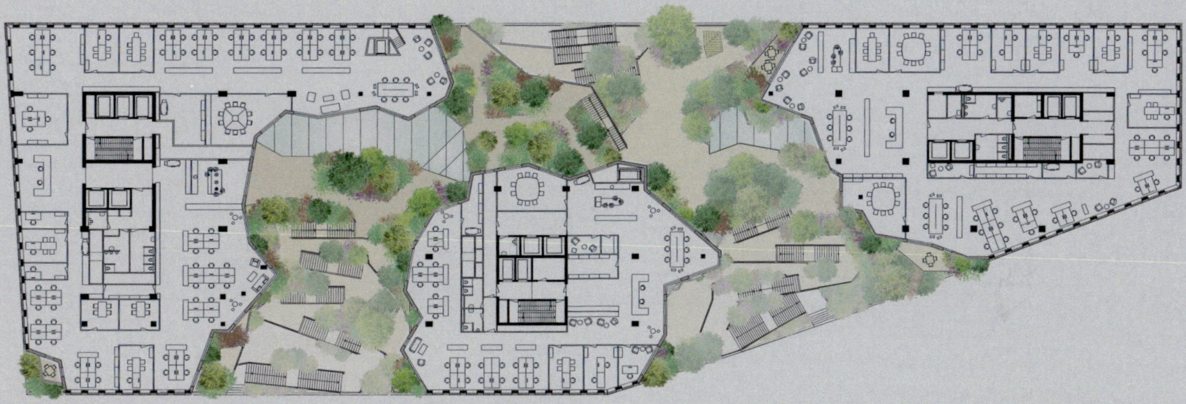

Jury statement

Valley is a project that "plays with the contrast between the sharp outer façade and the more randomized inner structure creating a livable vertical village. A project that animates and humanizes an otherwise cold business area." Parts of the building have been consciously opened to the public in such a way as to offer visitors views of the surroundings that would otherwise only be available to tenants. Valley brings the typology of a high-rise down to a very livable and individual scale, by ensuring that each apartment is unique thanks to the parametric design and enjoys its own greenery.

Jurystatement

Valley ist ein Projekt, das „mit dem Kontrast zwischen der strengen Außenfassade und der eher zufälligen inneren Struktur spielt und so ein lebenswertes vertikales Dorf entstehen lässt. Ein Projekt, das ein ansonsten kaltes Geschäftsviertel belebt und menschlicher macht." Teile des Gebäudes wurden bewusst für die Öffentlichkeit geöffnet, um Besucher:innen Einblicke in die Umgebung zu ermöglichen, die sonst nur den Bewohner:innen vorbehalten sind. Valley führt die Typologie des Hochhauses auf ein sehr wohnliches und individuelles Maß zurück, indem es dafür sorgt, dass jede Wohnung dank des parametrischen Entwurfs unterschiedlich gestaltet ist und über eine eigene Begrünung verfügt.

Powerhouse Company

Bunker Tower

Eindhoven, Netherlands Niederlande

The former student union building of Eindhoven University of Technology was built in 1969 in the Brutalist style, designed by Huig Maaskant, one of the most renowned Dutch architects of the 20th century. The building quickly developed into an important social center for students and soon became known as "De Bunker" because of its architecture. Thus, the structure combines significant architectural historical value with special social and cultural relevance.

Das ehemalige Studierendenwerk der Technischen Universität Eindhoven wurde 1969 nach den Plänen von Huig Maaskant, einem der bekanntesten niederländischen Architekten des 20. Jahrhunderts, im Stil des Brutalismus erbaut. Schnell entwickelte sich das Gebäude zu einem wichtigen sozialen Zentrum für die Studierenden und wurde bald wegen seiner Architektur nur noch „De Bunker" genannt. Somit vereint das Bauwerk einen großen architekturhistorischen Wert mit einer besonderen gesellschaftlich-kulturellen Relevanz.

84/1
Existing building The Bunker
Bestandsgebäude The Bunker

85/1
The new high-rise and the former student center form a well-harmonized unit.
Das neue Hochhaus und das ehemalige Studierendenzentrum ergeben eine gut harmonierende Einheit.

Architects Architekt:innen	**Powerhouse Company, Rotterdam, Netherlands** Niederlande
Project architects Projektarchitekt:innen	**Nanne de Ru, Stijn Kemper, Paul Stavert, Meagan Kerr, Daan Masmeijer**
Project team Projektteam	**Stefan de Meijer, Gerben Knol, Sanja Kralj, Martijn Ravia, Romano van den Dool, Thomas Ponds, Maarten Diederix, Stefan Prins, Erwin van Strien, Gert Ververs, Giovanni Coni, Bjørn Andreassen, Yoon Kyun (Peter) Lee, Ahmad Hallak, Robbert Verheij, Philip Weber, Lesia Topolnyk, Antonia Pohankova, Loz Mills, Sven Janse**
Client Bauherrschaft	**RED Company; Being Development**
Structural engineers Tragwerksplanung	**IMd Raadgevende Ingenieurs**
MEP Haustechnik	**Hoppenbrouwers Techniek; Deerns**
Landscape architects Landschaftsarchitekt:innen	**DELVA Landscape Architecture & Urbanism**
Height Höhe	**100 m**
Stories Geschosse	**32**
Site area Grundstücksfläche	**10 070 m²**
Building footprint Bebaute Fläche	**3406 m²**
Gross floor area Bruttogeschossfläche	**32 640 m²**
Structure Konstruktion	**Reinforced concrete** Stahlbeton
Completion Fertigstellung	**October 2022** Oktober 2022
Main use Hauptnutzung	**Residential, offices, restaurant** Wohnen, Büros, Restaurant

86/1
The proportion of glass on the northern façade is significantly higher than on the other façades.
An der nördlichen Fassade ist der Glasanteil deutlich höher als an den übrigen Fassaden.

86/2
Façade detail
Fassadendetail

86/3+4
The architecture of the tower echoes the sloping lines of The Bunker, transforming it vertically.
Die Architektur des Turms nimmt die schrägen Linien des Bunkers auf und transformiert ihn so in die Höhe.

Sustainability:
3,000 m² of the old structure were recycled in the new design; greened roof with 400 solar panels; apartments are connected to geothermal energy, so there is no need for gas; Bunker Park adds 13,000 m² to the city's green space

Nachhaltigkeit:
3.000 m² der alten Bausubstanz wurden im Neubau wiederverwendet; begrüntes Dach mit 400 Solarpaneelen; Versorgung der Wohnungen mit Geothermie ermöglicht kompletten Verzicht auf Gas; neuer Bunkerpark erweitert die städtischen Grünfläche um 13.000 m²

To save the aging building from demolition, Eindhoven University of Technology held a competition in 2016, which was won by the office Powerhouse Company. According to their winning design, the dilapidated concrete structure was carefully refurbished with sustainability in mind and complemented by a new residential tower providing 210 spacious rental and owner-occupied apartments. The construction of the tower not only created much-needed housing but also financed the elaborate restoration of the existing building.

The new high-rise echoes the sloping exterior walls and horizontal lines of "De Bunker's" façade as well as its color scheme, thus transforming the architectural language of the original structure into bold verticality. On the lower floors, solid bands of natural stone dominate the façade, which open up to allow for larger glass surfaces as the building rises. Simultaneously, the asymmetrical, slightly stepped volume of the tower tapers the higher it gets in analogy to the existing structure. The materials used in the high-rise, such as wood and glass, also reference Huig Maaskant's design. The natural stone used resembles concrete, further enhancing the ensemble effect of the new and existing buildings.

Following its transformation into a podium building, the former student union building (where Powerhouse Company founder Nanne de Ru also spent time as a student) now houses high-quality office spaces and a public restaurant, thus reviving one of its original social uses. Additionally, the underground parking garage built during the construction of the residential tower enabled the conversion of the adjacent parking lot into a public park that extends Eindhoven's northern green corridor called "de Karpen." The architectural language of the ensemble was also applied to the pathways, planting areas, and seating in the design of the open spaces.

Um das in die Jahre gekommene Gebäude vor dem Abriss zu bewahren, lobte die TU Eindhoven 2016 einen Wettbewerb aus, den das Büro Powerhouse Company für sich entscheiden konnten. Nach dessen Siegerentwurf wurde die marode Betonstruktur im Sinne der Nachhaltigkeit sorgfältig saniert und um einen neuen Wohnturm mit 210 großzügigen Miet- und Eigentumswohnungen ergänzt. Durch den Bau des Turms wurde nicht nur dringend benötigter Wohnraum geschaffen, sondern gleichzeitig die aufwendige Restaurierung des Bestandsgebäudes finanziert.

Das neue Hochhaus greift die geneigten Außenwände und horizontalen Linien der Fassade sowie die Farbigkeit des „Bunkers" auf und transformiert so die Architektursprache der ursprünglichen Struktur in die Höhe. In den unteren Etagen dominieren massive Bänder aus Naturstein die Fassade, die sich erst mit zunehmender Höhe zugunsten größerer Glasflächen öffnet. Gleichzeitig verjüngt sich die asymmetrische, leicht abgestufte Kubatur des Turms analog zum Bestand nach oben. Zudem orientieren sich die beim Hochhaus verwendeten Materialien wie Holz und Glas am Entwurf von Huig Maaskant. Der verbaute Naturstein mutet wie Beton an, wodurch die Ensemblewirkung von Neu- und Bestandsbau zusätzlich gestärkt wird.

Nach der Transformation zum Sockelgebäude beherbergt das ehemalige Studierendenwerk (in dem auch Nanne de Ru, Gründer von Powerhouse Company, als Student verkehrte) neben hochwertigen Büroräumen ein öffentliches Restaurant und damit wieder eine seiner ursprünglichen sozialen Nutzungen. Darüber hinaus ermöglichte die bei dem Bau des Wohnturms entstandene Tiefgarage die Umwandlung des angrenzenden Parkplatzes in einen öffentlichen Park, der Eindhovens nördliche Grünschneise De Karpen erweitert. Bei der Gestaltung der Freianlagen wurde die Formensprache des Ensembles auf die Wegeführung, die Pflanzflächen und Sitzgelegenheiten übertragen.

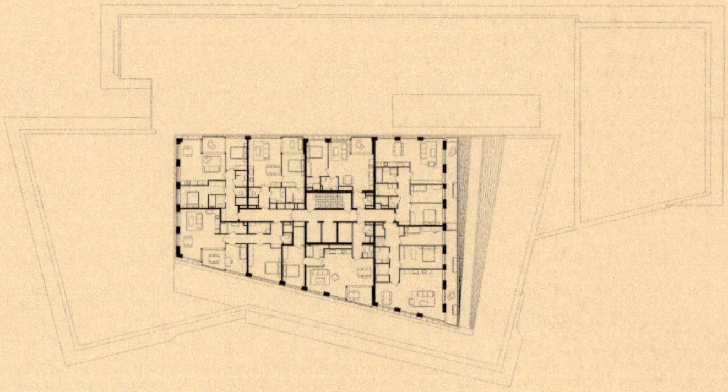

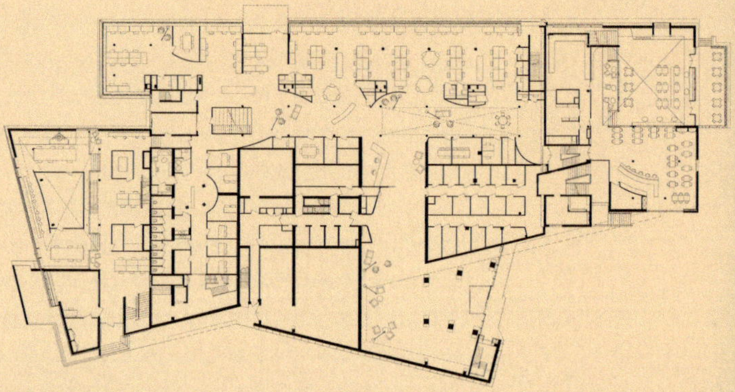

88/1
Concept pictogram
Konzeptpiktogramm

88/2
Entrance hall
Eingangshalle

88/3+4
18th floor and ground floor plans
Grundrisse 18. Obergeschoss und Erdgeschoss

88/5
On the lower floors, the inspiration is even more apparent than on the upper levels.
In den unteren Etagen ist die Inspiration noch deutlicher ersichtlich als in den oberen Stockwerken.

89/1
The design language of the old Bunker is also continued in the newly laid out park.
Auch in dem neu angelegten Park setzt sich die Formensprache des alten Bunkers fort.

Jury statement

The jury loved the idea of adapting to the site while preserving the local architectural legacy, transforming an old structure in a talented way. This sensitivity to heritage is visible in the choice of materials, with the focus on natural stone and wood, such that the high-rise is actually far more refined as a building than might be noticed at first glance. The former student center has been essentially extruded upwards to create a monumental and contemporary building. With its angled walls and insistence on horizontal lines despite its clear verticality, the Bunker Tower evolves a quite unique formal appearance all of its own, proving "the power of a clear, uncompromising idea."

Jurystatement

Der Jury gefiel die Idee, das Projekt an den Standort anzupassen und gleichzeitig das lokale architektonische Erbe durch die geschickte Umgestaltung der alten Gebäudeform zu bewahren. Diese Sensibilität für das Erbe spiegelt sich auch in der Wahl der Materialien wider: Der Schwerpunkt liegt auf Naturstein und Holz, sodass das Hochhaus tatsächlich ein viel raffinierteres Bauwerk ist, als man auf den ersten Blick vermuten würde. Das ehemalige Studierendenzentrum wurde gewissermaßen in die Höhe gezogen, um ein monumentales und modernes Gebäude entstehen zu lassen. Mit seinen geneigten Außenwänden und dem Beharren auf horizontalen Linien trotz klarer Vertikalität entwickelt der Bunker Tower eine ganz eigene Formensprache und beweist die „Stärke einer klaren, kompromisslosen Idee."

31

	Location Lage	Architects Architekt:innen	Detailed information Ausführliche Informationen
Lighthouse *Out of Competition Außer Konkurrenz*	**Aarhus, Denmark** Dänemark	**3XN** **Copenhagen, Denmark** Kopenhagen, Dänemark	**Page 92** Seite 92
Central Park Tower	**New York NY, USA**	**Adrian Smith + Gordon Gill Architecture** **Chicago IL, USA**	**Page 94** Seite 94
611 West 56th Street	**New York NY, USA**	**Álvaro Siza** **Porto, Portugal**	**Page 96** Seite 96
Tours Duo	**Paris, France** Frankreich	**Ateliers Jean Nouvel** **Paris, France** Frankreich	**Page 98** Seite 98
CapitaSpring *Prize Winner Preisträger*	**Singapore** Singapur	**BIG – Bjarke Ingels Group** **Copenhagen, Denmark/New York NY, USA** Kopenhagen, Dänemark/New York NY, USA; **CRA – Carlo Ratti Associati** **Turin, Italy/New York NY, USA** Turin, Italien/New York NY, USA	**Page 16** Seite 16
IQON Residences *Finalist*	**Quito, Ecuador**	**BIG – Bjarke Ingels Group** **Copenhagen, Denmark/New York NY, USA** Kopenhagen, Dänemark/New York NY, USA	**Page 66** Seite 66
The Spiral	**New York NY, USA**	**BIG – Bjarke Ingels Group** **Copenhagen, Denmark/New York NY, USA** Kopenhagen, Dänemark/New York NY, USA	**Page 100** Seite 100
555 Collins Street	**Melbourne, Australia** Australien	**COX Architecture** **Sydney, Australia** Australien; **Gensler** **San Francisco CA, USA**	**Page 102** Seite 102
Varso Tower	**Warsaw, Poland** Warschau, Polen	**Foster + Partners** **London, UK** Großbritannien	**Page 104** Seite 104
Alberni	**Vancouver, Canada** Kanada	**Kengo Kuma & Associates** **Tokyo, Japan** Tokio, Japan	**Page 106** Seite 106
320 Granville	**Vancouver, Canada** Kanada	**Kohn Pedersen Fox Associates** **New York NY, USA**	**Page 108** Seite 108
Atlantis The Royal Resort	**Dubai, UAE** VAE	**Kohn Pedersen Fox Associates** **New York NY, USA**	**Page 110** Seite 110
Citymark Tower	**Shenzhen, China**	**Kohn Pedersen Fox Associates** **New York NY, USA**	**Page 112** Seite 112
Shenzhen Women & Children's Center *Finalist*	**Shenzhen, China**	**MVRDV** **Rotterdam, Netherlands** Niederlande	**Page 72** Seite 72
Valley *Finalist*	**Amsterdam, Netherlands** Niederlande	**MVRDV** **Rotterdam, Netherlands** Niederlande	**Page 78** Seite 78
One Za'abeel Tower	**Dubai, UAE** VAE	**Nikken Sekkei** **Tokyo, Japan** Tokio, Japan	**Page 114** Seite 114

Nominations
Nominierungen

	Location Lage	**Architects** Architekt:innen	**Detailed information** Ausführliche Informationen
Eagle + West	**New York NY, USA**	**OMA Office for Metropolitan Architecture** **Rotterdam, Netherlands** Niederlande	**Page 116** Seite 116
Hangzhou Prism	**Hangzhou, China**	**OMA Office for Metropolitan Architecture** **Rotterdam, Netherlands** Niederlande	**Page 118** Seite 118
Mori JP Tower	**Tokyo, Japan** Tokio, Japan	**Pelli Clarke & Partners** **New Haven CT, USA**	**Page 120** Seite 120
Bunker Tower ***Finalist***	**Eindhoven, Netherlands** Niederlande	**Powerhouse Company** **Rotterdam, Netherlands** Niederlande	**Page 84** Seite 84
Qianhai Telecommunication Center	**Shenzhen, China**	**schneider + schumacher** **Frankfurt am Main, Germany** Deutschland	**Page 122** Seite 122
Hangzhou Wangchao Center	**Hangzhou, China**	**Skidmore, Owings & Merrill** **Chicago IL, USA**	**Page 124** Seite 124
Karlatornet	**Gothenburg, Sweden** Göteborg, Schweden	**Skidmore, Owings & Merrill** **Chicago IL, USA**	**Page 126** Seite 126
One and Two Manhattan West	**New York NY, USA**	**Skidmore, Owings & Merrill** **Chicago IL, USA**	**Page 128** Seite 128
Airside	**Hong Kong, China** Hongkong, China	**Snøhetta** **Oslo, Norway** Norwegen	**Page 130** Seite 130
Nanjing Vertical Forest	**Nanjing, China**	**Stefano Boeri Architetti** **Milan, Italy** Mailand, Italien	**Page 132** Seite 132
11 Hoyt	**New York NY, USA**	**Studio Gang** **Chicago IL, USA**	**Page 134** Seite 134
The One	**Vienna, Austria** Wien, Österreich	**StudioVlayStreeruwitz** **Vienna, Austria** Wien, Österreich	**Page 136** Seite 136
Pan Pacific Orchard	**Singapore** Singapur	**WOHA** **Singapore** Singapur	**Page 138** Seite 138
Heritage Lanes, 80 Ann Street	**Brisbane, Australia** Australien	**Woods Bagot** **Adelaide, Australia** Australien	**Page 140** Seite 140
Tokyu Kabukicho Tower	**Tokyo, Japan** Tokio, Japan	**Yuko Nagayama & Associates** **Tokyo, Japan** Tokio, Japan	**Page 142** Seite 142
The Henderson	**Hong Kong, China** Hongkong, China	**Zaha Hadid Architects** **London, UK** Großbritannien	**Page 144** Seite 144

Lighthouse

Aarhus, Denmark Dänemark

Architects Architekt:innen	**3XN Copenhagen, Denmark** Kopenhagen, Dänemark
Project architects Projektarchitekt:innen	**Jes John Tønsgaard**
Client Bauherrschaft	**Lighthouse United**
Structural engineers Tragwerksplanung	**Ramboll**
MEP Haustechnik	**Ramboll**
Landscape architects Landschaftsarchitekt:innen	**Schønherr**
Height Höhe	**142 m**
Stories Geschosse	**45**
Site area Grundstücksfläche	**11 227 m²**
Gross floor area Bruttogeschossfläche	**44 600 m²**
Structure Konstruktion	**Reinforced concrete** Stahlbeton
Completion Fertigstellung	**January 2024** Januar 2024
Main use Hauptnutzung	**Residential, commercial** Wohnen, Gewerbe

At the tip of the Aarhus Harbor promenade, Denmark's tallest building combines private and subsidized housing with elements such as catering and retail spaces along with a public rooftop restaurant that bring the area to life.

All apartments boast a south orientation and a north view, and they all feature a private balcony or outdoor terrace from which to enjoy the spectacular views. The building's façade texture is inspired by the waves and reflections of the sea. It unites the slender high-rise with the adjoining terraced wings. The private courtyard serves as a quiet retreat for residents away from the bustling public spaces, fostering a sense of community.

An der Spitze der Hafenpromenade von Aarhus gelegen, vereint das höchste Gebäude Dänemarks privates und gefördertes Wohnen mit belebenden Elementen wie Gastronomie und Einzelhandelsflächen sowie einem öffentlichen Dachrestaurant.

Alle Wohnungen des Projekts verfügen über eine Süd- und Nordausrichtung sowie Zugang zu einem privaten Balkon oder einer Außenterrasse, von der aus sich die spektakuläre Aussicht genießen lässt. Die Fassadentextur des Projekts ist von den Wellen und Reflexionen des Meeres inspiriert. Sie vereint das schlanke Hochhaus mit den terrassenförmig angelegten Seitenflügeln. Der private Innenhof dient den Bewohner:innen als ruhiger Rückzugsort abseits der belebten öffentlichen Plätze und stärkt so das Gemeinschaftsgefühl.

92/1
As the name suggests, the high-rise building is surrounded by water and offers an unobstructed view out to sea.
Wie schon der Name vermuten lässt, ist das Hochhaus von Wasser umgeben und gewährt freie Sicht hinaus aufs Meer.

93/1
Section
Schnitt

93/2+3
While the new waterfront promenade is popular with joggers and walkers, the outdoor space enclosed by the base is reserved for residents.
Während die neue Uferpromenade bei Jogger:innen und Spaziergänger:innen beliebt ist, ist der vom Sockel umschlossene Außenraum den Bewohner:innen vorbehalten.

93/4
The terraced wings of the base building rise toward the tower.
Stufenartig steigen die Flügel des Sockelgebäudes gen Wasser zum Turm hin auf.

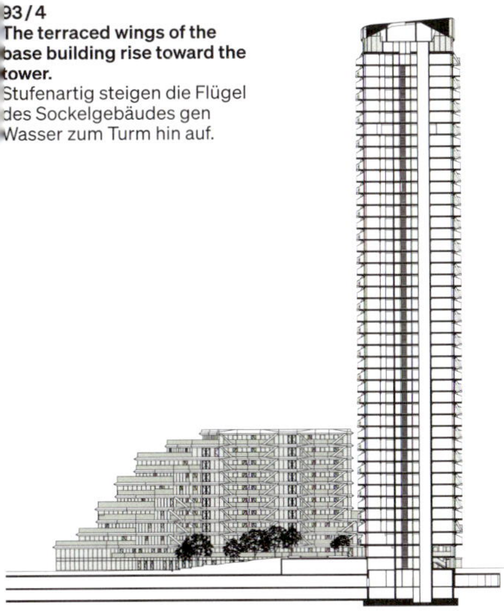

Adrian Smith + Gordon Gill Architecture

Central Park Tower

New York NY, USA

As part of the famed Billionaires' Row, Central Park Tower is a high-rise of superlatives. As the tallest residential building in the world, it is topped in New York only by the antenna of the One World Trade Center. Above the luxury department store at the base, plenty of amenities for the residents are provided up to the 31st floor. These include childcare, a laundry service, a fitness center with spa, an indoor and outdoor pool, as well as a cinema. The extensive offerings are complemented by a private club restaurant on the 100th floor.

The sizes of the 179 apartments, each boasting a unique view, range from 133 square meters to 1,626 square meters and sell for an average price of 22 million USD. The penthouse, spanning the top three floors, was even put on the market for 250 million USD.

Sustainability:
efficient use of land due to high-density design; water reuse system reduces water consumption by at least 25% through gray water recycling or condensate collection; optimized natural lighting

Nachhaltigkeit:
effiziente Flächennutzung durch hochverdichtete Bauweise; Wasserwiederverwendungssystem reduziert den Wasserverbrauch um mindestens 25% durch Grauwasserrecycling oder Kondensatsammlung; Optimierung der natürlichen Belichtung

Als Teil der bekannten Billionaires' Row ist der Central Park Tower ein Turm der Superlative. Als höchstes Wohngebäude der Welt wird er in New York nur von der Antenne des One World Trade Centers überragt. Über dem Luxuskaufhaus im Sockel stapeln sich bis zur 31. Etage die Annehmlichkeiten für die Bewohner:innen. Sie umfassen unter anderem eine Kinderbetreuung, eine Reinigung, ein Fitnesscenter mit Spa, einen In- und Outdoorpool sowie ein Kino. Ergänzt wird das umfangreiche Angebot durch ein privates Club-Restaurant im 100. Stockwerk. Die Wohnungsgrößen der 179 Apartments mit einzigartigem Ausblick reichen von 133 Quadratmetern bis zu 1.626 Quadratmetern und haben einen durchschnittlichen Preis von 22 Millionen US-Dollar. Das die drei obersten Etagen umfassende Penthouse wurde sogar für 250 Millionen US-Dollar auf den Markt gebracht.

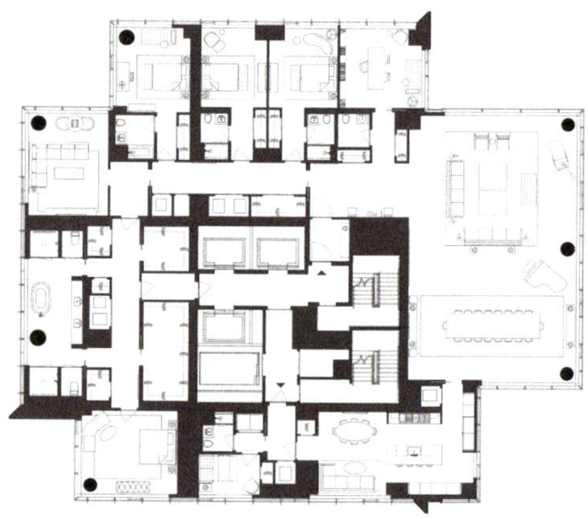

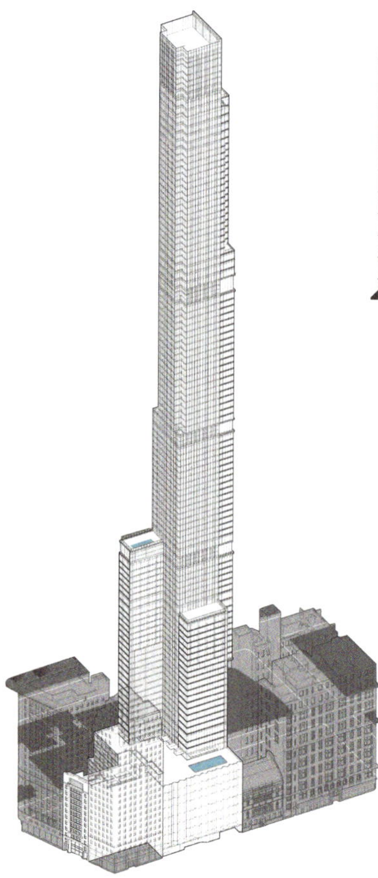

Architects Architekt:innen	**Adrian Smith + Gordon Gill Architecture Chicago IL, USA**
Project architects Projektarchitekt:innen	**Adrian Smith, Gordon Gill, Robert Forest**
Architects of record Lokale Architekt:innen	**Adamson Associates Architects**
Client Bauherrschaft	**Extell Development Company**
Structural engineers Tragwerksplanung	**WSP Global**
MEP Haustechnik	**AKF Engineers**
Landscape architects Landschaftsarchitekt:innen	**HM White**
Height Höhe	**472 m**
Stories Geschosse	**131**
Site area Grundstücksfläche	**3716 m²**
Building footprint Bebaute Fläche	**3150 m²**
Gross floor area Bruttogeschossfläche	**119 409 m²**
Structure Konstruktion	**Steel** Stahl
Completion Fertigstellung	**December 2021** Dezember 2021
Main use Hauptnutzung	**Residential, retail** Wohnen, Einzelhandel

94/1+95/1
Central Park Tower clearly rises above many of its neighbors in the western part of Manhattan.
Deutlich überragt der Central Park Tower seine vielen Nachbarn im westlichen Teil Manhattans.

94/2
Axonometric view
Axonometrie

94/3
Standard floor plan
Grundriss Regelgeschoss

95/2
The undulating façade of the Nordstrom department store at the base contrasts with the flat façade of the residential tower.
Die gewellte Fassade des Kaufhauses Nordstrom im Sockel bildet einen Kontrast zur flachen Fassade des Wohnturms.

95/3+4
The unique views over Central Park, extending far beyond Manhattan, are unparalleled.
Die einzigartigen Ausblicke auf den Central Park bis weit über Manhattan hinaus suchen ihresgleichen.

95/5
A striking cantilever 88 meters above the ground extends the tower eastward.
Eine markante Auskragung 88 Meter über dem Boden erweitert den Turm nach Osten.

Álvaro Siza

611 West 56th Street

New York NY, USA

Named after its address, the building at 611 West 56th Street is the first high-rise building by the 1992 Pritzker Prize laureate and the first project completed by Álvaro Siza in the USA. In Manhattan's vibrant Hell's Kitchen neighborhood, the slender high-rise emerges from a base that extends across the entire width of the plot and culminates in a 16-meter-tall setback at its top.

The minimalist façade made of light-colored limestone, typical of Siza, sets the building apart from its mostly dark and glass-clad neighbors, lending it a certain presence despite its modest height. Additionally, Manhattan's road network served as inspiration for the strictly gridded façade, which unites the 80 different residential units (ranging from studio apartments to Maisonette duplexes and penthouses) into a cohesive structure.

Das nach seiner Adresse benannte Gebäude 611 West 56th Street ist das erste Hochhaus des Pritzker-Preisträgers von 1992 und zugleich das erste von Álvaro Siza fertiggestellte Projekt in den USA. In Manhattans pulsierendem Bezirk Hell's Kitchen entwächst das schlanke Hochhaus einem über die gesamte Grundstücksbreite reichenden Sockel und endet an seiner Spitze mit einem weiter zurückspringenden, 16 Meter hohen Abschluss.

Die reduzierte Fassade aus hellem, für Siza typischen Kalkstein hebt dabei das Hochhaus von seinen meist dunklen sowie verglasten Nachbarn ab und verleiht ihm trotz seiner bescheidenen Höhe eine gewisse Präsenz. Zudem diente das Straßennetz Manhattans als Inspiration für die streng gerasterte Fassade, die die 80 unterschiedlichen Wohneinheiten (Einzimmerwohnung bis Maisonette-Penthouse) zu einem einheitlichen Baukörper vereint.

96/1
Viewed from the east, the building's small footprint becomes apparent.
Aus östlicher Blickrichtung offenbart sich die geringe Grundfläche des Gebäudes.

96/2
Unobstructed view from the rooftop terrace over the Hudson River
Freier Blick von der Dachterrasse auf den Hudson River

96/3
View over Hell's Kitchen toward Lower Manhattan
Blick über Hell's Kitchen auf Lower Manhattan

97/1
The tower's grid-like façade blends unobtrusively into its surroundings.
Zurückhaltend gliedert sich die gerasterte Hochhausfassade in die Umgebung ein.

97/2
Elevations
Ansichten

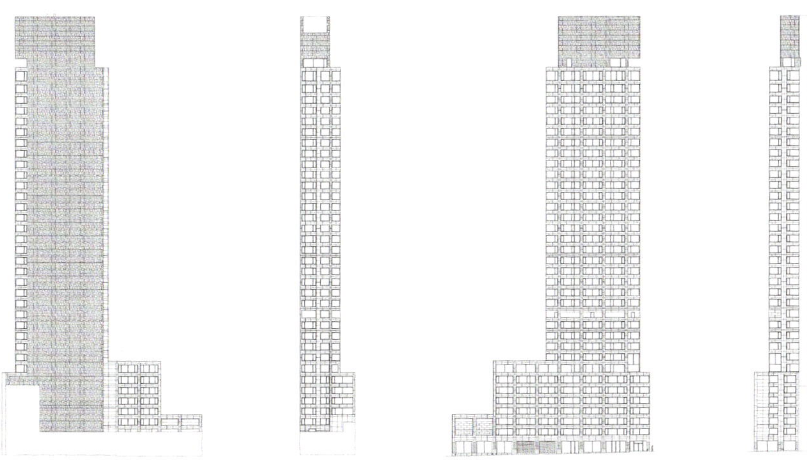

Architects Architekt:innen	**Álvaro Siza** **Porto, Portugal**
Project architects Projektarchitekt:innen	**Álvaro Siza**
Architects of record Lokale Architekt:innen	**SLCE Architects**
Client Bauherrschaft	**Sumaida & Khurana;** **Leny**
Structural engineers Tragwerksplanung	**McNamara Salvia**
MEP Haustechnik	**Stantec Engineering**
Height Höhe	**138 m**
Stories Geschosse	**39**
Site area Grundstücksfläche	**992 m²**
Building footprint Bebaute Fläche	**892 m²**
Gross floor area Bruttogeschossfläche	**15 173 m²**
Structure Konstruktion	**Reinforced concrete** Stahlbeton
Completion Fertigstellung	**June 2020** Juni 2020
Main use Hauptnutzung	**Residential, commercial** Wohnen, Gewerbe

Ateliers Jean Nouvel

Tours Duo

Paris, France Frankreich

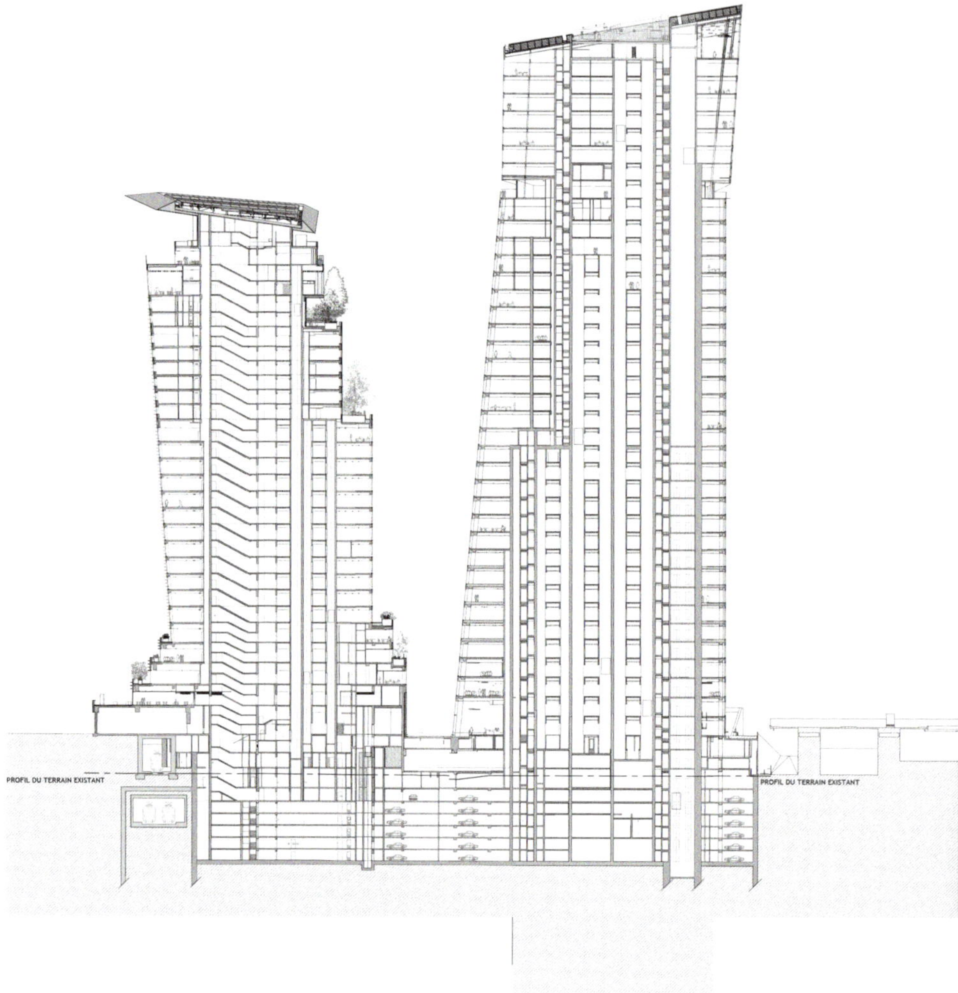

Architects Architekt:innen	**Ateliers Jean Nouvel** **Paris, France** Frankreich
Project architects Projektarchitekt:innen	**Didier Brault, Vincent Chaigneau, Laure Frachet**
Client Bauherrschaft	**Ivanhoé Cambridge; Natixis Assurances; Hines France; Semapa**
Structural engineers Tragwerksplanung	**Aedis; Egis Group**
MEP Haustechnik	**Artelia**
Landscape architects Landschaftsarchitekt:innen	**Ateliers Jean Nouvel**
Height Höhe	**180 m; 125 m**
Stories Geschosse	**39; 29**
Site area Grundstücksfläche	**8794 m²**
Building footprint Bebaute Fläche	**4717 m²**
Gross floor area Bruttogeschossfläche	**140 000 m²**
Structure Konstruktion	**Reinforced concrete** Stahlbeton
Completion Fertigstellung	**September 2022**
Main use Hauptnutzung	**Mixed use comprising offices, hotel, restaurant, retail** Mischnutzung aus Büros, Hotel, Restaurant, Einzelhandel

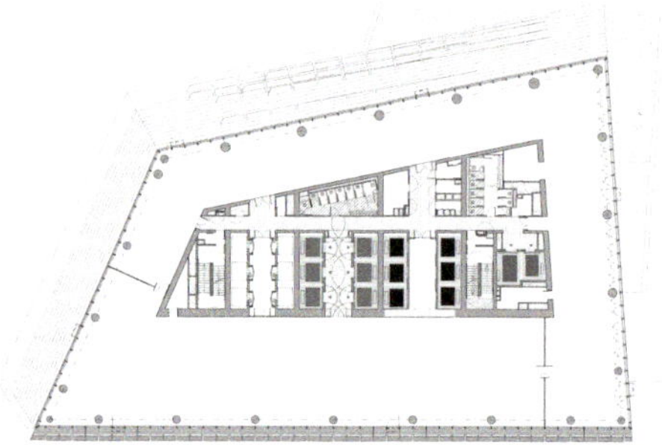

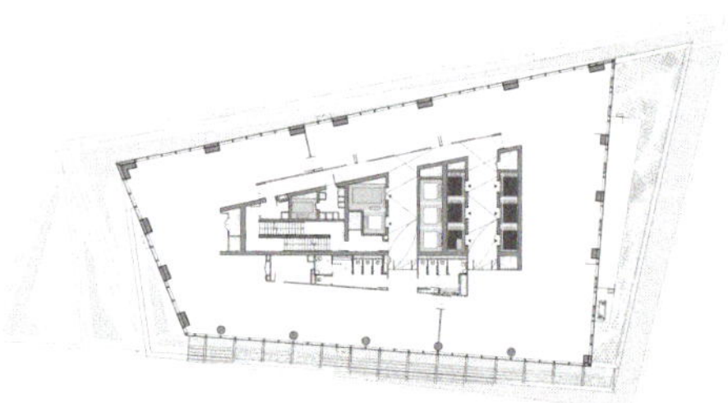

Sustainability certifications:
NF BT HQE™;
Passeport Bâtiment Durable – Exceptionnel;
EFFINERGIE +;
WELL – Platinum
Sustainability:
systems optimizing water and energy efficiency; use of renewable energy; stormwater management; V-shaped arrangement of buildings allows for better exposure to sunlight and natural lighting

Nachhaltigkeitszertifizierung:
NF BT HQE™;
Passeport Bâtiment Durable – Exceptionnel;
EFFINERGIE +;
WELL – Platinum
Nachhaltigkeit:
Systeme zur Optimierung der Wasser- und Energieeffizienz; Nutzung erneuerbarer Energien; Regenwasserbewirtschaftung; v-förmige Anordnung der Gebäude ermöglicht bessere Sonneneinstrahlung und natürliche Belichtung

98/1
Section
Schnitt

98/2+3
Standard floors Tours Duo 1+2
Regelgeschosse Tours Duo 1+2

98/4
Terrace below the head of the taller Tours Duo 1
Terrasse im Knick des höheren Tours Duo 1

99/1
Tours Duo marks the traffic hub at Avenue de France in the southeast of Paris.
Die Tours Duo markieren den Verkehrsknotenpunkt Avenue de France im Südosten von Paris.

99/2
Façade panels for light control
Fassadenpaneele zur Lichtsteuerung

In the southeast of Paris, Tours Duo has emerged as an identity-generating pair of towers. The two high-rises of unequal height crane their "heads" upward in a conspiratorial manner, while also engaging in a dialogue with their dynamic surroundings. Bordering on Avenue de France, rail lines, and the ring road, the double-sloped façades play with the reflections of traffic flows. A new central plaza emerges between the two high-rises, housing shops in the form of large kiosks. The resulting V-shape allows the rising sun to shine through and simultaneously suggests the opening of historic Paris to its suburbs.

Im Südosten von Paris ist mit Tours Duo ein identitätsstiftender Doppelturm entstanden. Die beiden ungleich großen Türme recken komplizenhaft ihre „Köpfe" in die Höhe und treten in einen Dialog mit ihrer dynamischen Umgebung. Gelegen am Rande der Avenue de France, der Eisenbahn und der Ringstraße, spielen die doppelt geneigten Fassaden mit den Reflexionen der Verkehrsflüsse. Zwischen den beiden Hochhäusern entsteht ein neuer zentraler Platz, der Geschäfte in Form von großen Kiosken beherbergt. Die resultierende V-Form lässt die aufgehende Sonne hindurch und deutet zugleich die Öffnung des historischen Paris zu seinen Vorstädten an.

BIG – Bjarke Ingels Group

The Spiral

New York NY, USA

Architects Architekt:innen	**BIG – Bjarke Ingels Group Copenhagen, Denmark/ New York NY, USA** Kopenhagen, Dänemark/ New York NY, USA
Project architects Projektarchitekt:innen	**Bjarke Ingels, Daniel Sundlin, Thomas Christoffersen, Douglass Alligood, Nicholas Potts, Carolien Schippers, Dominyka Voelkle, Jennifer Wood, Armen Menendian**
Architects of record Lokale Architekt:innen	**Adamson Associates**
Client Bauherrschaft	**Tishman Speyer**
Structural engineers Tragwerksplanung	**WSP Cantor Seinuk**
MEP Haustechnik	**Consentini**
Landscape architects Landschaftsarchitekt:innen	**BIG – Bjarke Ingels Group**
Height Höhe	**317 m**
Stories Geschosse	**66**
Site area Grundstücksfläche	**6266 m²**
Building footprint Bebaute Fläche	**5458 m²**
Gross floor area Bruttogeschossfläche	**241 498 m²**
Structure Konstruktion	**Composite construction** Verbundbauweise
Completion Fertigstellung	**July 2022** Juli 2022
Main use Hauptnutzung	**Offices** Büros

As one of the last high-rises to be completed in the Hudson Yards megaproject, The Spiral extends the New York High Line upwards in the form of a ribbon of terraces spiraling around the building. These terraces structure the façade of the supertall, which tapers as it rises, while at the same time providing access to fresh air and daylight on all floors. The greenery on the 13,000 square meters of terrace space varies with increasing height and is adjusted to external factors such as wind and sunlight.

Inside the building, the ribbon of terrace is reflected in the form of two-story atriums. These allow natural light to penetrate deeper into the individual floors and also promote communication and short distances between the different levels. Thus, the project's stepped design transforms the typical setbacks of New York high-rises into a forward-looking concept.

Als eines der zuletzt fertiggestellten Hochhäuser des Megaprojekts Hudson Yards verlängert The Spiral die New Yorker High Line in Form eines spiralförmig umlaufenden Terrassenbandes in die Höhe. Dabei strukturieren die Terrassen die Fassade des sich nach oben verjüngenden Supertalls und bieten gleichzeitig auf allen Etagen Zugang zu Frischluft und Tageslicht. Die Begrünung der insgesamt 13.000 Quadratmeter Terrassenfläche variiert mit ansteigender Höhe und ist auf äußere Faktoren wie Wind und Sonneneinstrahlung abgestimmt.

Im Inneren des Gebäudes bildet sich das Terrassenband als zweigeschossige Atrien ab. Diese ermöglichen einen tieferen Einfall von natürlichem Licht in die einzelnen Etagen und fördern darüber hinaus die Kommunikation und kurze Wege zwischen den verschiedenen Stockwerken. Somit transformiert das Projekt die für New Yorker Hochhäuser typischen Rücksprünge (*setbacks*) in ein zukunftsweisendes Konzept.

Sustainability certifications: LEED Gold
Sustainability: cascading terraces with interior and exterior greenery; use of native plants; water management system including rainwater utilization; generous ceiling heights and specially selected glass coatings enable deeper penetration of natural light

Nachhaltigkeitszertifizierung: LEED Gold
Nachhaltigkeit: abgestufte Terrassen mit Innen- und Außenbegrünung; Nutzung einheimischer Pflanzen; Wassermanagement-system einschließlich Regenwassernutzung; großzügige Deckenhöhen und spezielle Glasbeschichtungen ermöglichen tieferes Eindringen des natürlichen Lichts

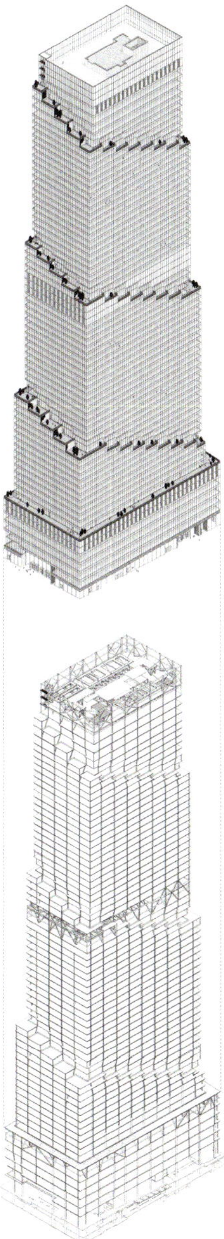

100/1+2
Outdoor terraces
Außenterrassen

101/1
The stringent concept of The Spiral is already noticeable at street level.
Das stringente Konzept von The Spiral ist schon auf Straßenebene erlebbar.

101/2
Concept pictogram
Konzeptpiktogramm

101/3
Like the steps of a spiral staircase, the terraces wrap around the building, which tapers as it rises.
Wie die Stufen einer Wendeltreppe legen sich die Terrassen um das sich nach oben verjüngende Gebäude.

101/4+5
Ground and 26th floor plans
Grundrisse Erdgeschoss und 26. Obergeschoss

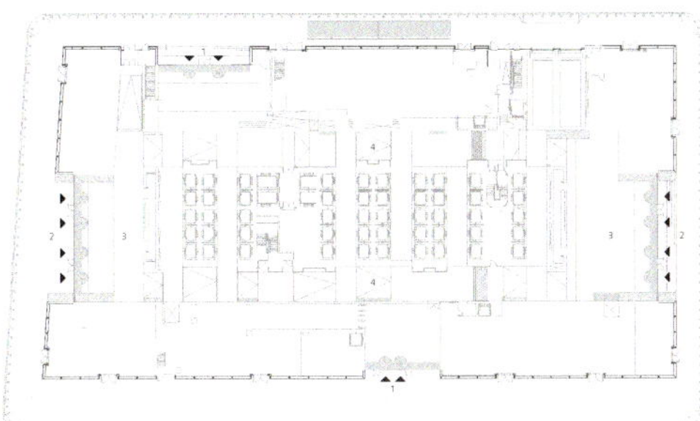

COX Architecture; Gensler

555 Collins Street

Melbourne, Australia Australien

Sustainability certifications: Green Star – 6 Stars; NABERS Energy – 5.5 Stars; WELL Platinum; NABERS Waste – 6 Stars; Climate Active Carbon Neutral Standard
Sustainability: use of eco-concrete resulting in a 20% reduction of carbon emissions; platform for the integration of building services, enabling implementation of the latest innovative technologies; high-efficiency central cold and hot water system; waste water treatment and rainwater harvesting; photovoltaic system

Nachhaltigkeitszertifizierung: Green Star – 6 Stars; NABERS Energy – 5.5 Stars; WELL Platinum; NABERS Waste – 6 Stars; Climate Active Carbon Neutral Standard
Nachhaltigkeit: Nutzung von Ökobeton führt zu einer 20-prozentigen Reduktion der Kohlenstoffemissionen; Plattform zur Implementierung neuester innovativer Technologien in die Haustechnik; hocheffiziente zentrale Kalt- und Warmwasseranlage; Brauchwasseraufbereitung und Regenwassernutzung; Photovoltaikanlage

102/1
The high-rise building has a classic structure with a base, mid-section, and top section.
Das Hochhaus ist ganz klassisch in Sockelzone, Mittelteil und oberen Abschluss gegliedert.

103/1–3
Floor plans of ground floor, standard floors in the mid-section, and standard floors in the top section
Grundrisse Erdgeschoss, Regelgeschoss Mittelteil und Regelgeschoss oberer Abschluss

103/4
As is often the case in Australia, new architecture meets historical buildings here.
Wie so oft in Australien trifft hier neue Architektur auf historische Bausubstanz.

Architects Architekt:innen	**COX Architecture Sydney, Australia** Australien; **Gensler San Francisco CA, USA**
Project architects Projektarchitekt:innen	**Simon Haussegger, Tom Owens, Johannes Lupolo-Chan**
Client Bauherrschaft	**Charter Hall**
Structural engineers Tragwerksplanung	**Robert Bird Group**
MEP Haustechnik	**Floth**
Landscape architects Landschaftsarchitekt:innen	**Aspect Studios**
Height Höhe	**128 m**
Stories Geschosse	**34**
Site area Grundstücksfläche	**2200 m²**
Building footprint Bebaute Fläche	**2000 m²**
Gross floor area Bruttogeschossfläche	**66 400 m²**
Structure Konstruktion	**Reinforced concrete** Stahlbeton
Completion Fertigstellung	**July 2023** Juli 2023
Main use Hauptnutzung	**Offices, retail** Büros, Einzelhandel

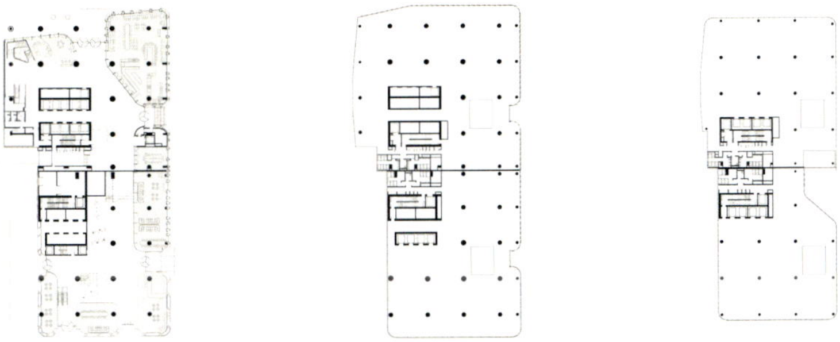

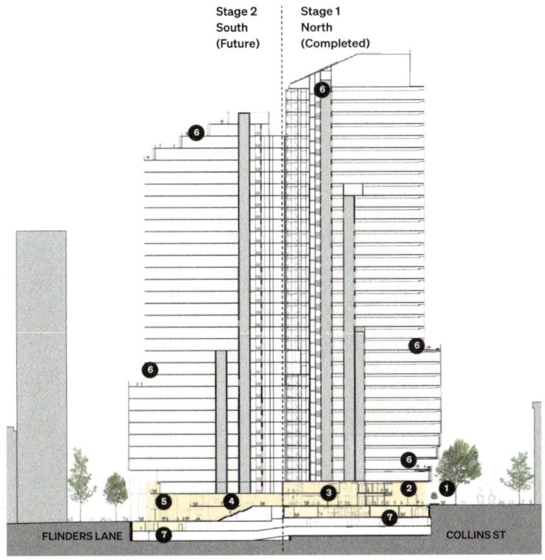

Vertical community Vertikale Community
❶ **New urban plaza** Neuer urbaner Platz ❷ **Urban living room** Urbanes Wohnzimmer
❸ **International laneway network** Internationales Wegenetz ❹ **Amphitheater** Amphitheater
❺ **Market hall** Markthalle ❻ **Terraces** Terrassen ❼ **Wellness center** Wellnesscenter

103/5
Façade detail mid-section
Fassadendetail Mittelteil

103/6
Entrance hall
Eingangshalle

103/7
Section
Schnitt

103/8
Façade detail base zone
Fassadendetail Sockelzone

Following the demolition of the historical Federal Coffee Palace, one of the grandest buildings of the Marvellous Melbourne era, an urban wound had been gaping at the western end of Melbourne's CBD since 1972. The new building aims to restore both the scale and grandeur of its predecessor with its three main street frontages and to revitalize the entire Midtown precinct. In terms of scale and materiality, the base of the building echoes the surrounding context. It is articulated by a series of deep, masonry portals whose sculptural forms invite people to enter and linger. The high-rise emerges from this base as a vertical campus.

Nach dem Abriss des historischen Federal Coffee Palace, eines der prächtigsten Gebäude der *Marvellous Melbourne*-Ära, klaffte seit 1972 eine urbane Wunde am westlichen Ende von Melbournes CBD. Der Neubau zielt mit den drei Hauptstraßenfronten darauf ab, sowohl die Größe und Erhabenheit der Adresse wiederherzustellen als auch den gesamten Midtown-Bezirk wiederzubeleben. Der Sockel des Gebäudes setzt in Maßstab und Materialität den Umgebungskontext fort. Gegliedert wird er durch eine Reihe von tiefen, gemauerten Portalen, die mit ihren skulpturalen Formen zum Eintreten und Verweilen einladen. Darüber erhebt sich das Hochhaus als vertikaler Campus.

Foster + Partners

Varso Tower

Warsaw, Poland Warschau, Polen

Sustainability certifications:
BREEAM Outstanding;
WELL Gold
Sustainability:
triple-glazed façade; sky garden with sixteen trees; landscaped lobby

Nachhaltigkeitszertifizierung:
BREEAM Outstanding;
WELL Gold
Nachhaltigkeit:
dreifach verglaste Fassade; Dachgarten mit sechzehn Bäumen; begrünte Eingangshalle

Varso Tower, the tallest building in the European Union, is the final component of Varso Place, a mixed-use mega-project comprising several high-rises in the immediate vicinity of Warsaw's main train station. In the middle of this metropolitan area, a 10-meter-high entrance hall leads to a green and glass-enclosed plaza which offers a place to stay and at the same time connects the building with its neighbors. Public roof gardens at the top of the tower, where a panoramic restaurant and a bar are located, are the second part of the green concept surrounding the office floors.

Der Varso Tower, das höchste Gebäude in der Europäischen Union, bildet den finalen Baustein des Varso Place, eines mischgenutzten Großprojekts, das in unmittelbarer Nähe zu Warschaus Hauptbahnhof unter anderem mehrere Hochhäuser umfasst. Inmitten dieses großstädtischen Zentrums gelangt man durch eine 10 Meter hohe Eingangshalle auf einen begrünten und verglasten Platz, der eine Möglichkeit zum Aufenthalt bietet und gleichzeitig das Gebäude mit seinen Nachbarn verbindet. Öffentliche Dachgärten an der Spitze des Turms, wo sich ein Panoramarestaurant sowie eine Bar befinden, bilden den zweiten Teil des die Büroetagen umschließenden Grünkonzepts.

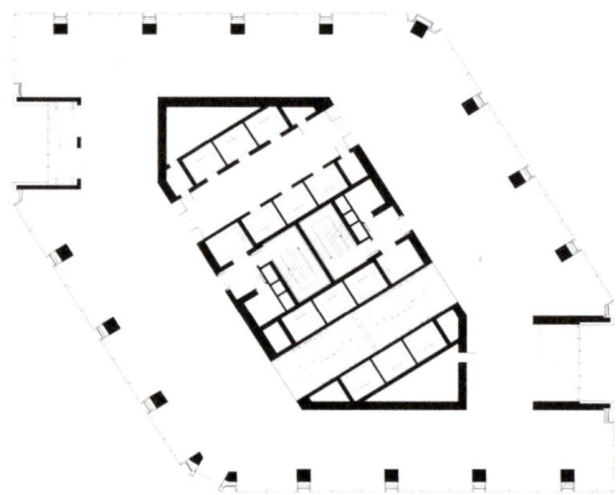

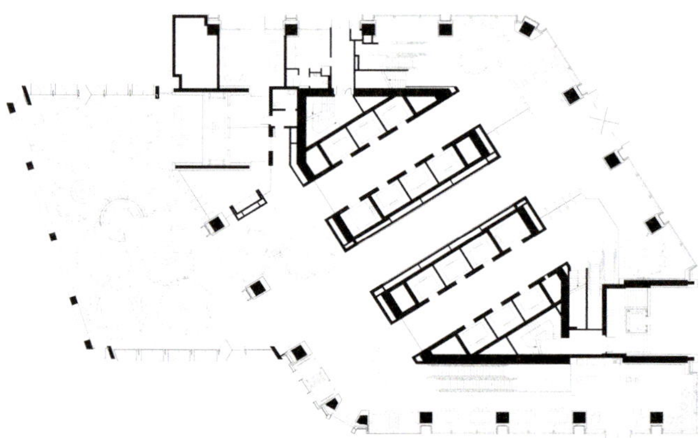

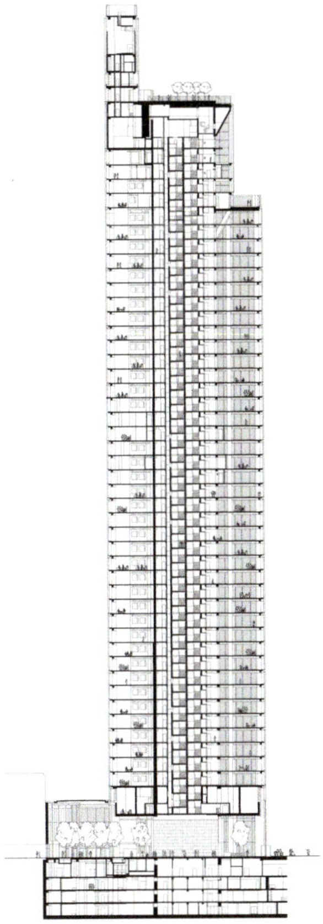

Architects Architekt:innen	**Foster + Partners** **London, UK** Großbritannien
Architects of record Lokale Architekt:innen	**Epstein**
Client Bauherrschaft	**HB Reavis**
Structural engineers Tragwerksplanung	**Buro Happold**
MEP Haustechnik	**Buro Happold**
Landscape architects Landschaftsarchitekt:innen	**RS Architektura**
Height Höhe	**310 m**
Stories Geschosse	**53**
Site area Grundstücksfläche	**3506 m²**
Building footprint Bebaute Fläche	**2577 m²**
Gross floor area Bruttogeschossfläche	**70 000 m²**
Structure Konstruktion	**Reinforced concrete** Stahlbeton
Completion Fertigstellung	**October 2022** Oktober 2022
Main use Hauptnutzung	**Offices** Büros

104/1
Green plaza on the ground floor
Begrünter Platz im Erdgeschoss

104/2+3
Ground and 6th floor plans
Grundrisse Erdgeschoss und 6. Obergeschoss

105/1
Section
Schnitt

105/2
Located in the immediate vicinity of Warsaw's main station, the new tower has excellent public transport connections.
In unmittelbarer Nachbarschaft zum Warschauer Hauptbahnhof ist der neue Turm bestens an den ÖPNV angebunden.

105/3
Entrance hall
Eingangshalle

105/4
Viewing platform
Aussichtsplattform

Kengo Kuma & Associates

Alberni

Vancouver, Canada Kanada

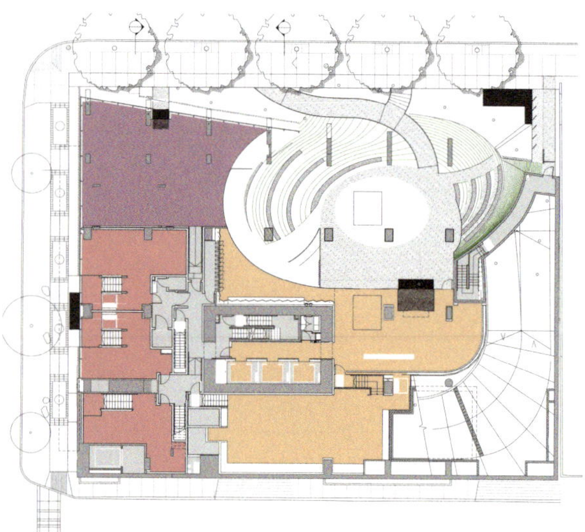

106/1
Due to the reflective panels on the façade, the appearance of the building changes with the seasons and times of the day.
Durch die reflektierenden Paneele der Fassade wechselt das Gewand des Gebäudes mit den Jahres- und den Tageszeiten.

106/2+5
Ground and 40th floor plans
Grundrisse Erdgeschoss und 40. Obergeschoss

106/3+4
The areas seemingly carved out of the overall volume make the building's total cubature difficult to grasp.
Die scheinbar aus dem Gesamtvolumen herausgeschnitzten Bereiche machen die Gesamtkubatur des Gebäudes schwer fassbar.

107/1+2
Sections
Schnitte

107/3
Open-air stage with grand piano
Freiluftbühne mit Flügel

Sustainability:
FSC-certified wood throughout the building; bamboo forest at the base of the building; passive shading calibrated per sun exposure per cardinal direction; district heating supply

Nachhaltigkeit:
FSC-zertifiziertes Holz im gesamten Gebäude; Bambuswald am Fuß des Gebäudes; passiver Sonnenschutz kalibriert je nach Sonneneinstrahlung und Himmelsrichtung; Fernwärmenutzung

The characteristic silhouette of the building, which the architecture studio itself describes as "Boolean scoop," results from the existing view corridors of the adjacent buildings to the harbor and the mountains beyond. Thus, the interweaving with the surroundings and interaction with the neighbors are crucial to Kuma's architecture. In this spirit, the interior opens up on the ground floor in the form of a moss-covered amphitheater where open-air music and theater performances take place.

The exterior façades made of glass and countless aluminum and grille panels reflect the ever-changing light of the Pacific Northwest. Together, they create a distinctive, shimmering presence on Vancouver's skyline, giving the shape of the building an elusive character.

Die charakteristische Silhouette des Gebäudes, die das Architekturbüro selbst als „Boolesche Schaufel" bezeichnet, resultiert aus bestehenden Aussichtskorridoren der angrenzenden Gebäude zum Hafen und zu den Bergen dahinter. So sind die Verwebung mit der Umgebung sowie die Interaktion mit den Nachbarn maßgeblich für Kumas Architektur. In diesem Sinne öffnet sich auch das Innere des Gebäudes zum Erdgeschoss in Form eines mit Moos bewachsenen Amphitheaters, in dem Musik- und Theateraufführungen unter freiem Himmel stattfinden.

Die äußeren Fassaden aus Glas, unzähligen Aluminium- und Gitterpaneelen reflektieren das ständig wechselnde Licht des pazifischen Nordwestens. Gemeinsam erzeugen sie eine unverwechselbare, flimmernde Präsenz in der Skyline von Vancouver, die die Form des Baukörpers nur schwer erfassen lässt.

Architects Architekt:innen	**Kengo Kuma & Associates Tokyo, Japan** Tokio, Japan
Project architects Projektarchitekt:innen	**Kengo Kuma, Balázs Bognár**
Architects of record Lokale Architekt:innen	**Merrick Architecture**
Client Bauherrschaft	**Westbank Development**
Structural engineers Tragwerksplanung	**Glotman Simpson Consulting Engineers**
MEP Haustechnik	**Nemetz (S/A) & Associates; Norman Disney & Young**
Landscape architects Landschaftsarchitekt:innen	**PFS Studio**
Height Höhe	**132 m**
Stories Geschosse	**43**
Site area Grundstücksfläche	**1921 m²**
Building footprint Bebaute Fläche	**1843 m²**
Gross floor area Bruttogeschossfläche	**26 612 m²**
Structure Konstruktion	**Reinforced concrete** Stahlbeton
Completion Fertigstellung	**June 2023** Juni 2023
Main use Hauptnutzung	**Residential** Wohnen

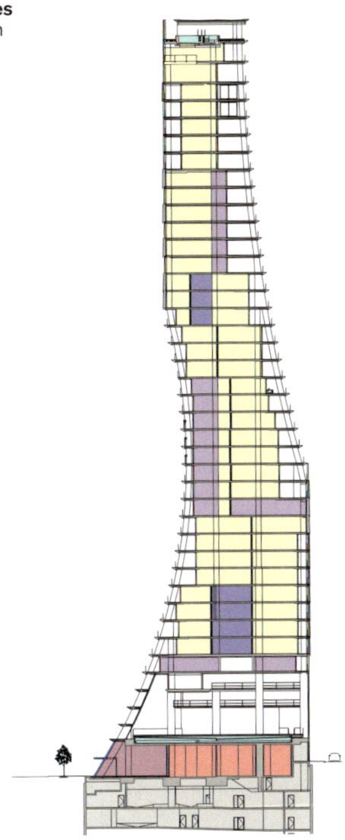

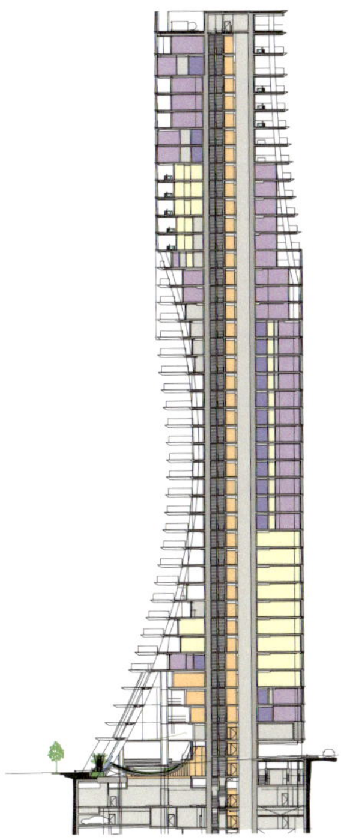

Kohn Pedersen Fox Associates

320 Granville

Vancouver, Canada Kanada

Located directly at Waterfront Station, one of the most important transportation hubs in downtown Vancouver, the high-rise stands on a sloping site not far from the harbor basin. The tower's proximity to the waterfront is formally emphasized by the concave and convex undulating façade. The three curved corners of the building, together with the slightly varying shape of the floor slabs, evoke associations with the waves of the sea.

To achieve the best possible views of the harbor and the sea as well as the mountain ranges to the north, the offices are finished with floor-to-ceiling glazing, and the building core is offset to the south of the center. Additionally, the first five floors feature a rich array of recreational and break rooms, restaurants, and shopping facilities, completing the unique working environment.

Direkt an der Waterfront Station, einem der wichtigsten Verkehrsknoten im Stadtzentrum von Vancouver, steht das Hochhaus auf einem abfallenden Grundstück unweit des Hafenbeckens. Die Nähe des Wolkenkratzers zum Wasser wird formal durch die konkav und konvex gewellte Fassade betont. Die drei abgerundeten Ecken des Gebäudes wecken gemeinsam mit der leicht variierenden Form der Geschossplatten Assoziationen an den Wellengang des Meeres.

Um eine bestmögliche Aussicht auf den Hafen und das Meer sowie die Bergketten im Norden zu ermöglichen, sind die Büros raumhoch verglast, der Gebäudekern ist aus der Mitte heraus nach Süden versetzt. Auf den fünf untersten Etagen rundet darüber hinaus ein reichhaltiges Angebot an Erholungs- und Pausenräumen, Gastronomie sowie Einkaufsmöglichkeiten das besondere Arbeitsumfeld ab.

Sustainability certifications:
LEED Gold

Nachhaltigkeitszertifizierung:
LEED Gold

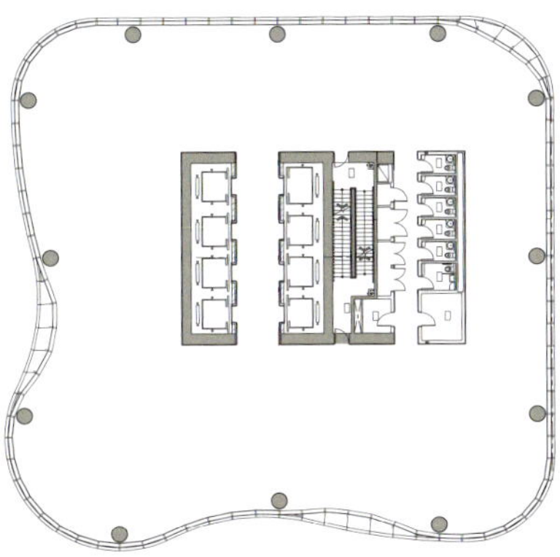

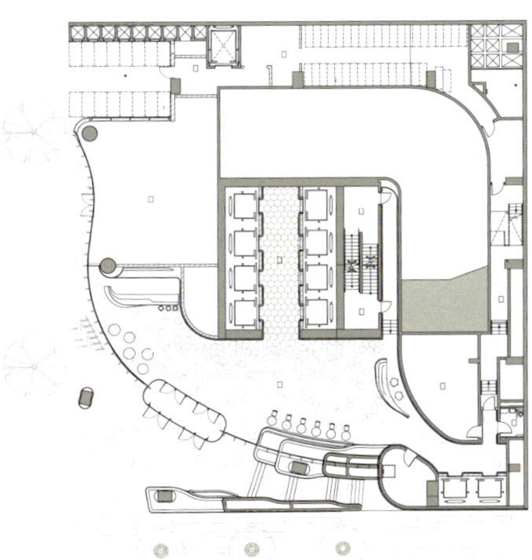

108/1
Situated in a prime location, the sculptural tower is a new eye-catcher in Vancouver's skyline.
In bester Lage stellt der skulpturale Turm einen neuen Blickfang in der Skyline Vancouvers da.

108/2
Façade detail
Fassadendetail

108/3+4
Entrance hall and arrival situation
Eingangshalle und Ankunftssituation

109/1
The undulating façade with its light-colored profiles evokes associations with foamy waves.
Die gewellte Fassade mit den hellen Profilen weckt Assoziationen an schäumende Wellen.

109/2+3
20th and ground floor plans
Grundrisse 20. Obergeschoss und Erdgeschoss

Architects Architekt:innen	**Kohn Pedersen Fox Associates** **New York NY, USA**
Project architects Projektarchitekt:innen	**James von Klemperer**
Architects of record Lokale Architekt:innen	**Chris Dikeakos Architects**
Client Bauherrschaft	**Bosa Development Corporation**
Structural engineers Tragwerksplanung	**Glotman Simpson Group**
MEP Haustechnik	**Enersolv Design and Build; Nemetz & Associate**
Height Höhe	**114 m**
Stories Geschosse	**30**
Site area Grundstücksfläche	**1450 m²**
Gross floor area Bruttogeschossfläche	**34 819 m²**
Structure Konstruktion	**Reinforced concrete** Stahlbeton
Completion Fertigstellung	**May 2021** Mai 2021
Main use Hauptnutzung	**Offices** Büros

Atlantis The Royal Resort

Dubai, UAE VAE

Architects Architekt:innen	**Kohn Pedersen Fox Associates New York NY, USA**
Project architects Projektarchitekt:innen	**James von Klemperer, Elie Gamburg**
Architects of record Lokale Architekt:innen	**DEC Dynamic Design Studio; IBI Group Architects**
Client Bauherrschaft	**Kerzner International**
Structural engineers Tragwerksplanung	**Arup; WSP**
MEP Haustechnik	**Arup; WSP**
Landscape architects Landschaftsarchitekt:innen	**SKS Studio; 40NORTH**
Height Höhe	**178 m**
Stories Geschosse	**43**
Site area Grundstücksfläche	**92 816 m²**
Gross floor area Bruttogeschossfläche	**406 000 m²**
Structure Konstruktion	**Reinforced concrete** Stahlbeton
Completion Fertigstellung	**October 2022** Oktober 2022
Main use Hauptnutzung	**Hotel, residential** Hotel, Wohnen

On the outer ring of Palm Jumeirah, an artificial island off the coast of Dubai in the shape of a palm tree, the architects realized Atlantis The Royal, a second resort to complement the existing Atlantis The Palm.

The two building sections, made up of stepped cubes stacked on top of each other, programmatically separate the hotel and residential uses. They are connected by a central "Skybridge," which is punctuated with pools, lounges, and cabanas creating a lush oasis and frames a large gateway between the two building sections. Green courtyards and terraces between the cubes further break up the building volume and afford views in both directions – toward the skyline and the Gulf of Dubai.

Sustainability certifications: LEED Certified, EarthCheck Silver

Auf dem Außenring der Palm Jumeirah, einer vor der Küste Dubais künstlich aufgeschütteten Insel in Form einer Palme, realisierten die Architekt:innen mit dem Atlantis The Royal ein zweites Resort in Ergänzung zum bestehenden Atlantis The Palm.

In zwei Gebäudeteilen aus abgetreppt gestapelten Kuben sind die Nutzungen Hotel und Wohnen programmatisch voneinander getrennt. Verbunden sind die Gebäudeteile über eine zentrale Skybridge, die wie eine üppige Oase Pools, Lounges und Cabañas beherbergt und ein großes Tor zwischen den beiden Stapelungen bildet. Begrünte Innenhöfe und Terrassen zwischen den Kuben lockern das Gebäudevolumen zusätzlich auf und geben den Blick in beide Richtungen – auf die Skyline und den Golf von Dubai – frei.

Nachhaltigkeitszertifizierung: LEED Certified, EarthCheck Silber

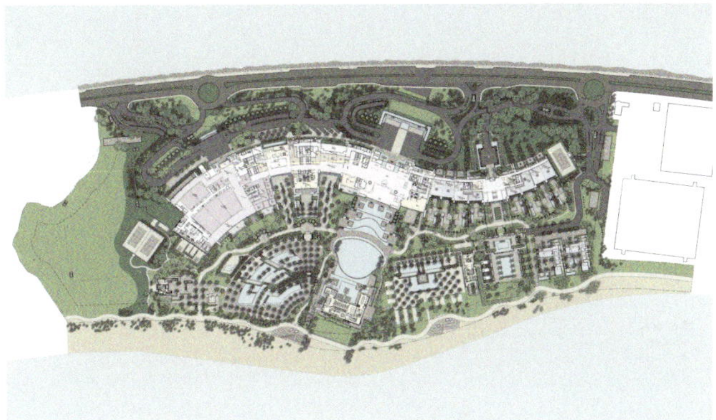

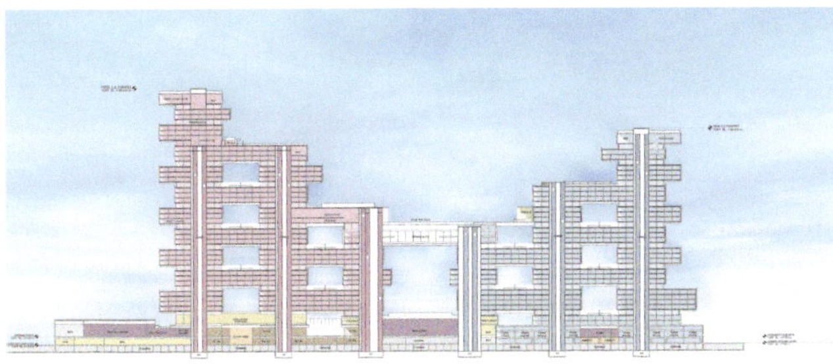

110/1
On the outer ring of the artificial island Palm Jumeirah stands the impressive megastructure off the coast of Dubai.
Auf dem Außenring der künstlich angelegten Insel Palm Jumeirah steht die beeindruckende Megastruktur vor der Küste Dubais.

111/1+2
The stacked cubes not only boast private balconies but also form a multitude of large terraces.
Die gestapelten Kuben verfügen nicht nur über private Balkone, sondern formen eine Vielzahl von großen Terrassen aus.

111/3
Infinity pool in the middle of the building
Infinitypool in der Mitte des Bauwerks

111/4
Site plan
Lageplan

111/5
Section
Schnitt

Kohn Pedersen Fox Associates

Citymark Tower

Shenzhen, China

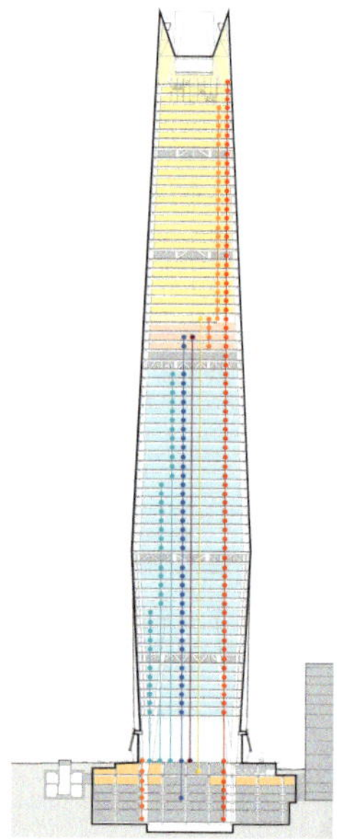

The appearance of the 388-meter-high Citymark Tower in northeast Shenzhen has an aerodynamic feel. The pyramidal tapering of the building above a distinctive horizontal kink and the cut-back corner edges in the vertical axis characterize the high-rise.

The interior accommodates a classic mix of uses: on a square floor plan, the lower floors provide office spaces, while the smaller floors above house residential units. These apartments have terraces in the recessed corners, enhancing the building's aerodynamic look. The high-rise, defined as a landmark in the master plan for the Citymark Center, culminates in a rooftop garden.

Das Erscheinungsbild des 388 Meter hohen Citymark Towers im Nordosten von Shenzhen mutet aerodynamisch an. Die pyramidenförmige Verjüngung des Baukörpers über einem prägnanten Knick in der Horizontalen und aufbrechende Eckkanten in der Vertikalen charakterisieren das Hochhaus.

Im Inneren findet sich klassische Mischnutzung: Auf quadratischem Grundriss beherbergen die unteren Etagen Büroflächen, in den kleineren Stockwerken darüber befinden sich Wohnappartements. Ihnen sind in den eingeschnittenen Ecken Terrassen vorgelagert, die das aerodynamische Antlitz des Gebäudes verstärken. Gekrönt wird das im Masterplan für das Citymark Center als Landmarke definierte Hochhaus von einem Dachgarten.

Sustainability certifications:
LEED Gold; WELL Gold;
Green Building – 2 Stars
Sustainability:
glass curtain wall maximizes natural daylighting and enhances energy efficiency; greened areas

Nachhaltigkeitszertifizierung: LEED Gold; WELL Gold; Green Building – 2 Stars
Nachhaltigkeit: Glasvorhangfassade maximiert natürlichen Lichteinfall und verbessert die Energieeffizienz; begrünte Bereiche

112 / 1
In the coming years, the fourth tallest building in Shenzhen will be surpassed by four more skyscrapers in the city.
In den nächsten Jahren wird das vierthöchste Gebäude Shenzhens noch von vier weiteren Hochhäusern in der Stadt übertroffen werden.

112 / 2
Section
Schnitt

113 / 1
Balcony of residential floors
Balkon der Wohnetagen

113 / 2
Entrance hall
Eingangshalle

113 / 3
The dimensions of the building are impressive even at ground level.
Die Dimensionen des Gebäudes sind auch am Boden eindrucksvoll.

113 / 4 + 5
Standard floor plans offices and living
Grundrisse Regelgeschosse Büros und Wohnen

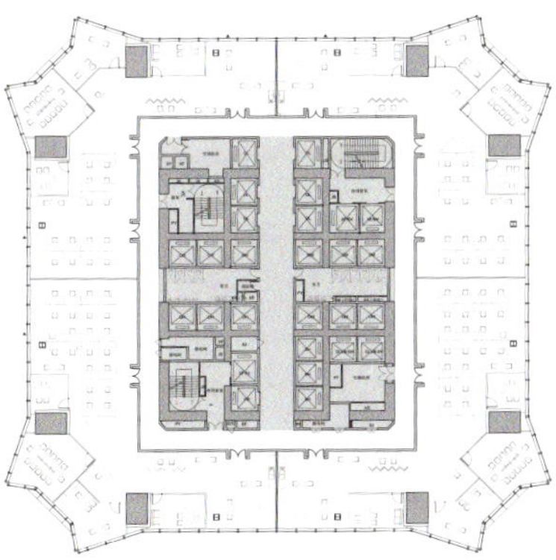

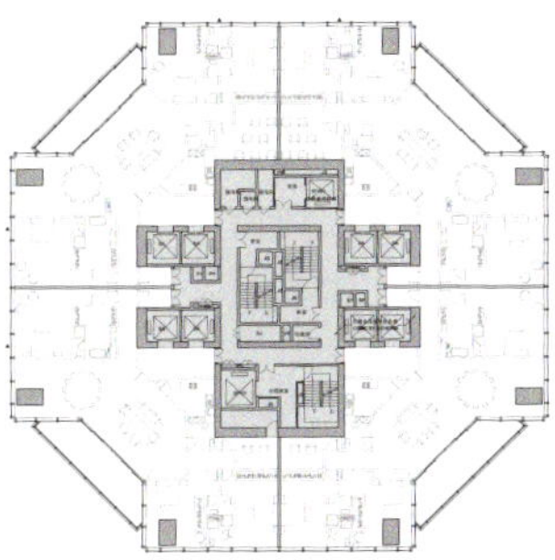

Architects Architekt:innen	**Kohn Pedersen Fox Associates New York NY, USA**
Project architects Projektarchitekt:innen	**Josh Chaiken**
Architects of record Lokale Architekt:innen	**Zhubo Design**
Client Bauherrschaft	**Shenzhen Maiyuan Real Estate; Shenzhen Citymark Holding**
Structural engineers Tragwerksplanung	**Thornton Tomasetti**
MEP Haustechnik	**WSP**
Landscape architects Landschaftsarchitekt:innen	**AECOM**
Height Höhe	**388 m**
Stories Geschosse	**70**
Site area Grundstücksfläche	**9202 m²**
Gross floor area Bruttogeschossfläche	**177 973 m²**
Structure Konstruktion	**Composite construction** Verbundbauweise
Completion Fertigstellung	**July 2023** Juli 2023
Main use Hauptnutzung	**Offices, residential** Büros, Wohnen

Nikken Sekkei

One Za'abeel Tower

Dubai, UAE VAE

Architects Architekt:innen	**Nikken Sekkei** **Tokyo, Japan** Tokio, Japan
Project architects Projektarchitekt:innen	**Koko Nakamura**
Architects of record Lokale Architekt:innen	**WSP Middle East**
Client Bauherrschaft	**ICD Investment Corporation of Dubai**
Structural engineers Tragwerksplanung	**WSP Middle East**
MEP Haustechnik	**WSP Middle East**
Landscape architects Landschaftsarchitekt:innen	**Cracknell**
Height Höhe	**301 m; 238 m**
Stories Geschosse	**67; 58**
Site area Grundstücksfläche	**31 100 m²**
Building footprint Bebaute Fläche	**25 700 m²**
Gross floor area Bruttogeschossfläche	**530 700 m²**
Structure Konstruktion	**Composite construction** Verbundbauweise
Completion Fertigstellung	**January 2024** Januar 2024
Main use Hauptnutzung	**Mixed use comprising offices, hospitality, residential** Mischnutzung aus Büros, Hotels, Wohnen

One Za'abeel Tower is intended as an interface between the International Airport and the new center of Dubai. Visible from afar, the linear, asymmetrical silhouette prominently marks the boundary between the old and new city on the skyline. Since the highway connecting both parts of the city runs through the site, two towers housing offices, hotels, residential spaces, and commercial premises have been built on either side of the arterial road. Both high-rises are connected 100 meters above the ground by a horizontal, cantilevered structure called The Link. To span the highway below, the structure was pre-assembled and then lifted to its final height in two stages using the incremental launch method.

Sustainability certifications:
LEED Gold
Sustainability:
use of regionally sourced materials with low VOC (Volatile Organic Compounds) emissions; green roofs with native planting; drip irrigation using treated sewage and HVAC condensate; airlocks at entrances to minimize cooling losses; bicycle parking and EV charging stations

Der One Za'abeel Tower versteht sich als Schnittstelle zwischen dem internationalen Flughafen und dem neuen Zentrum von Dubai. Die lineare, asymmetrische Silhouette verweist in der Skyline weithin sichtbar auf die Grenze zwischen der alten und neuen Stadt. Da die Autobahn, die beide Teile Dubais miteinander verbindet, mitten durch das Grundstück führt, sind zwei Türme mit Büros, Hotels, Wohnflächen und Geschäftsräumen links und rechts des Highways entstanden. Durch eine horizontale, freitragende Struktur namens The Link sind beide Hochhäuser 100 Meter über dem Boden miteinander verbunden. Um die darunterliegende Autobahn zu überspannen, wurde der Baukörper mit der „Incremental Launch"-Methode (Taktschiebeverfahren) vormontiert und anschließend in zwei Etappen auf seine endgültige Höhe angehoben.

Nachhaltigkeitszertifizierung:
LEED Gold
Nachhaltigkeit:
Verwendung regionaler Materialien mit geringen VOC-Emissionen (flüchtige organische Verbindungen); mit einheimischen Pflanzen begrünte Dächer; Tröpfchenbewässerung mit aufbereitetem Grauwasser und HLK-Kondensat; Luftschleusen an den Eingängen zur Minimierung von Kühlverlusten; Fahrradparkplätze und Ladestationen für Elektrofahrzeuge

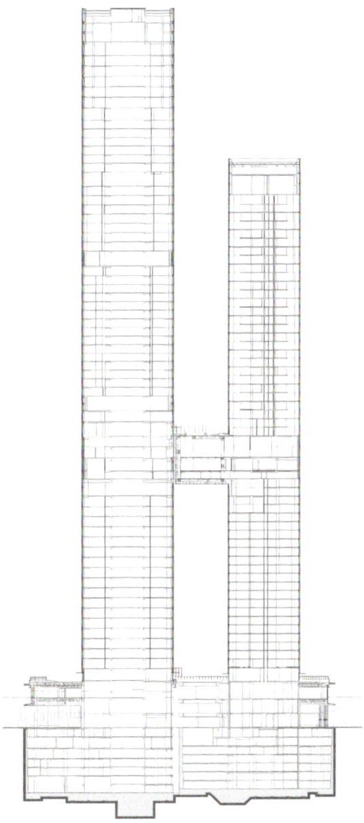

114/1
At 230 meters long, The Link is only five meters shorter than the smaller of the two skyscrapers.
Mit 230 Metern Länge ist The Link nur fünf Meter kürzer als der kleinere der beiden Wolkenkratzer.

115/1+4
Crowned by a huge infinity pool, the 67.5-meter cantilever is the longest in the world.
Von einem riesigen Infinitypool gekrönt, ist der Ausleger mit 67,5 Metern der längste weltweit.

115/2
Section
Schnitt

115/3
Site plan
Lageplan

115/5
Glass floor of The Link
Gläserner Boden von The Link

115/6
Floor plan of The Link
Grundriss The Link

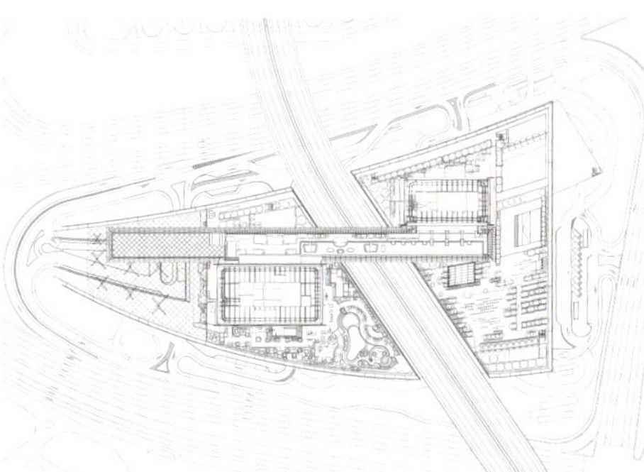

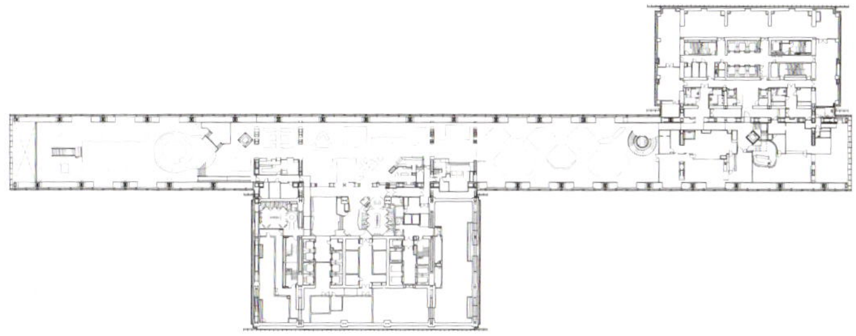

OMA Office for Metropolitan Architecture

Eagle + West

New York NY, USA

At the northernmost tip of Brooklyn, the significant complex marks the start of the development of a counterpart to the Manhattan skyline. The two towers and the connecting podium appear to have been carved out of a single block. The division of the volumes into seven- to eight-story segments echoes the scale of the surroundings. The relief of the façade is reminiscent of the shingle cladding that is common for Greenpoint's townhouses.

Various open spaces with numerous facilities for residents and 2,800 square meters of newly created public space are intended to symbolically contribute to the transformation from a post-industrial periphery to an open, lively waterfront district.

Sustainability certifications:
LEED Silver
Sustainability:
incorporation of green spaces to enhance biodiversity, mitigate heat island effects, and improve urban microclimate

An der nördlichsten Spitze Brooklyns markiert der signifikante Komplex den Start zur Entwicklung eines Gegenparts zur Skyline von Manhattan. Die beiden Türme sowie der verbindende Sockel wirken wie aus einem einzigen Block herausgebrochen. Die Unterteilung der Volumen in sieben bis acht Geschosse pro Segment greift dabei den Maßstab der Umgebung auf. Das Relief der Fassade erinnert an die Schindelverkleidung, die für die Stadthäuser in Greenpoint charakteristisch ist.

Verschiedene Freiflächen mit zahlreichen Angeboten für die Bewohner:innen sowie 2.800 Quadratmeter neu entstandener öffentlicher Raum sollen sinnbildlich zum Wandel vom postindustriellen Rand zu einem offenen, belebten Quartier am Wasser beitragen.

Nachhaltigkeitszertifizierung:
LEED Silver
Nachhaltigkeit:
Integration von Grünflächen zur Förderung der Biodiversität, zur Minderung von Hitzeinseln und zur Verbesserung des städtischen Mikroklimas

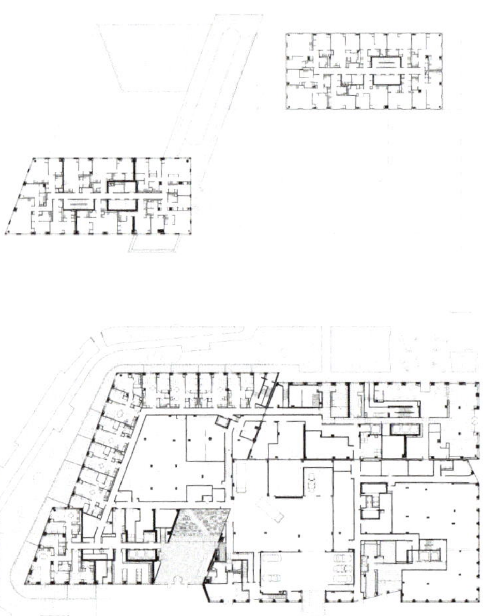

Architects Architekt:innen	**OMA Office for Metropolitan Architecture Rotterdam, Netherlands** Niederlande
Project architects Projektarchitekt:innen	**Jason Long, Yusef Ali Dennis, Christine Yoon**
Architects of record Lokale Architekt:innen	**Beyer Blinder Belle Architects & Planners**
Client Bauherrschaft	**Brookfield Properties**
Structural engineers Tragwerksplanung	**DeSimone Consulting Engineers**
MEP Haustechnik	**Cosentini Associates**
Landscape architects Landschaftsarchitekt:innen	**Field Operations; Marmol Radziner**
Height Höhe	**122 m; 92 m**
Stories Geschosse	**40; 30**
Site area Grundstücksfläche	**11 420 m²**
Building footprint Bebaute Fläche	**5790 m²**
Gross floor area Bruttogeschossfläche	**79 970 m²**
Structure Konstruktion	**Reinforced concrete** Stahlbeton
Completion Fertigstellung	**December 2022** Dezember 2022
Main use Hauptnutzung	**Residential** Wohnen

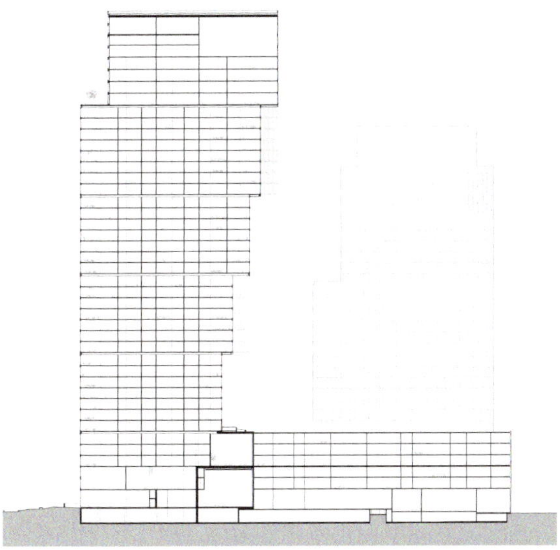

116/1
At present, the complex stands relatively isolated on the eastern shore of the East River. However, this will change very soon.
Noch steht der Komplex relativ frei am östlichen Ufer des East Rivers. Dies wird sich aber schon sehr bald ändern.

116/2+3
22nd and ground floor plans
Grundrisse 22. Obergeschoss und Erdgeschoss

116/4
The arrangement of the towers of varying heights creates a dialogue between them.
Durch die Anordnung der unterschiedlich hohen Türme ergibt sich ein Dialog zwischen beiden.

117/1+2
Breaking up the strict rectangularity makes the building appear less massive.
Das Aufbrechen der strengen Rechtwinkligkeit lässt das Gebäude weniger massiv erscheinen.

117/3
Section
Schnitt

OMA Office for Metropolitan Architecture

Hangzhou Prism

Hangzhou, China

Architects Architekt:innen	**OMA Office for Metropolitan Architecture Rotterdam, Netherlands** Niederlande
Project architects Projektarchitekt:innen	**Chris van Duijn, Michael Hadjistyllis**
Architects of record Lokale Architekt:innen	**LPA**
Client Bauherrschaft	**Zhejiang Xinhu Haichuang Real Estate Development**
Structural engineers Tragwerksplanung	**LPA**
MEP Haustechnik	**LPA**
Landscape architects Landschaftsarchitekt:innen	**IPD Integrated Planning and Design**
Height Höhe	**107 m**
Stories Geschosse	**22**
Site area Grundstücksfläche	**7533 m²**
Building footprint Bebaute Fläche	**5350 m²**
Gross floor area Bruttogeschossfläche	**80 650 m²**
Structure Konstruktion	**Composite structure** Verbundbauweise
Completion Fertigstellung	**April 2024**
Main use Hauptnutzung	**Mixed use comprising residential, office, hotel** Mischnutzung aus Wohnen, Büros, Hotel

Hangzhou Prism is conceived as an homage to the Chinese proverb that "there is paradise in heaven, and there is Hangzhou on earth." Two radical oblique cuts in the building envelope create terraced lofts with their own private balconies – attractive living spaces designed to draw new economy workers to the capital of Zhejiang Province, which now competes with Beijing and Shanghai.

Another incision within the building volume creates a large, semi-open atrium with a publicly accessible garden. This atrium serves as a thermal buffer, protecting the tower's interiors from overheating in summer and from heat loss in winter. To emphasize its prism-like effect, the pixel window façade is clad in blue glass, while the vertical curtain façade is covered with gray glass.

Sustainability:
large atrium acts as thermal buffer; limited glass windows feature natural light and enhance thermal performance to reduce energy consumption

Hangzhou Prism begreift sich als Hommage an das chinesische Sprichwort, wonach „im Himmel das Paradies liegt und auf Erden Hangzhou". Zwei radikale Schrägschnitte in der Gebäudehülle lassen terrassenförmige Lofts mit eigenen privaten Balkonen entstehen – attraktiver Wohnraum, der Arbeitskräfte der neuen Wirtschaft in die Hauptstadt der Provinz Zhejiang locken soll, die inzwischen mit Peking und Shanghai konkurriert.

Ein weiterer Einschnitt innerhalb des Baukörpers schafft ein großes, halb im Freien liegendes Atrium mit öffentlich zugänglichem Garten. Es dient als Wärmepuffer, der die Innenräume des Turms im Sommer vor Überhitzung und im Winter vor Wärmeverlust schützt. Um die Wirkung als Prisma zu betonen, ist die Pixelfensterfassade mit blauem Glas und die vertikale Vorhangfassade mit grauem Glas verkleidet.

Nachhaltigkeit:
großes Atrium fungiert als thermischer Puffer; Fenster mit begrenzter Glasfläche sorgen für natürliche Belichtung und verbessern gleichzeitig die Wärmeleistung, um den Energieverbrauch zu senken

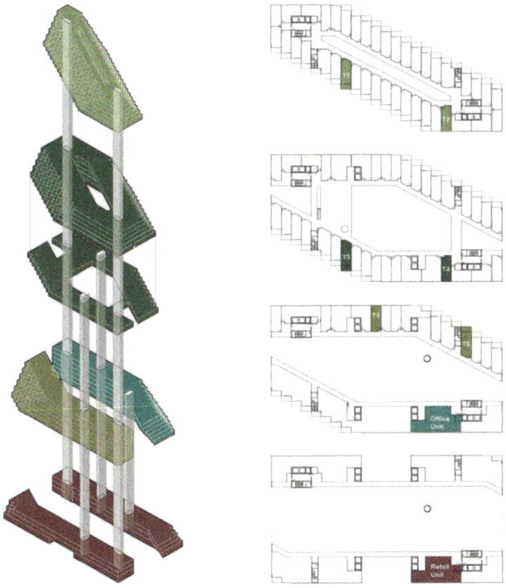

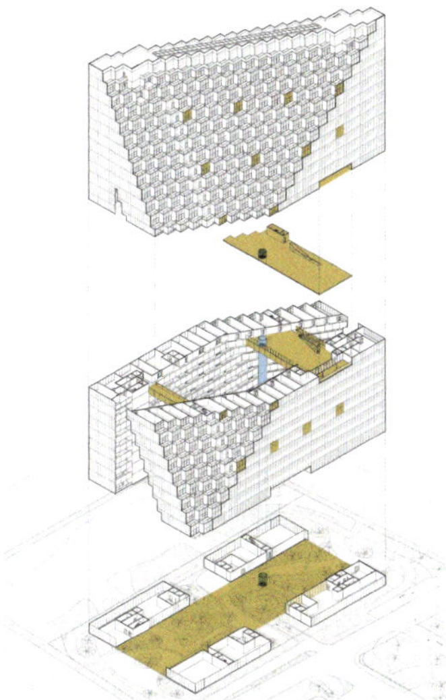

118/1
The unusual cubature is difficult to grasp at first glance.
Die ungewöhnliche Kubatur lässt sich auf den ersten Blick nur schwer erfassen.

119/1
Distribution of uses
Nutzungsverteilung

119/2
Exploded-view diagram
Explosionsdiagramm

119/3
Hangzhou is one of China's metropolitan areas that is currently undergoing rapid change.
Hangzhou ist eine der Metropolen Chinas, die sich aktuell rasant verändern.

119/4
View into the (not yet greened) atrium
Blick in das (noch nicht begrünte) Atrium

119/5
Still quite unusual for China, almost all residential units as well as the office spaces have their own balconies.
Noch recht ungewöhnlich für China verfügen fast alle Wohneinheiten sowie die Büroflächen über eigene Balkone.

Pelli Clarke & Partners

Mori JP Tower

Tokyo, Japan Tokio, Japan

In the Tokyo skyline, Mori JP Tower is unique not only for its height of 330 meters but also for its immense floor space of up to 6,400 square meters per story. Modeled on a bundle of four towers, the design creates generous layouts for retail, work, and residential spaces. The steel-glass façade wraps around the building's silhouette, which tapers toward both the top and the ground, like a garment. This shape plays with the concept of *mukuri*, which in traditional Japanese design expresses a gentle curve in the form of an inviting gesture. At the top, the high-rise unfolds like a lotus flower, while at the base, it opens up to the public space, a roughly 24,000-square-meter green area with a market hall designed by Heatherwick Studio.

In der Skyline von Tokio macht den Mori JP Tower nicht nur seine Höhe von 330 Metern einzigartig, sondern auch seine immense Grundfläche von bis zu 6.400 Quadratmetern. Indem der Turm einem Bündel von vier Türmen nachempfunden ist, entstehen großzügige Grundrisse für Einzelhandel, Arbeiten und Wohnen. Dabei umschmiegt die Stahl-Glas-Fassade wie ein Textilgewand die minimal taillierte und sich nach oben leicht verjüngende Silhouette des Baukörpers. Die Form spielt so mit dem *mukuri*, das im traditionellen japanischen Design eine sanfte Kurve in Form einer einladenden Geste ausdrückt. An der Spitze entfaltet sich das Hochhaus wie eine Lotusblume, nach unten öffnet es sich zum öffentlichen Raum, einer rund 24.000 Quadratmeter umfassenden Grünfläche mit Markthalle gestaltet von Heatherwick Studio.

120/1–3
Despite its enormous size, the tower is well integrated into the surrounding context at ground level.
Trotz seiner enormen Größe ist der Turm am Boden gut mit dem umliegenden Kontext verzahnt.

120/4
At the same time, a project of this scale is hardly conceivable outside of Asia.
Zugleich ist ein Projekt solchen Ausmaßes außerhalb Asiens kaum denkbar.

121/1
Entrance hall
Eingangshalle

121/2+3
Standard floor plans living and offices
Grundrisse Regelgeschosse Wohnen und Büros

121/4
Section
Schnitt

Architects Architekt:innen	**Pelli Clarke & Partners** **New Haven CT, USA**
Project architects Projektarchitekt:innen	**Fred Clarke**
Architects of record Lokale Architekt:innen	**Nihon Sekkei**
Client Bauherrschaft	**Mori Building; Toranomon-Azabudai District Urban Redevelopment**
Structural engineers Tragwerksplanung	**Nihon Sekkei**
MEP Haustechnik	**Nihon Sekkei**
Landscape architects Landschaftsarchitekt:innen	**Heatherwick Studio**
Height Höhe	**330 m**
Stories Geschosse	**64**
Site area Grundstücksfläche	**24 000 m²**
Building footprint Bebaute Fläche	**15 200 m²**
Gross floor area Bruttogeschossfläche	**461 800 m²**
Structure Konstruktion	**Steel** Stahl
Completion Fertigstellung	**June 2023** Juni 2023
Main use Hauptnutzung	**Mixed use comprising offices, residential, retail** Mischnutzung aus Büros, Wohnen, Gewerbe

Sustainability certifications:
LEED BD+C Platinum;
LEED ND Platinum;
WELL Core
Sustainability:
use of 100% zero-emission, renewable energy; rainwater reuse; use of heat from sewage to reduce carbon emissions across the district by about 70 t per year; water-saving equipment throughout the complex reduces water consumption to 40%

Nachhaltigkeitszertifizierung:
LEED BD+C Platinum;
LEED ND Platinum;
WELL Core
Nachhaltigkeit:
Nutzung von 100 % emissionsfreier, erneuerbarer Energien; Regenwassernutzung; Nutzung aus Abwasserwärme zur Verringerung der CO_2-Emissionen im gesamten Bezirk um etwa 70 t pro Jahr; wassersparende Geräte im gesamten Komplex reduzieren den Wasserverbrauch auf 40 %

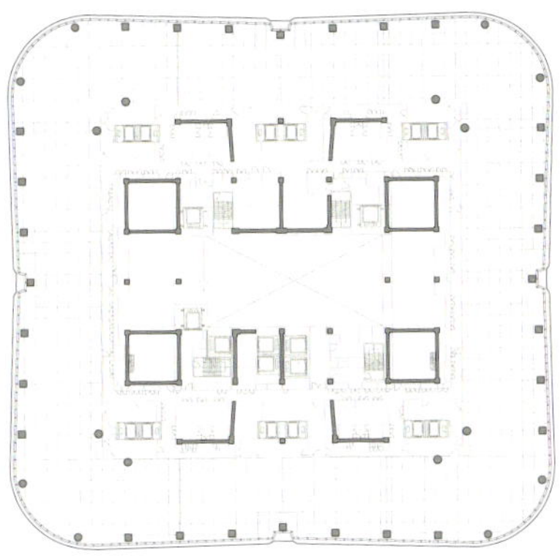

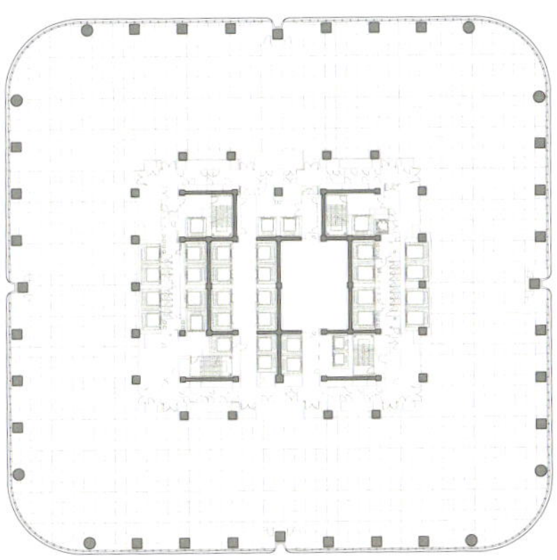

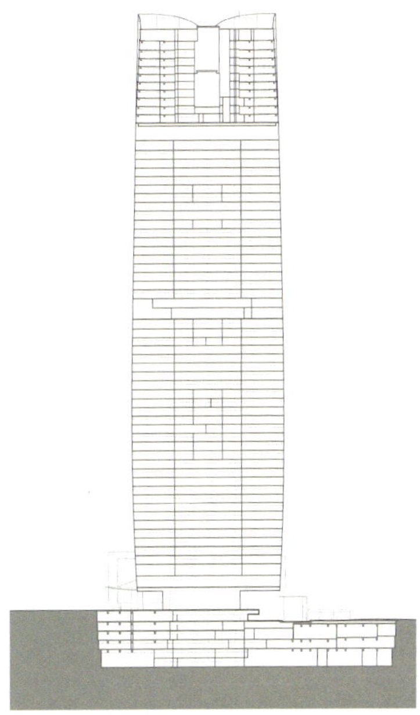

schneider + schumacher

Qianhai Telecommunication Center

Shenzhen, China

Architects Architekt:innen	**schneider + schumacher Frankfurt am Main, Germany** Deutschland
Project architects Projektarchitekt:innen	**Michael Schumacher, Till Schneider, Wang Nan, Joachim Wendt**
Architects of record Lokale Architekt:innen	**China Northeast Architectural Design and Research Institute**
Client Bauherrschaft	**Shenzhen Qianhai Investment Holding Group**
Structural engineers Tragwerksplanung	**China Northeast Architectural Design and Research Institute**
MEP Haustechnik	**China Northeast Architectural Design and Research Institute**
Landscape architects Landschaftsarchitekt:innen	**Rehwaldt Landschaftsarchitekten**
Height Höhe	**110 m**
Stories Geschosse	**17**
Site area Grundstücksfläche	**7682 m²**
Building footprint Bebaute Fläche	**6273 m²**
Gross floor area Bruttogeschossfläche	**68 610 m²**
Structure Konstruktion	**Reinforced concrete** Stahlbeton
Completion Fertigstellung	**April 2024**
Main use Hauptnutzung	**Data center** Rechenzentrum

122/1
Even though the data center in the form of a high-rise building is still a kind of prototype, we will see more of this typology in the future.
Auch wenn das Rechenzentrum in Form eines Hochhauses noch eine Art Prototyp ist, wird uns diese Typologie in Zukunft vermehrt begegnen.

122/2
The public use of the ground floor links the otherwise closed building with its surroundings.
Die öffentliche Nutzung des Erdgeschosses vernetzt das ansonsten verschlossene Gebäude mit der Umgebung.

123/1
Elevator lobby
Aufzugsvorraum

123/2
Constant air circulation is essential for cooling the building.
Eine ständige Luftzirkulation ist für die Kühlung des Gebäudes maßgeblich.

123/3
Standard floor plan
Grundriss Regelgeschoss

123/4
View of a computing floor
Blick in eine Rechenetage

123/5
Section
Schnitt

Qianhai Telecommunication Center in Shenzhen is the world's first high-rise data center. The majority of the floors are occupied by 3,515 mainframe computers, while the lower floors of the building are designed as a spacious, publicly accessible lobby with a post office.

The otherwise predominantly windowless façade is clad with movable elements that represent the universal number Pi in binary code. This façade design thus reflects the building's technical theme while simultaneously creating a dynamic and interactive exterior. At the same time, the cladding reflects sunlight and provides a natural buffer zone around the building, efficiently cooling the high-performance computers inside in an energy- and resource-saving way. The top floor features a large glass front and terrace, providing a comfortable working environment for staff working in the control rooms.

Das Qianhai Telecommunication Center in Shenzhen ist das erste Rechenzentrum der Welt in Form eines Hochhauses. Dabei belegen 3.515 Großrechner den überwiegenden Teil der Stockwerke, während das Gebäude am Boden mit einer Postfiliale sowie einer großzügigen Lobby für die Öffentlichkeit zugänglich ist.

Die ansonsten überwiegend fensterlose Fassade ist mit beweglichen Elementen verkleidet, die die universelle Zahl Pi in ihrer binären Darstellung bilden. Somit greift die Fassade das technische Thema des Gebäudes auf, während gleichzeitig eine lebendige und interaktive Gebäudefront geschaffen wird. Zugleich reflektiert sie die Sonnenstrahlen und bildet eine natürliche Pufferzone, um das Gebäude und die darin befindlichen Hochleistungsrechner energie- und ressourcenschonend zu kühlen. Im obersten Stockwerk bieten die große Glasfront sowie die dort befindliche Terrasse dem Personal in den Kontrollräumen ein komfortables Arbeitsumfeld.

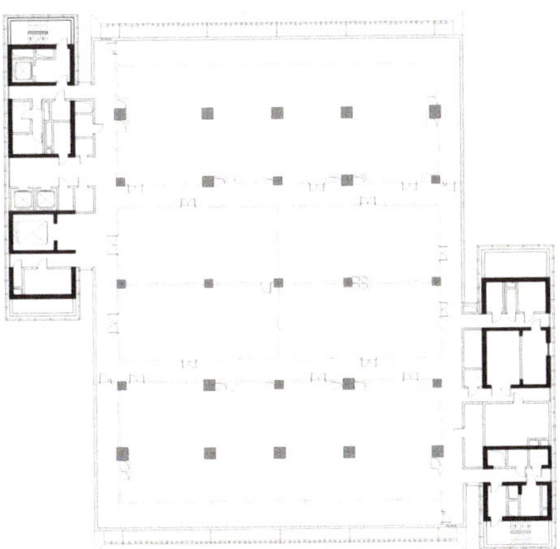

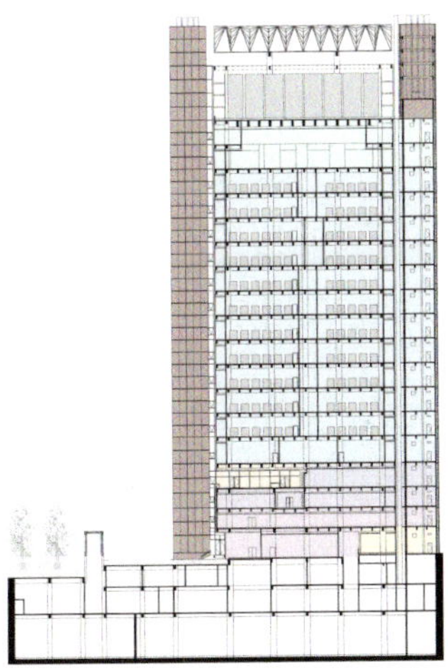

Skidmore, Owings & Merrill

Hangzhou Wangchao Center

Hangzhou, China

Architects Architekt:innen	**Skidmore, Owings & Merrill Chicago IL, USA**
Project architects Projektarchitekt:innen	**Gary Haney, Brant Coletta, Daniel Cashen, Charles Besjak, Eric Van Epps**
Client Bauherrschaft	**Dadao Qiyun**
Structural engineers Tragwerksplanung	**Skidmore, Owings & Merrill**
MEP Haustechnik	**Skidmore, Owings & Merrill**
Landscape architects Landschaftsarchitekt:innen	**T.R.O.P Terrains + Open Space**
Height Höhe	**280 m**
Stories Geschosse	**54**
Site area Grundstücksfläche	**10 419 m²**
Building footprint Bebaute Fläche	**5000 m²**
Gross floor area Bruttogeschossfläche	**125 000 m²**
Structure Konstruktion	**Composite construction** Verbundbauweise
Completion Fertigstellung	**December 2023** Dezember 2023
Main use Hauptnutzung	**Offices** Büros

Hangzhou Wangchao Center in the eastern Chinese city of Hangzhou, known as China's Silicon Valley, complements the city's expansion into an international commercial center as a flagship project. Eight mega-columns, alternately inclined outwards, lend the glass façade a flowing character, making the high-rise appear to elegantly twist upwards. Inside, column-free, flexible floor plans are created to facilitate mixed uses.

In contrast to the office towers in the neighborhood, Hangzhou Wangchao Center does not occupy the entire plot, leaving space for precious public areas. The lobby design allows for pedestrian traffic to flow around the travertine-clad core, which the ultra-clear glass façade highlights as a sculptural focal point.

Sustainability certifications: LEED Platinum
Sustainability: high-performance glazing; rainwater reuse; green spaces at ground level; link to public transport

Das Hangzhou Wangchao Center in der ostchinesischen Stadt Hangzhou, die als das Silicon Valley Chinas gilt, ergänzt als Leuchtturmprojekt die Stadterweiterung zum internationalen Handelszentrum. Acht abwechselnd nach außen geneigte Megasäulen verleihen der Glasfassade einen fließenden Charakter; das Hochhaus scheint sich elegant in die Höhe zu drehen. Im Inneren entstehen stützenfreie, flexible Grundrisse für eine gemischte Nutzung.

Im Gegensatz zu den Bürotürmen in der Nachbarschaft nimmt das Hangzhou Wangchao Center nicht die Fläche des gesamten Grundstücks ein, sondern lässt Platz für wertvollen öffentlichen Raum. Die Lobby ermöglicht einen 360-Grad-Fußgängerfluss um den mit Travertin verkleideten Kern, den die ultraklare Glasfassade als skulpturalen Blickfang hervortreten lässt.

Nachhaltigkeitszertifizierung: LEED Platinum
Nachhaltigkeit: Hochleistungsverglasung; Regenwassernutzung; ebenerdige Grünflächen; Anbindung an öffentliche Verkehrsmittel

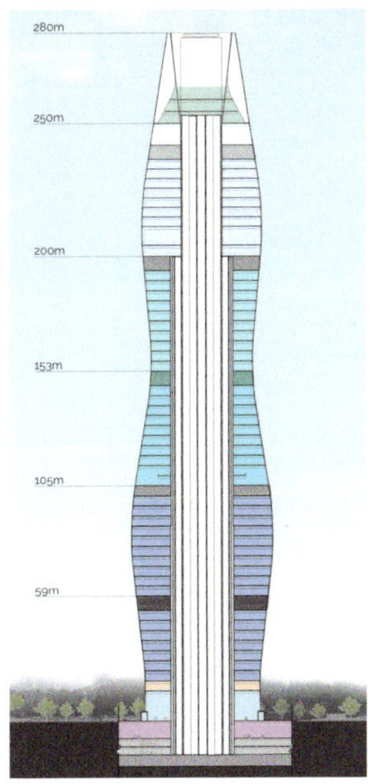

124/1+125/5
Only the massive building core and the eight mega-columns at the building's edges support the entire structure.
Lediglich der massive Gebäudekern und die acht Megastützen an den Gebäudekanten tragen das gesamte Gebäude.

125/1
The sculptural building is the new landmark of Qianjiang Century City, the new CBD of Hangzhou.
Das skulpturale Gebäude ist das neue Wahrzeichen der Qianjiang Century City, des neuen CBD Hangzhous.

125/2
Façade detail
Fassadendetail

125/3+4
Ground and standard floor plans
Grundrisse Erdgeschoss und Regelgeschoss

125/6
Section
Schnitt

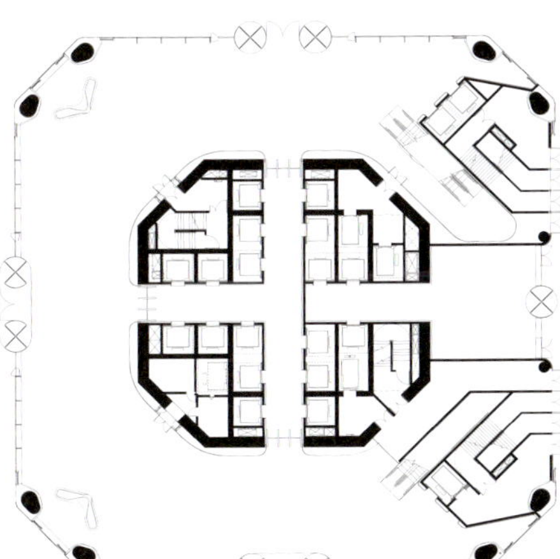

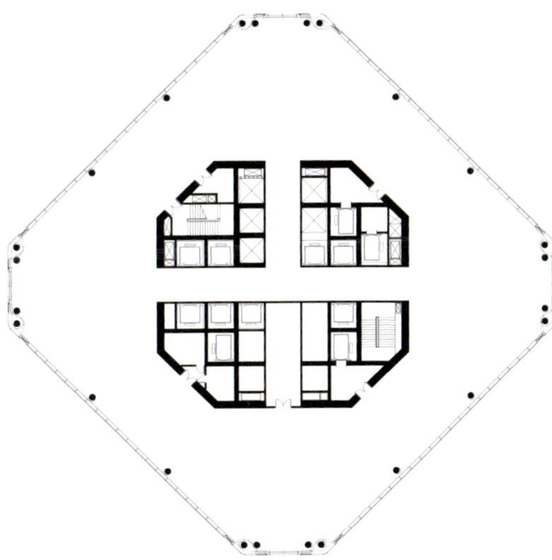

Skidmore, Owings & Merrill

Karlatornet

Gothenburg, Sweden Göteborg, Schweden

Architects Architekt:innen	**Skidmore, Owings & Merrill Chicago IL, USA**
Project architects Projektarchitekt:innen	**Kent Jackson, Peter Jackson**
Architects of record Lokale Architekt:innen	**Semrén & Månsson**
Client Bauherrschaft	**Serneke Group**
Structural engineers Tragwerksplanung	**VBK Konsulterande Ingenjörer**
MEP Haustechnik	**Bengt Dahlgren**
Height Höhe	**246 m**
Stories Geschosse	**74**
Site area Grundstücksfläche	**32 000 m² (wider master plan** gesamter Masterplan **143 000 m²)**
Building footprint Bebaute Fläche	**980 m²**
Gross floor area Bruttogeschossfläche	**97 000 m²**
Structure Konstruktion	**Composite construction** Verbundbauweise
Completion Fertigstellung	**August 2023**
Main use Hauptnutzung	**Mixed use comprising residential, hotel, offices, restaurants** Mischnutzung aus Wohnen, Hotel Büros, Gastronomie

126/1
Karlatornet still seems to be out of scale with Lindholmen. But according to SOM's master plan, further towers will soon create a transition to the surrounding area.
Noch scheint Karlatornet den Maßstab von Lindholmen zu sprengen. Doch gemäß dem Masterplan von SOM schaffen schon bald weitere Türme einen Übergang zur Umgebung.

126/2
The imposing twist of the façade gives the tower its sculptural appearance.
Durch die imposante Drehung der Fassade erlangt der Turm sein skulpturales Erscheinungsbild.

127/1
Section
Schnitt

127/2
Loggias stacked over the entire height further emphasize the verticality of the slender tower by dividing it into four sections.
Über die gesamte Höhe gestapelte Loggien betonen die Vertikale des schlanken Turms zusätzlich, indem sie ihn in vier Teile unterteilen.

127/3
Standard floor plan
Grundriss Regelgeschoss

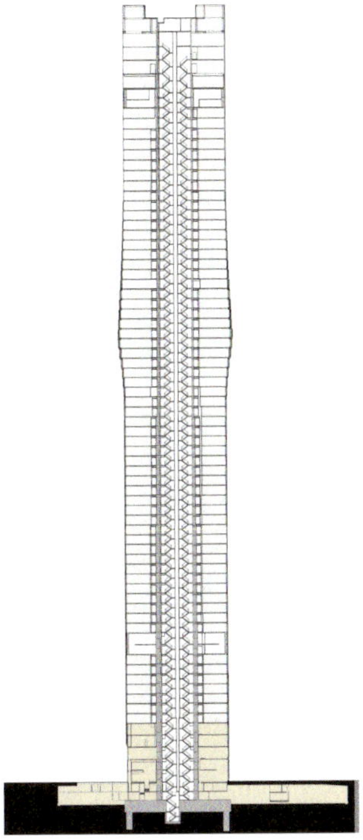

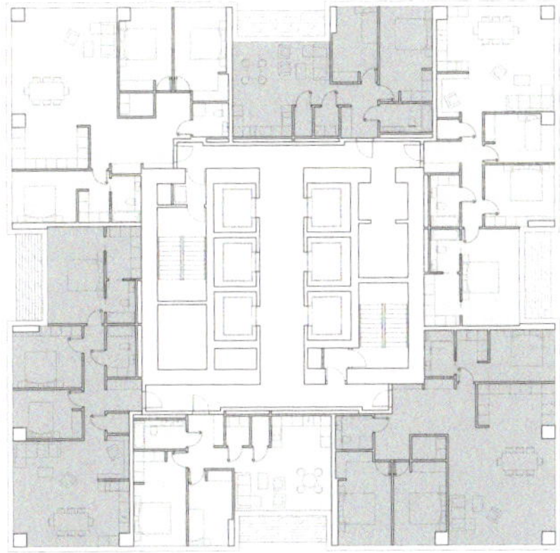

Sustainability:
high-performance building envelope with integrated triple-glazed windows; CO_2 reduction of 400 t by using concrete with lower cement content; significant embodied carbon savings through optimized lateral systems

Nachhaltigkeit:
hochleistungsfähige Gebäudehülle mit integrierten Dreifachverglasungen; Beton mit geringerem Zementanteil ermöglicht Einsparung von 400 t CO_2; erhebliche Einsparungen an gebundenem Kohlenstoff durch innovatives Tragwerk

Karlatornet is the centerpiece of the major Karlastaden master plan for Lindholmen, a former industrial district in Gothenburg's prime riverside location. With over 600 apartments, a hotel, and a restaurant along with a public viewing platform, Karlatornet acts as a revitalizing catalyst in the district, which was previously dominated by the Lindholmen Technology and Science Park. Following its transformation into an urban quarter, Scandinavia's tallest building will be flanked by several smaller high-rises in the future. The striking twist in the façade makes the tower not only an identity-forming building for Lindholmen but also a special landmark for Gothenburg as a whole.

Der Karlatornet bildet das Herzstück des großen Masterplans Karlastaden für Lindholmen, einen ehemaligen Industriebezirk in bester Wasserlage Göteborgs. Mit seinen über 600 Wohnungen, einem Hotel und einem Restaurant sowie einer öffentlichen Aussichtsplattform fungiert Karlatornet als belebender Katalysator in dem bisher durch den Lindholmen Technologie- und Wissenschaftspark geprägten Bezirk. Nach der vollzogenen Umwandlung in ein urbanes Stadtquartier soll das höchste Gebäude Skandinaviens zukünftig von mehreren kleineren Hochhäusern flankiert werden. Der markante Twist in der Fassade macht das Hochhaus nicht nur zu einem identitätsstiftenden Gebäude für Lindholmen, sondern zu einem besonderen Wahrzeichen für ganz Göteborg.

Skidmore, Owings & Merrill

One and Two Manhattan West

New York NY, USA

The towers, clad in high-performance glass, assert themselves confidently in the skyline of Hudson Yards with their clear appearance featuring rounded corners and slightly diverging silhouettes. Their unique location above active rail lines required complex foundations and a special structural framework.

At One Manhattan West, this resulted in a transparent and column-free lobby, as the load-bearing columns slope inward toward the travertine-clad core, which stands directly on bedrock.

At Two Manhattan West, the sculpted columns splay out in such a way that they transfer the load of the tower precisely between the underground tracks.

Die mit Hochleistungsglas verkleideten Türme behaupten sich in ihrem klaren Erscheinungsbild mit den abgerundeten Ecken und leicht auseinanderlaufenden Silhouetten selbstbewusst in der Skyline der Hudson Yards. Ihr besonderer Standort über aktiven Bahnlinien erforderte eine komplizierte Gründung und ein besonderes Tragwerk.

Bei One Manhattan West resultierte daraus eine transparente und stützenfreie Lobby, da sich die tragenden Säulen nach innen zum mit Travertin verkleideten Kern, der direkt auf dem felsigen Untergrund steht, neigen. Bei Two Manhattan West spreizen sich die skulpturalen Säulen so auf, dass sie das Gewicht des Turms genau zwischen die unterirdischen Gleise abtragen.

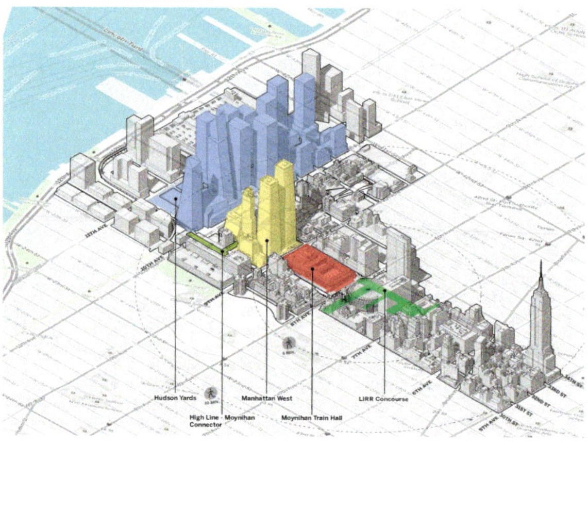

128/1
Site plan
Lageplan

128/2+3+129/1
The rounded corners lend the two towers a dynamic presence in the skyline.
Die abgerundeten Ecken verleihen den beiden Türmen eine dynamische Präsenz in der Skyline.

128/4+129/2
A public green space connects the entrance halls of both towers.
Eine öffentliche Grünfläche verbindet die Eingangshallen der beiden Türme miteinander.

129/3
Entrance hall of Two Manhattan West
Eingangshalle von Two Manhattan West

129/4
Load transfer of the twin towers
Lastenabtrag der beiden Zwillingstürme

Sustainability certifications: LEED Gold
Sustainability: buildings powered by 100% renewable energy; expected 80% reduction in direct carbon emissions; landscaping features native species; rainwater reuse; beehives; pedestrian connection to Moynihan Train Hall and Penn Station

Nachhaltigkeitszertifizierung: LEED Gold
Nachhaltigkeit: Gebäudebetrieb mit 100 % erneuerbarer Energie; erwartete Reduzierung der direkten Kohlenstoffemissionen um 80 %; Landschaftsgestaltung mit einheimischen Pflanzen; Regenwassernutzung; Bienenstöcke; fußläufige Verbindung zur Moynihan Train Hall und Penn Station

Architects Architekt:innen	**Skidmore, Owings & Merrill Chicago IL, USA**
Project architects Projektarchitekt:innen	**Gary Haney, Kenneth Lewis, Julia Murphy, Kim Van Holsbeke, Charles Besjak, Preetam Biswas**
Client Bauherrschaft	**Brookfield Properties**
Structural engineers Tragwerksplanung	**Skidmore, Owings & Merrill**
MEP Haustechnik	**Jaros, Baum & Bolles**
Height Höhe	**303 m; 285 m**
Stories Geschosse	**67; 58**
Site area Grundstücksfläche	**11 776 m²**
Building footprint Bebaute Fläche	**9405 m²**
Gross floor area Bruttogeschossfläche	**352 656 m²**
Structure Konstruktion	**Composite construction** Verbundbauweise
Completion Fertigstellung	**January 2024** Januar 2024
Main use Hauptnutzung	**Offices** Büros

Snøhetta

Airside

Hong Kong, China Hongkong, China

In the newly developed business district of Kai Tak, named after the airport that once stood on this site, five volumes combine to form a structure consisting of a chamfered podium and a high-rise building. In between, a landscaped rooftop garden, which is accessed via a spectacular public atrium, mediates between them.

Drawing on Hong Kong's tradition of textile manufacturing, the architecture evokes various aspects of tailoring. The shape of the chamfered edges is inspired by textile cuttings, while the ribbed glass of the façade is an allusion to the drapes of fabrics. In this way, the building illustrates the transformation of both the developer and Hong Kong itself from textile industry to real estate development, finance, and technology.

Im neu erschlossenen Geschäftsviertel von Kai Tak, benannt nach dem einst an dieser Stelle befindlichen Flughafen, fügen sich fünf Teilvolumen zu einer Kombination aus abgekantetem Sockel und Hochhaus zusammen. Zwischen beiden vermittelt eine begrünte Dachlandschaft, die über ein spektakuläres öffentliches Atrium erschlossen ist.

Angelehnt an Hongkongs Tradition der Textilherstellung, greift die Architektur des Projekts verschiedene Aspekte der Schneiderei auf. Die Form der abgeschrägten Kanten ist von Textilzuschnitten inspiriert, während das geriffelte Glas der Fassade eine Anspielung auf das Drapieren von Stoffen ist. Somit verdeutlicht das Gebäude sowohl den Wandel des Bauträgers als auch Hongkongs selbst: von der Textilherstellung hin zu Immobilienentwicklung, Finanzen und Technologie.

Sustainability certifications:
LEED Core and Shell Platinum; BEAM Plus NB Platinum; BEAM Plus NH Platinum; WELL Core Platinum; China Green Building Design – 3 Stars; Smart Core Platinum, Wired Score Platinum
Sustainability:
extensive greenery; rainwater reuse; bicycle parking facilities; heat recovery; lift regenerative drives; energy-efficient heating and cooling systems; comprehensive smart waste management

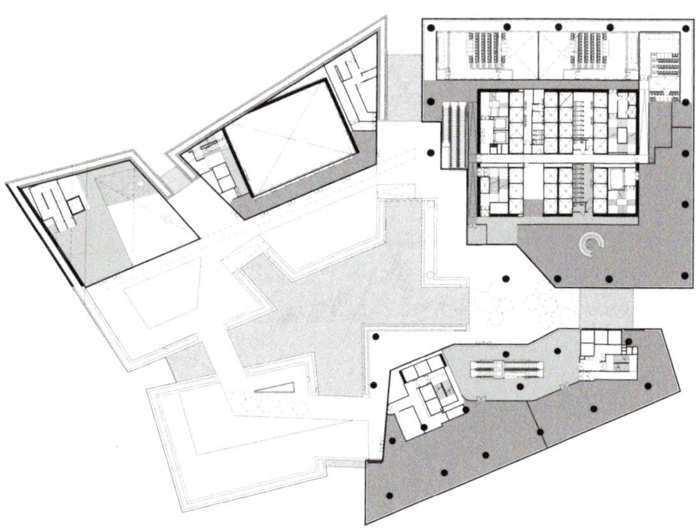

130/1
The tiered structure of the building volumes and the green rooftop garden mediate between the high-rise and the promenade along the banks of the Kai Tak River.
Durch die Abstufung der einzelnen Baukörper und den begrünten Dachgarten wird zwischen dem Hochhaus und der Uferpromenade des Kai Tak Rivers vermittelt.

130/2
Mall in the podium
Mall im Sockelgebäude

130/3
Rooftop landscape with water mist cooling
Dachlandschaft mit Wassernebelkühlung

131/1
Entrance hall of office floors
Eingangshalle Büronutzung

131/2+3
10th and 36th floor plans
Grundrisse 10. und 36. Obergeschoss

131/4
6th floor plan
Grundriss 6. Obergeschoss

Nachhaltigkeitszertifizierung: LEED Core and Shell Platinum; BEAM Plus NB Platinum; BEAM Plus NH Platinum; WELL Core Platinum; China Green Building Designn – 3 Stars; Smart Core Platinum, Wired Score Platinum
Nachhaltigkeit: umfangreiche Begrünung; Regenwassernutzung; Fahrradparkplätze; Wärmerückgewinnung; Aufzüge mit regenerativem Antrieb; energieeffiziente Heiz- und Kühlsysteme; umfassendes intelligentes Abfallmanagement

Architects Architekt:innen	**Snøhetta** **Oslo, Norway** Norwegen
Project architects Projektarchitekt:innen	**Robert Greenwood**
Architects of record Lokale Architekt:innen	**Ronald Lu & Partners**
Client Bauherrschaft	**Nan Fung Group**
Structural engineers Tragwerksplanung	**Arup; J. Roger Preston**
MEP Haustechnik	**Arup**
Landscape architects Landschaftsarchitekt:innen	**Urbis**
Height Höhe	**213 m**
Stories Geschosse	**47**
Site area Grundstücksfläche	**19 044 m²**
Building footprint Bebaute Fläche	**11 239 m²**
Gross floor area Bruttogeschossfläche	**176 000 m²**
Structure Konstruktion	**Composite construction** Verbundbauweise
Completion Fertigstellung	**September 2023**
Main use Hauptnutzung	**Mixed use comprising offices, retail, restaurants, public gardens** Mischnutzung aus Büros, Einzelhandel, Gastronomie, öffentliche Gärten

Stefano Boeri Architetti

Nanjing Vertical Forest

Nanjing, China

Sustainability: urban afforestation with 4,500 m² of greenery

Nachhaltigkeit: städtische Aufforstung durch 4.500 m² Grünflächen

132/1
The project is intended to serve as a prototype for China's densely built-up megacities. The plants make an important contribution to biodiversity in big cities.
Das Projekt soll als Prototyp für Chinas dicht bebaute Megacitys dienen. Die Pflanzen leisten einen wichtigen Beitrag zur Biodiversität in der Großstadt.

132/2+3
Façade details: the greenery is expected to steadily increase over time and become denser.
Fassadendetails: Das Grün soll mit der Zeit stetig zunehmen und immer dichter werden.

133/1
The two towers share a common podium, which houses a mall with a wide range of offerings.
Die beiden Türme teilen sich einen gemeinsamen Sockel, in dem sich eine Mall mit weitreichendem Angebot befindet.

133/2
Standard floor plan Tower A
Grundriss Regelgeschoss Turm A

133/3
Section
Schnitt

Nanjing Vertical Forest is Stefano Boeri's second project in China. The façades of the two towers are segmented into circumferential bands of balconies and plant troughs, clad with red terracotta panels. They host over 800 trees as well as more than 2,500 shrubs, perennials, and climbing plants, creating a new vertical forest that contributes to the regeneration of local biodiversity by planting 27 native species.

Nanjing Vertical Forest represents another advancement in the adaptability of the Vertical Forest typology, which includes several examples in various climate zones, each addressing regional and specific needs.

Nanjing Vertical Forest ist das zweite Projekt von Stefano Boeri in China. Die Fassaden der beiden Türme gliedern sich in umlaufende Bänder aus Balkonen und Pflanztrögen, die mit Platten aus rotem Terrakotta verkleidet sind. Sie beherbergen über 800 Bäume sowie über 2.500 Sträucher, Stauden und Kletterpflanzen. So entsteht ein neuer vertikaler Wald, der durch die Anpflanzung von 27 einheimischen Arten zur Regeneration der lokalen Artenvielfalt beiträgt.

Der Nanjing Vertical Forest stellt einen weiteren Fortschritt in Bezug auf die Anpassungsfähigkeit der Vertical-Forest-Typologie dar, die mehrere Beispiele in verschiedenen Klimazonen umfasst, von denen jedes auf regionale, spezifische Bedürfnisse eingeht.

Architects Architekt:innen	**Stefano Boeri Architetti Milan, Italy** Mailand, Italien
Project architects Projektarchitekt:innen	**Stefano Boeri, Yibo Xu, Pietro Chiodi**
Architects of record Lokale Architekt:innen	**Nanjing Yangtze River Urban Architectural Design**
Client Bauherrschaft	**Nanjing Yang Zi State-owned Investment Group**
Structural engineers Tragwerksplanung	**Arup; Nanjing Yangtze River Urban Architectural Design**
MEP Haustechnik	**Nanjing Yangtze River Urban Architectural Design**
Landscape architects Landschaftsarchitekt:innen	**Studio Laura Gatti**
Height Höhe	**200 m; 108 m**
Stories Geschosse	**35; 19**
Site area Grundstücksfläche	**18 760 m²**
Building footprint Bebaute Fläche	**10 124 m²**
Gross floor area Bruttogeschossfläche	**80 970 m²**
Structure Konstruktion	**Reinforced concrete** Stahlbeton
Completion Fertigstellung	**April 2024**
Main use Hauptnutzung	**Mixed use comprising offices, museum, education, retail, restaurant** Mischnutzung aus Büros, Museum, Bildung, Einzelhandel, Restaurant

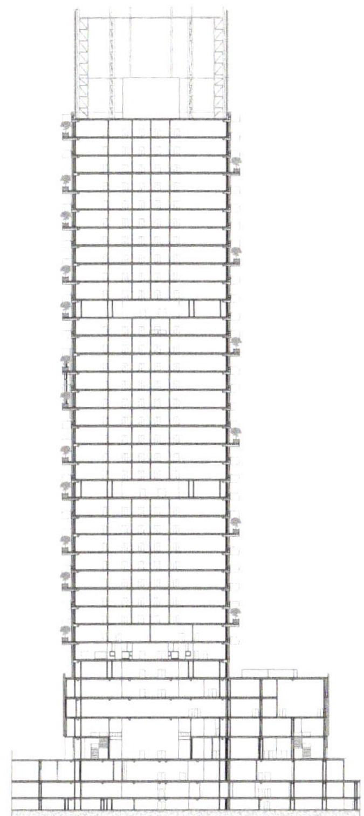

Studio Gang

11 Hoyt

New York NY, USA

Sustainability certifications: LEED Gold; NYC Energy Efficiency Ratings – A
Sustainability: high-performance façade reduces energy consumption by 43%; 2,500 m² of urban landscapes; rainwater reuse; low-flow fixtures; bicycle storage and EV-charging stations; reuse of existing parking garage for basement and part of ground floor slab reduces embodied carbon

Nachhaltigkeitszertifizierung: LEED Gold; NYC Energy Efficiency Ratings – A
Nachhaltigkeit: Hochleistungsfassade reduziert den Energieverbrauch um 43 %; 2500 m² Grünflächen; Regenwassernutzung; wassersparende Armaturen; Fahrradabstellplätze und Ladestationen für Elektrofahrzeuge; Einsparung von CO_2 durch Nutzung der bestehenden Tiefgarage für das Untergeschoss sowie einen Teil der Bodenplatte

On the former site of a parking garage, the tower with its scalloped edges and adjoining podium occupies the entire block. The "fifth façade" of the podium, visible from the street but screened from its activity, is lushly landscaped, creating a sustainable oasis in the middle of the city.

The tower's characteristically curved façade is inspired by the classic bay windows of traditional Brooklyn Brownstones and was constructed from a system of prefabricated double-shell concrete elements. The scalloped structure running across the façade forms numerous habitable window niches, resulting in more than 190 unique floor plans.

Auf dem ehemaligen Gelände eines Parkhauses nimmt der Turm mit seinen gewellten Kanten und dem anschließenden Podium den gesamten Block ein. Die von der Straße aus sichtbare, aber abgeschirmte „fünfte Fassade" des Podiums ist üppig begrünt und stellt eine nachhaltige Oase mitten in der Stadt dar.

Die charakteristisch geschwungene Fassade des Turms ist von den klassischen Erkern der traditionellen Brooklyner Brownstones inspiriert und wurde aus einem System von vorgefertigten Beton-Doppelschalungen zusammengefügt. Die Wellenstruktur, die sich über die Fassade zieht, formt eine Vielzahl an bewohnbaren Fensternischen aus, wodurch mehr als 190 individuelle Grundrisse entstehen.

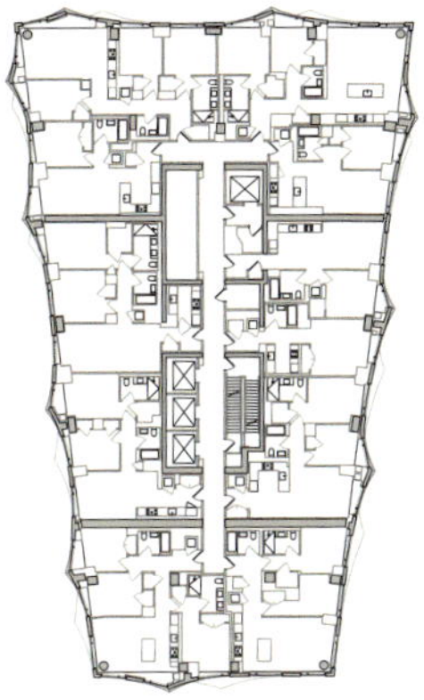

134 / 1
View up along the façade through the open roof of the podium
Aufblick entlang der Fassade durch das offene Dach des Podiums

134 / 2
The curved façade results not only in varying floor plans but also allows views in different directions.
Aus den Wellen der Fassade resultieren nicht nur variierende Grundrisse, sondern auch Aussichtsmöglichkeiten in verschiedene Richtungen.

135 / 1
Standard floor plan
Grundriss Regelgeschoss

135 / 2
Section
Schnitt

135 / 3
As the site was previously occupied by a parking garage, the compact footprint of the tower and the low height of the podium allow for more sunlight to reach the street.
Nachdem das Grundstück zuvor mit einem Parkhaus bebaut war, begünstigen die kompakte Grundfläche des Turms und die geringe Höhe des Podiums die Sonneneinstrahlung auf die Straße.

135 / 4
The communal garden on the podium's roof is a popular gathering spot for the residents.
Der gemeinschaftliche Garten auf dem Dach des Podiums ist ein beliebter Treffpunkt für die Bewohner:innen.

Architects Architekt:innen	**Studio Gang** **Chicago IL, USA**
Project architects Projektarchitekt:innen	**Jeanne Gang,** **Weston Walker,** **Arthur Liu**
Architects of record Lokale Architekt:innen	**Hill West**
Client Bauherrschaft	**Tishman Speyer**
Structural engineers Tragwerksplanung	**McNamara Salvia**
MEP Haustechnik	**Cosentini Associates**
Landscape architects Landschaftsarchitekt:innen	**Hollander Design**
Height Höhe	**189 m**
Stories Geschosse	**57**
Site area Grundstücksfläche	**5820 m²**
Building footprint Bebaute Fläche	**4349 m²**
Gross floor area Bruttogeschossfläche	**71 535 m²**
Structure Konstruktion	**Reinforced concrete** Stahlbeton
Completion Fertigstellung	**December 2021** Dezember 2021
Main use Hauptnutzung	**Residential** Wohnen

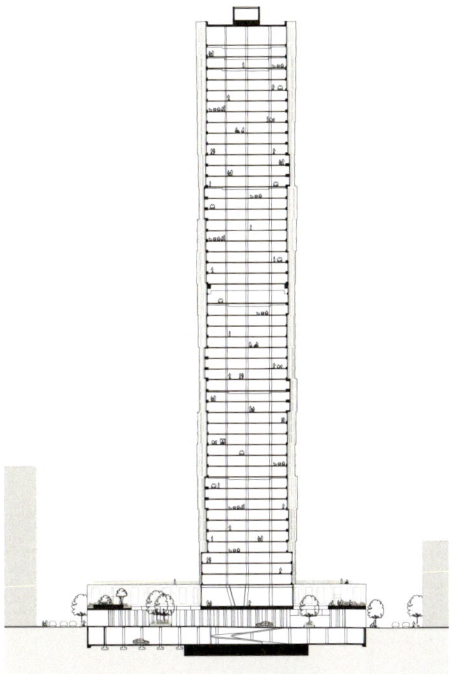

StudioVlayStreeruwitz

The One

Vienna, Austria Wien, Österreich

136/1
The One and the ensemble's central plaza
The One mit dem zentralen Quartiersplatz des Ensembles

136/2
Arcade with bicycle parking area
Arkade mit Fahrradgarage

136/3
Lighting concept in the entrance hall
Lichtkonzept in der Eingangshalle

137/1
Overall view of The Marks
Gesamtdarstellung The Marks

137/2
Concept diagram
Konzeptdiagramm

137/3
Section
Schnitt

137/4
At first glance, The One stands out from the other two towers in the ensemble thanks to its wrap-around balconies.
The One hebt sich durch die umlaufenden Balkone auf den ersten Blick von den beiden anderen Türmen des Ensembles ab.

137/5
A swimming pool atop the podium building is part of the communal areas for the residents.
Ein Schwimmbad auf dem Sockelgebäude ist Teil der Gemeinschaftsflächen für die Bewohner:innen.

In Vienna's diffuse Zwischenstadt ("in-between city"), the ensemble The Marks forms a new center with its three residential towers, which offer 50 percent of apartments at affordable rents in line with the city's vision. The One stands out from its two neighbors due to its meandering façade. The projections and recesses of the all-round balconies create a multifaceted image that changes depending on the viewing angle and incidence of light. At the same time, this design creates a transition from the apartments to the airy outdoor space.

At ground level, the high-rise buildings are interconnected by a continuous arcade. It forms a sequence of open plazas and accommodates spacious commercial areas and restaurants alongside a bicycle parking garage. Communal rooms and play areas on the green deck provide residents with potential open spaces outside their own apartments.

In Wiens diffuser Zwischenstadt bildet das Ensemble The Marks mit seinen drei Wohntürmen, die 50 Prozent leistbare Mieten im Sinne der Stadt anbieten, ein neues Zentrum. Dabei hebt sich The One durch die mäandrierende Fassade von seinen beiden Nachbarn ab. Dank der Vor- und Rücksprünge der umlaufenden Balkone verändert sich das vielschichtige Bild je nach Blickwinkel und Lichteinfall. Gleichzeitig wird so ein Übergang aus den Wohnungen in den luftigen Außenraum geschaffen.

Am Boden sind die Hochhäuser über eine durchgehende Arkade miteinander verbunden. Sie bildet eine Abfolge von offenen Plätzen und beherbergt neben einem Fahrradparkhaus großzügige Gewerbeflächen und Restaurants. Gemeinschaftsräume und Spielflächen auf dem Gründeck bieten den Bewohner:innen potenzielle Freiräume außerhalb der eigenen Wohnung.

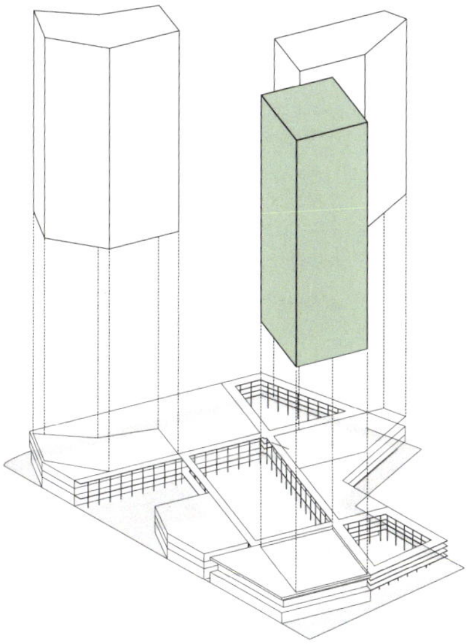

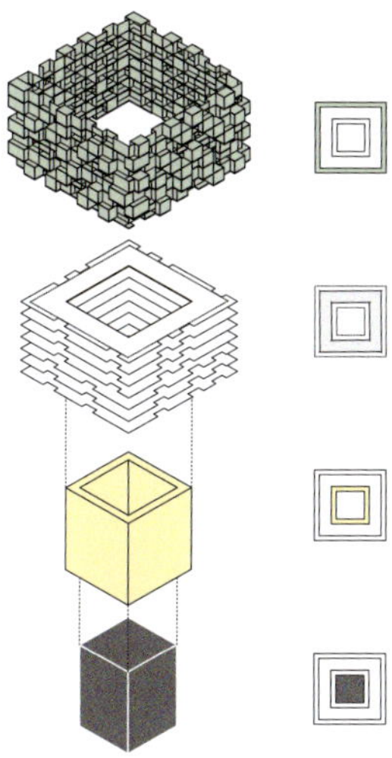

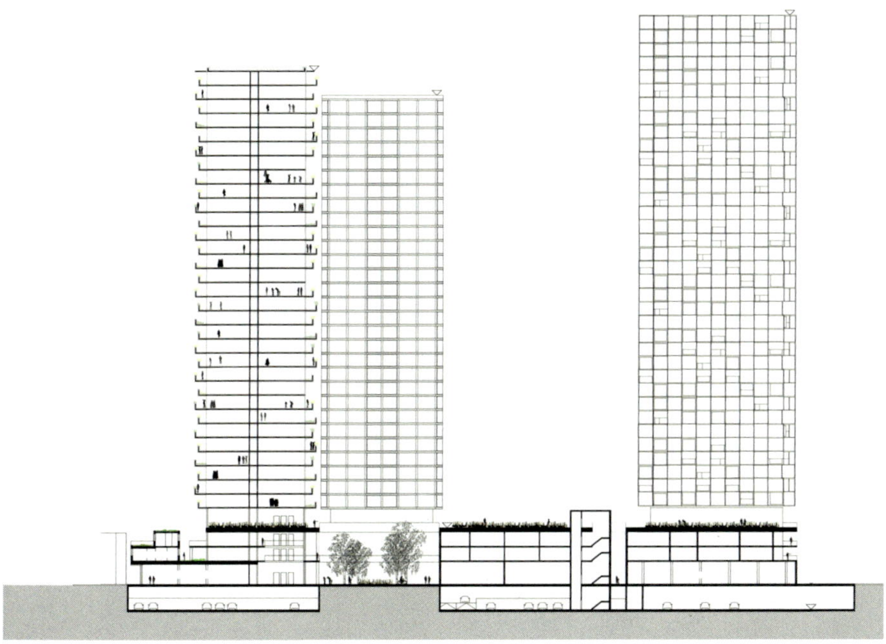

Architects Architekt:innen	**StudioVlayStreeruwitz** **Vienna, Austria** Wien, Österreich
Project architects Projektarchitekt:innen	**Lina Streeruwitz,** **Bernd Vlay**
Architects of record Lokale Architekt:innen	**puk architekten**
Client Bauherrschaft	**Neues Leben;** **WBV-GPA**
Structural engineers Tragwerksplanung	**Buschina & Partner** **Ziviltechniker**
MEP Haustechnik	**HTB-PLAN Haustechnik**
Landscape architects Landschaftsarchitekt:innen	**rajek barosch** **landschaftsarchitektur**
Height Höhe	**126 m**
Stories Geschosse	**38**
Site area Grundstücksfläche	**14 800 m²**
Building footprint Bebaute Fläche	**2230 m²**
Gross floor area Bruttogeschossfläche	**49 171 m²**
Structure Konstruktion	**Reinforced concrete** Stahlbeton
Completion Fertigstellung	**April 2023**
Main use Hauptnutzung	**Residential, retail** Wohnen, Einzelhandel

WOHA

Pan Pacific Orchard

Singapore Singapur

Architects Architekt:innen	**WOHA** **Singapore** Singapur
Project architects Projektarchitekt:innen	**Wong Mun Summ, Phua Hong Wei, Herbert Salim, Christina Ong, Sofwan, Yudhi Aristan, Victoria Tan, Chong Siew Way, Evanne Kok**
Client Bauherrschaft	**UOL Group Limited; Pan Pacific Hotels Group**
Structural engineers Tragwerksplanung	**DP Engineers; TEP Consultants**
MEP Haustechnik	**Beca Carter Hollings & Ferner**
Landscape architects Landschaftsarchitekt:innen	**WOHA**
Height Höhe	**141 m**
Stories Geschosse	**35**
Site area Grundstücksfläche	**3654 m²**
Building footprint Bebaute Fläche	**2850 m²**
Gross floor area Bruttogeschossfläche	**19 625 m²**
Structure Konstruktion	**Composite construction** Verbundbauweise
Completion Fertigstellung	**June 2023** Juni 2023
Main use Hauptnutzung	**Hotel**

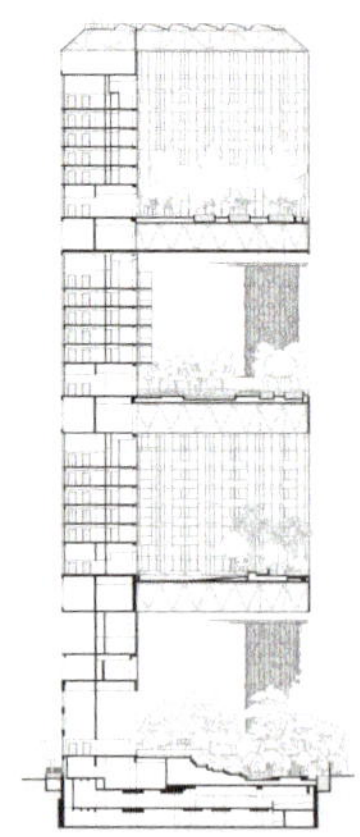

Sustainability certifications:
Green Mark Platinum
Sustainability:
natural ventilation; reflective ceilings

Pan Pacific Orchard is a prototype for vertical urban development, tripling the floor area compared to the previous building. The new high-rise consists of four stacked blocks, each with atrium-like recesses. These are designed as four lushly planted sky terraces themed around forest, beach, garden, and cloud. These open yet sheltered voids offer natural oases of tranquility and spaces for various outdoor activities and events in Singapore's equatorial climate, even during tropical rainfalls. Moreover, the densely built-up environment benefits both climatically and visually from the high proportion of green space (300 percent).

Nachhaltigkeitszertifizierung:
Green Mark Platinum
Nachhaltigkeit:
natürliche Belüftung;
reflektierende Decken

Pan Pacific Orchard stellt einen Prototyp für vertikalen Städtebau dar, der die Geschossfläche im Vergleich zur vorherigen Bebauung verdreifacht. Das neue Gebäude besteht aus vier übereinandergestapelten, atriumartig eingeschnittenen Blöcken. Diese formen vier üppig bepflanzte Himmelsterrassen zu den Themen Wald, Strand, Garten und Wolke aus. Die offenen und gleichzeitig geschützten Lufträume offerieren im äquatorialen Klima Singapurs naturnahe Ruheoasen sowie Raum für verschiedene Aktivitäten und Veranstaltungen im Freien, auch während tropischer Regenfälle. Darüber hinaus profitiert die stark verdichtete Umgebung klimatisch wie auch visuell von dem hohen Grünflächenanteil von 300 Prozent.

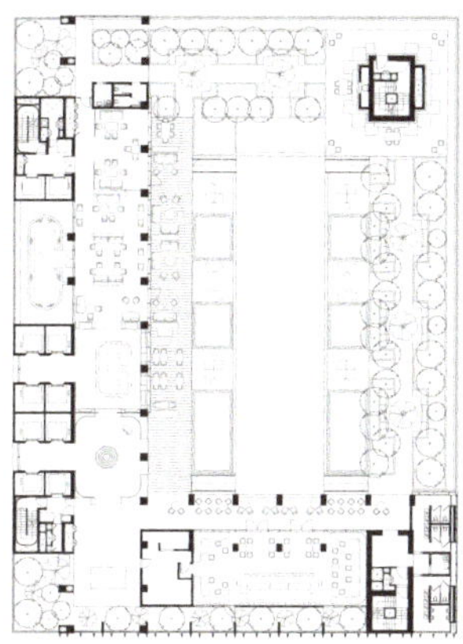

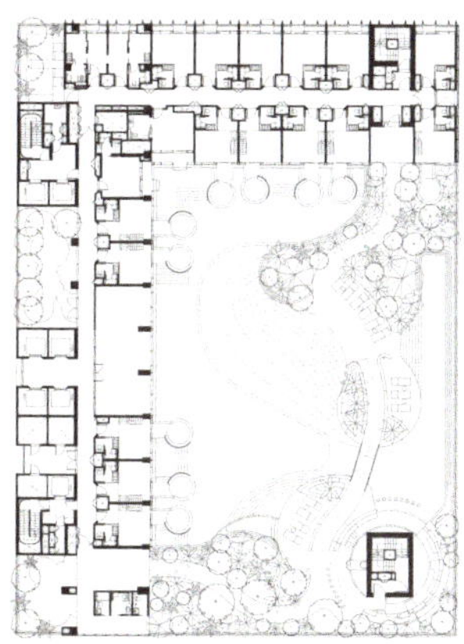

138/1
The garden terrace, reminiscent of a botanical garden, provides space for larger outdoor events.
Die Gartenterrasse, die an einen botanischen Garten erinnert, bietet Raum für größere Veranstaltungen im Grünen.

138/2
The beach terrace allows hotel guests to experience the feeling of a beach holiday while being in the city center.
Die Strandterrasse ermöglicht den Hotelgäst:innen das Gefühl eines Strandurlaubs, während sie sich im Zentrum der Stadt befinden.

138/3
Photovoltaic system on the rooftop of Pan Pacific Orchard
Photovoltaikanlage auf dem Dach von Pan Pacific Orchard

138/4
Section
Schnitt

139/1
The large open atriums characterize the unusual building structure.
Die großen offenen Lufträume charakterisieren die ungewöhnliche Gebäudestruktur.

139/2
Floor plan terrace level garden
Grundriss Terrassengeschoss Garten

139/3
Floor plan terrace level beach
Grundriss Terrassengeschoss Strand

Heritage Lanes, 80 Ann Street

Brisbane, Australia Australien

140/1
City garden in the podium
Stadtgarten im Sockel

140/2
The volume is divided into several cubes, creating open terraces at the intersections.
Das Volumen wird in mehrere Kuben unterteilt, wodurch an den Schnittstellen offene Terrassen entstehen.

141/1
The veil suspended in front of the podium opens up toward Ann Street, revealing a passageway to the elevated lobby – a permeable platform, a reinterpretation of the Queensland Veranda.
Der vorgehängte Schleier des Sockels lüftet sich zur Ann Street und öffnet einen Durchgang zur erhöhten Lobby – eine durchlässige Plattform, eine Neuinterpretation der Queensland Veranda.

141/2
Section
Schnitt

141/3+7+8
Ground floor, 1st floor, and standard floor plans
Grundrisse Erdgeschoss, 1. Obergeschoss und Regelgeschoss

141/4
Restaurant area
Restaurantbereich

141/5+6
Digital light installations in the form of LED ceilings, covering a total area of over 600 square meters, are installed both in the podium and on the rooftop.
Digitale Lichtinstallationen in Form von LED-Decken mit einer Gesamtfläche von über 600 Quadratmetern finden sich sowohl im Sockel als auch auf dem Dach.

Heritage Lanes is located in Brisbane's historical business district and is built upon the restored parts of the heritage-listed Fruit and Produce Exchange from 1906. In the subtropical climate of the city in northeastern Australia, not only the podium areas have been designed as an open marketplace and urban garden. Extensive greenery, interacting with immersive digital art, permeates the entire design of the office tower right up to the top of the building. Specially designed "breathable" office floors with garden terraces, access to daylight, and natural ventilation ensure a close connection between nature and technology.

Heritage Lanes befindet sich in einem historischen Geschäftsviertel von Brisbane und baut auf den restaurierten Teilen der denkmalgeschützten Fruit and Produce Exchange aus dem Jahr 1906 auf. Im subtropischen Klima der Stadt im Nordosten Australiens wurden nicht nur die Sockelflächen als offener Marktplatz und Stadtgarten konzipiert. Eine umfangreiche Begrünung, die mit immersiver digitaler Kunst interagiert, durchzieht die komplette Gestaltung des Büroturms bis zur Spitze des Gebäudes. Speziell „atmungsaktiv" angelegte Büroetagen mit Gartenterrassen, Zugang zu Tageslicht und natürlicher Belüftung schaffen eine enge Verbindung zwischen Natur und Technik.

Architects Architekt:innen	**Woods Bagot** **Adelaide, Australia** Australien
Project architects Projektarchitekt:innen	**David Lee**
Client Bauherrschaft	**Mirvac**
Structural engineers Tragwerksplanung	**Arup; AECOM**
MEP Haustechnik	**Arup; Ellis Air; Fredon**
Landscape architects Landschaftsarchitekt:innen	**ASPECT Studios**
Height Höhe	**143 m**
Stories Geschosse	**35**
Site area Grundstücksfläche	**5485 m²**
Building footprint Bebaute Fläche	**2800 m²**
Gross floor area Bruttogeschossfläche	**74 500 m²**
Structure Konstruktion	**Reinforced concrete** Stahlbeton
Completion Fertigstellung	**April 2022**
Main use Hauptnutzung	**Offices** Büros

Sustainability certifications:
NABERS Energy – 5.5 Stars;
NABERS Water – 4.5 Stars;
WELL Core and Shell Platinum;
Greenstar – 6 Stars
Sustainability:
restoration and integration of the former Brisbane Fruit and Produce Exchange from 1906; naturally ventilated podium; planted terraces

Nachhaltigkeitszertifizierung:
NABERS Energie – 5.5 Stars;
NABERS Wasser – 4.5 Stars;
WELL Core and Shell Platinum;
Greenstar – 6 Stars
Nachhaltigkeit:
Sanierung und Integration der ehemaligen Brisbane Fruit and Produce Exchange von 1906; natürlich belüftetes Sockelgebäude; begrünte Terrassen

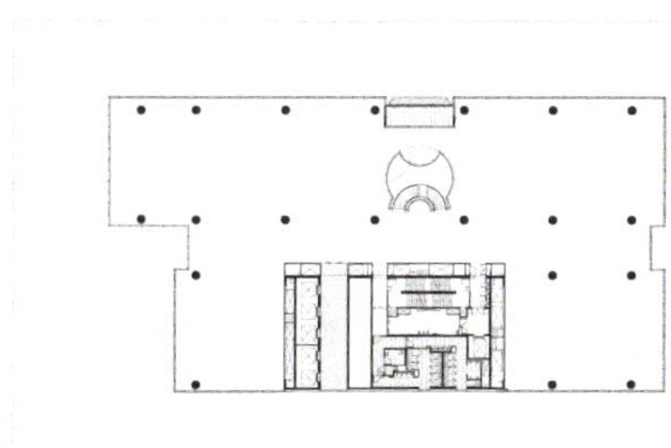

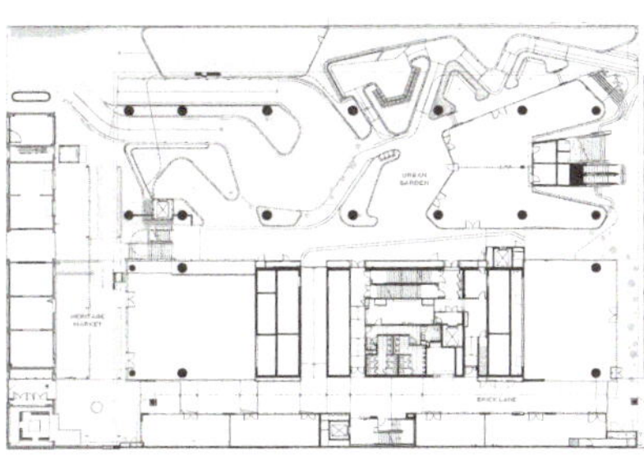

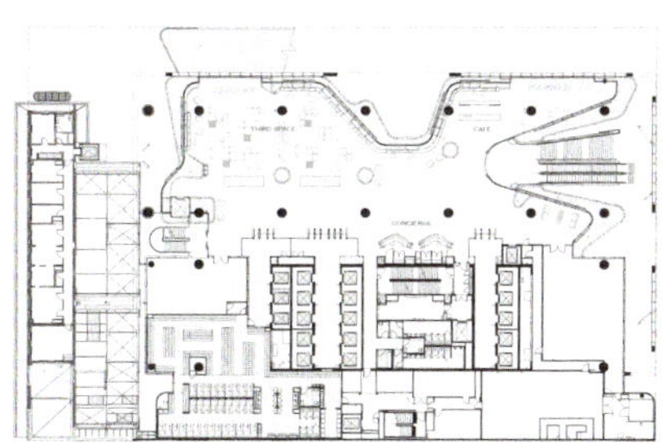

Yuko Nagayama & Associates

Tokyu Kabukicho Tower

Tokyo, Japan Tokio, Japan

Architects Architekt:innen	**Yuko Nagayama & Associates** **Tokyo, Japan** Tokio, Japan
Project architects Projektarchitekt:innen	**Yuko Nagayama**
Architects of record Lokale Architekt:innen	**Kume Sekkei; Tokyu Architects & Engineers**
Client Bauherrschaft	**Tokyu Corporation and Tokyu Recreation**
Structural engineers Tragwerksplanung	**Arup**
MEP Haustechnik	**Kume Sekkei**
Lighting design Lichtplaner:innen	**ICE Illumination of City Environment**
Height Höhe	**225 m**
Height Höhe	**126 m**
Stories Geschosse	**45**
Site area Grundstücksfläche	**4604 m²**
Building footprint Bebaute Fläche	**3171 m²**
Gross floor area Bruttogeschossfläche	**87 400 m²**
Structure Konstruktion	**Steel** Stahl
Completion Fertigstellung	**January 2023** Januar 2023
Main use Hauptnutzung	**Mixed use comprising hotel, restaurants, cinema, theater, entertainment** Mischnutzung aus Hotel, Restaurants, Kino, Theater, Unterhaltung

Named after the nightlife area in Tokyo's vibrant Shinjuku district, Tokyu Kabukicho Tower, with its hotels, restaurants, theaters, game arcades, and clubs, is the largest entertainment complex in Japan. Its undulating glass façade, printed with an arch pattern made up of countless ceramic dots, resembles a giant animated water fountain. It recalls the many fountains that sprang from Kabukicho's former swamps and ultimately defined the plaza now built over by the high-rise. The movement of the splashing water symbolizes the vitality and energy that emanates from the people in Kabukicho, deliberately contrasting with the austere architectural vocabulary of the surrounding office buildings.

Sustainability certifications:
BELS – 4 Stars

Nachhaltigkeitszertifizierung:
BELS – 4 Stars

Benannt nach dem Ausgehviertel in Tokios pulsierendem Bezirk Shinjuku, ist der Tokyu Kabukicho Tower mit seinen Hotels, Restaurants, Theatern, Spielhallen und Clubs der größte Vergnügungskomplex Japans. Seine gewellte Glasfassade, die mit einem Bogenmuster aus unzähligen Keramikpunkten bedruckt ist, gleicht einer riesigen animierten Wasserfontäne. Sie erinnert an die vielen Brunnen, die aus den ehemaligen Sümpfen Kabukichos entsprangen und zuletzt den mit dem Hochhaus überbauten Platz prägten. Dabei steht die Bewegung des spritzenden Wassers symbolisch für die Vitalität und Energie der Menschen in Kabukicho und bildet so bewusst einen Kontrast zu der strengen Formensprache der umliegenden Bürogebäude.

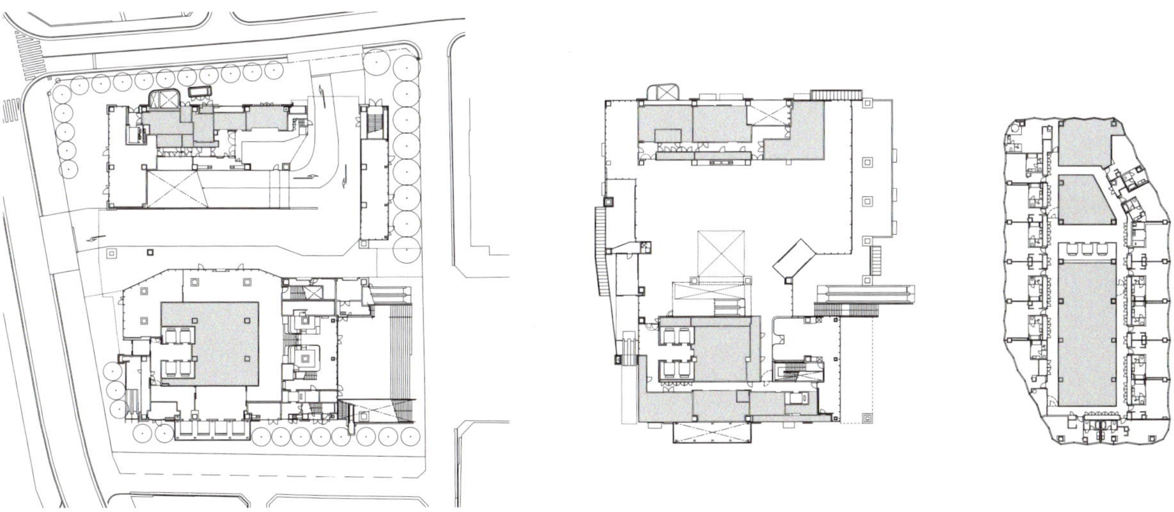

142/1
Façade with ceramic arch pattern
Fassade mit Bogenmuster aus Keramik

143/1
The building, shaped like a giant water fountain, is the new landmark of the entertainment district.
Das Gebäude in Form einer riesigen Wasserfontäne fungiert als neues Wahrzeichen des Vergnügungsviertels.

143/2
Entrance to a part of the building
Eingang zu einem Teilbereich

143/3
Ground floor, 6th floor, and standard floor plans
Grundrisse Erdgeschoss, 6. Obergeschoss und Regelgeschoss

143/4
In contrast to the uniform glass façade, the base of the building clearly suggests its special use.
Der Gebäudesockel suggeriert im Gegensatz zur einheitlichen Glasfassade die besondere Nutzung recht deutlich.

Zaha Hadid Architects

The Henderson

Hong Kong, China Hongkong, China

Sustainability certifications:
LEED Platinum;
WELL Platinum;
China Green Building – 3 Stars
Sustainability:
4-ply, double-laminated, double-curved insulated glass units; 26% reduction in electricity demand through optimized chiller plant, high-efficiency HVAC equipment and daylight sensors; automated management system adjusts ventilation, temperature, humidity, and fresh air volume based on occupancy, thus optimizing energy consumption; real-time monitoring of outdoor conditions; solar-responsive ventilators (SRV) powered by photovoltaics regulate solar radiative heat

Nachhaltigkeitszertifizierung:
LEED Platinum;
WELL Platinum;
China Green Building – 3 Stars
Nachhaltigkeit:
vierfach verglaste, doppelt laminierte, doppelt gebogene Isolierglasscheiben; 26 % Reduktion des Strombedarfs durch optimierte Kühlanlagen; hocheffiziente HLK-Anlagen und Tageslichtsensoren; automatisiertes Gebäudemanagementsystem zur Anpassung der Belüftung, Temperatur, Luftfeuchtigkeit und Frischluftzufuhr basierend auf Belegung optimiert den Energieverbrauch; Echtzeitüberwachung der Außenbedingungen; solargestützte Ventilatoren (SRV), die mittels Photovoltaik betrieben werden, regulieren die Aufheizung durch Sonnenlicht

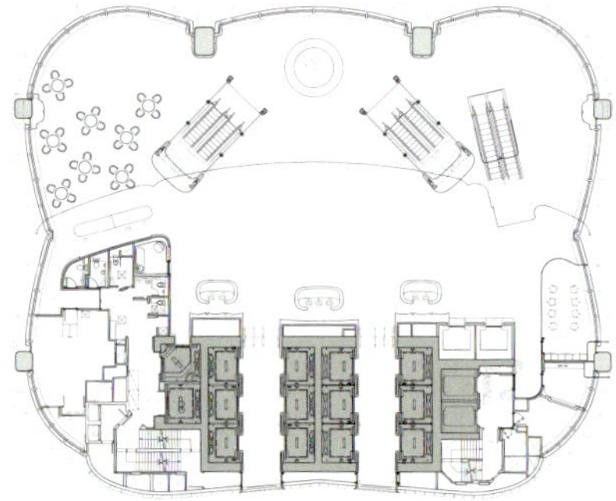

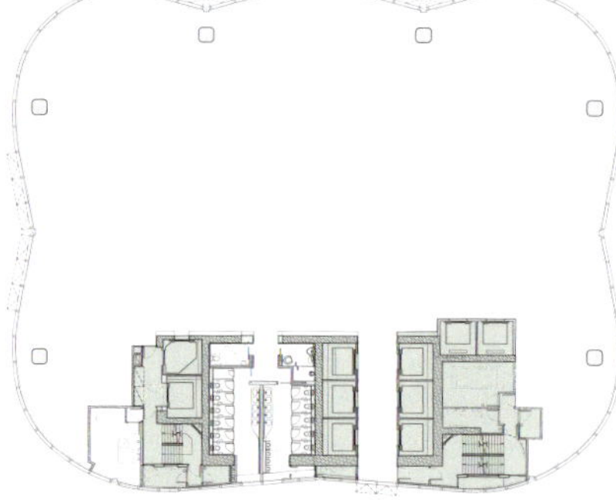

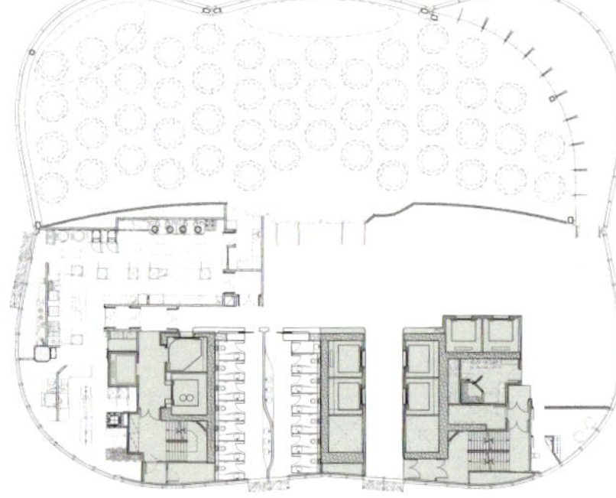

The design vocabulary of the high-rise is inspired by the structure and layering of a Bauhinia bud just before it blooms. This plant, known as the Hong Kong orchid tree, was first cultivated in the city's botanical gardens above Murray Road, where the high-rise is situated in the heart of Hong Kong's financial district.

Organic shapes, natural light, and greenery dominate the spacious foyer, extending over two floors to welcome visitors and employees. The vertical core is located on the east side to optimize the views from the office floors and the banquet hall at the top of the tower. The façade is made of four-layer, double-laminated, double-curved insulating glass – the first of its kind in Hong Kong.

Die Formensprache des Hochhauses orientiert sich an der Struktur und Schichtung einer Bauhinia-Knospe kurz vor dem Erblühen. Die als Hongkonger Orchideenbaum bekannte Pflanze wurde erstmals in den botanischen Gärten der Stadt oberhalb der Murray Road – an ihr liegt das Hochhaus im Herzen des Finanzdistrikts von Hongkong – vermehrt.

Organische Formen, natürliches Licht und Begrünung dominieren das weitläufige Foyer, das Besucher:innen und Mitarbeiter:innen über zwei Etagen empfängt. Der vertikale Kern befindet sich auf der Ostseite, um den Ausblick aus den Büroetagen und dem Festsaal an der Spitze des Turms zu optimieren. Die Fassade besteht aus vierlagigem, doppelt laminiertem, doppelt gekrümmtem Isolierglas – das erste seiner Art in Hongkong.

144/1
The plot at 2 Murray Road, in the immediate vicinity of the Bank of China high-rise by I. M. Pei, reportedly had the highest price per square meter in the world and cost a total of 3 billion US dollars.
Das Grundstück in der 2 Murray Road, in unmittelbarer Nachbarschaft zum Hochhaus der Bank of China von I. M. Pei, war Berichten zufolge das Grundstück mit dem höchsten Quadratmeterpreis der Welt mit einem Gesamtpreis von 3 Milliarden US-Dollar.

144/2+145/1
Façade details
Fassadendetails

144/3–5
3rd floor, standard floor, and top floor plans
Grundrisse 3. Obergeschoss, Regelgeschoss, Dachgeschoss

Architects Architekt:innen	**Zaha Hadid Architects** **London, UK** Großbritannien
Project architects Projektarchitekt:innen	**Patrik Schumacher, Jim Heverin, Sara Klomps, Chris Lepine, Simon Yu**
Architects of record Lokale Architekt:innen	**Ronald Lu & Partners**
Client Bauherrschaft	**Henderson Land**
Structural engineers Tragwerksplanung	**LERA Consulting Structural Engineers; C M Wong & Associates; Eckersley O'Callaghan**
MEP Haustechnik	**WSP**
Landscape architects Landschaftsarchitekt:innen	**PWP Landscape Architecture; Earthasia**
Height Höhe	**190 m**
Stories Geschosse	**36**
Site area Grundstücksfläche	**2880 m²**
Building footprint Bebaute Fläche	**2880 m²**
Gross floor area Bruttogeschossfläche	**43 200 m²**
Structure Konstruktion	**Composite construction** Verbundbauweise
Completion Fertigstellung	**April 2024**
Main use Hauptnutzung	**Offices** Büros

The International High-Rise Award 2004–2024

Internationaler Hochhaus Preis 2004–2024

#

3D/International, **Houston TX, USA**
Carl B. Stokes Federal Courthouse, Cleveland OH, USA
Submission 2004 *Einreichung 2004*

3XN, **Copenhagen, Denmark**
Kopenhagen, Dänemark

Quay Quarter Tower, Sydney, Australia
Australien
Prize Winner 2022 *Preisträger 2022*

Lighthouse, Aarhus, Denmark Dänemark
Out of competition *Außer Konkurrenz*

A

ABB Architekten
Frankfurt am Main, Germany
Deutschland
Bocom Financial Towers, Shanghai, China
Submission 2004 *Einreichung 2004*

Adjaye Associates
London, UK / New York NY, USA
London, Großbritannien / New York NY, USA
130 William, New York NY, USA
Nomination 2022 *Nominierung 2022*

Adrian Smith + Gordon Gill Architecture
Chicago IL, USA
Central Park Tower, New York NY, USA
Nomination 2024 *Nominierung 2024*

Aedas
London, UK Großbritannien
Al Bahr Towers, Abu Dhabi, UAE VAE
Nomination 2014 *Nominierung 2014*

Aflalo & Gasperini Arquitectos
São Paulo, Brazil Brasilien
Ventura Corporate Tower, Rio de Janeiro, Brazil Brasilien
Nomination 2012 *Nominierung 2012*

AL_A
London, UK Großbritannien
Central Embassy, Bangkok, Thailand
Nomination 2018 *Nominierung 2018*

Álvaro Siza
Porto, Portugal
611 West 56th Street, New York NY, USA
Nomination 2024 *Nominierung 2024*

Amateur Architecture Studio
Hangzhou, China
Vertical Courtyard, Hangzhou, China
Nomination 2008 *Nominierung 2008*

Andrea Maffei Architects
Milan, Italy
Mailand, Italien
Allianz Tower, Milan, Italy
Mailand, Italien
Nomination 2016 *Nominierung 2016*

Arata Isozaki & Associates
Tokyo, Japan Tokio, Japan
Allianz Tower, Milan, Italy
Mailand, Italien
Nomination 2016 *Nominierung 2016*

Arc Studio Architecture + Urbanism
Singapore Singapur

Pinnacle@Duxton, Singapore Singapur
Finalist 2012

Architectus
Sydney, Australia Australien

1 Bligh Street, Sydney, Australia
Australien
Prize Winner 2012 *Preisträger 2012*

Architekturbüro Magnus Kaminiarz & Cie
Frankfurt am Main, Germany
Deutschland
Grand Tower, Frankfurt am Main, Germany Deutschland
Nomination 2020 *Nominierung 2020*

Arquitectonica International Corporation
Miami FL, USA

Landmark East, Hong Kong, China
Hongkong, China
Nomination 2010 *Nominierung 2010*

Torun Tower, Istanbul, Turkey Türkei
Nomination 2016 *Nominierung 2016*

Atelier Christian de Portzamparc
Paris, France Frankreich
One57, New York NY, USA
Nomination 2014 *Nominierung 2014*

Ateliers Jean Nouvel
Paris, France Frankreich

Torre Agbar, Barcelona, Spain Spanien
Prize Winner 2006 *Preisträger 2006*

Doha Tower, Doha, Qatar Katar
Nomination 2014 *Nominierung 2014*

One Central Park, Sydney, Australia
Australien
Finalist 2014

Renaissance Barcelona Fira Hotel, Barcelona, Spain Spanien
Finalist 2014

Le Nouvel Ardmore, Singapore Singapur
Nomination 2016 *Nominierung 2016*

Le Nouvel KLCC, Kuala Lumpur, Malaysia
Nomination 2018 *Nominierung 2018*

La Marseillaise, Marseille, France
Frankreich
Nomination 2020 *Nominierung 2020*

Tours Duo, Paris, France Frankreich
Nomination 2024 *Nominierung 2024*

Atkins
London, UK Großbritannien

Bahrain World Trade Center, Manama, Bahrain
Nomination 2008 *Nominierung 2008*

Landmark 81, Ho Chi Minh City, Vietnam
Ho-Chi-Minh-Stadt, Vietnam
Nomination 2020 *Nominierung 2020*

Audrius Ambrasas Architects
Vilnius, Lithuania Litauen
Europa Tower, Vilnius, Lithuania Litauen
Submission 2004 *Einreichung 2004*

B

Baumschlager-Eberle
Lustenau, Austria Österreich
PopMoma, Beijing, China
Peking, China
Nomination 2008 *Nominierung 2008*

BIG – Bjarke Ingels Group
Copenhagen, Denmark/ New York NY, USA
Kopenhagen, Dänemark/ New York NY, USA

VIA 57 West, New York NY, USA
Prize Winner 2016 *Preisträger 2016*

Omniturm, Frankfurt am Main, Germany
Deutschland
Finalist 2020

Shenzhen Energy Headquarters, Shenzhen, China
Nomination 2020 *Nominierung 2020*

Telus Sky, Calgary, Canada Kanada
Nomination 2022 *Nominierung 2022*

Vancouver House, Vancouver, Canada
Kanada
Finalist 2022

CapitaSpring, Singapore Singapur
Prize Winner 2024 *Preisträger 2024*

IQON Residences, Quito, Ecuador
Finalist 2024

The Spiral, New York NY, USA
Nomination 2024 *Nominierung 2024*

Boeri Studio
Milan, Italy
Mailand, Italien

Bosco Verticale, Milan, Italy
Mailand, Italien
Prize Winner 2014 *Preisträger 2014*

Building Design (Pvt) Ltd.
Colombo, Sri Lanka
HNB Towers, Colombo, Sri Lanka
Submission 2004 *Einreichung 2004*

Büro Ole Scheeren
Beijing, China
Peking, China

CCTV Headquarters, Beijing, China
Peking, China
Nomination 2014 *Nominierung 2014*

DUO, Singapore Singapur
Nomination 2018 *Nominierung 2018*

MahaNakhon, Bangkok, Thailand
Finalist 2018

C

C. Y. Lee & Partners
Taipei, Taiwan
Taipei 101, Taipei, Taiwan
Nomination 2006 *Nominierung 2006*

Carlos Zapata Studio
New York NY, USA
Bitexco Financial Tower, Ho Chi Minh City, Vietnam
Ho-Chi-Minh-Stadt, Vietnam
Nomination 2012 *Nominierung 2012*

CCDI Group
Shenzhen, China
Shenzhen Baidu Headquarters, Shenzhen, China
Nomination 2020 *Nominierung 2020*

CetraRuddy Architecture
New York NY, USA

One Madison Park, New York NY, USA
Nomination 2012 *Nominierung 2012*

ARO, New York NY, USA
Nomination 2020 *Nominierung 2020*

Cook + Fox Architects
New York NY, USA
The Bank of America Tower, New York NY, USA
Nomination 2010 *Nominierung 2010*

Coop Himmelb(l)au
Vienna, Austria
Wien, Österreich
ECB – European Central Bank, Frankfurt am Main, Germany Deutschland
Nomination 2016 *Nominierung 2016*

COX Architecture
Sydney, Australia Australien

Metro Residences Chatswood, Sydney, Australia Australien
Nomination 2016 *Nominierung 2016*

555 Collins Street, Melbourne, Australia
Australien
Nomination 2024 *Nominierung 2024*

CPG Consultants
Singapore Singapur

Singapore State Courts, Singapore
Singapur
Finalist 2022

CRA – Carlo Ratti Associati
Turin, Italy/New York NY, USA
Turin, Italien/New York NY, USA

CapitaSpring, Singapore Singapur
Prize Winner 2024 *Preisträger 2024*

Cyrus Moser Architekten
Frankfurt am Main, Germany
Deutschland
Senckenberg Quartier, Frankfurt am Main, Germany Deutschland
Nomination 2022 *Nominierung 2022*

D

(designed by) Erick van Egeraat
Rotterdam, Netherlands Niederlande
Mercury City Tower, Moscow, Russia
Moskau, Russland
Nomination 2012 *Nominierung 2012*

Dam & Partners Architecten
Amsterdam, Netherlands Niederlande
Maastoren, Rotterdam, Netherlands
Niederlande
Nomination 2010 *Nominierung 2010*

David Chipperfield Architects
London, UK Großbritannien

Amorepacific Headquarters, Seoul, South Korea Südkorea
Nomination 2018 *Nominierung 2018*

The Bryant, New York NY, USA
Finalist 2022

Delugan Meissl Associated Architects
Vienna, Austria
Wien, Österreich

Delugan Meissl Tower, Vienna, Austria
Wien, Österreich
Finalist 2006

Diller Scofidio + Renfro
New York NY, USA
15 Hudson Yards, New York NY, USA
Nomination 2010 *Nominierung 2010*

Dina Ammar – Avraham Curiel Architects
Haifa, Israel
The Sail Tower, Haifa, Israel
Submission 2004 *Einreichung 2004*

Dominique Perrault Architecture
Paris, France Frankreich

ME Barcelona Hotel, Barcelona, Spain
Spanien
Nomination 2010 *Nominierung 2010*

Fukoku Tower, Osaka, Japan
Nomination 2012 *Nominierung 2012*

DC Tower I, Vienna, Austria
Wien, Österreich
Nomination 2014 *Nominierung 2014*

5th Extension of the European Court of Justice, Luxembourg Luxemburg
Nomination 2010 *Nominierung 2010*

Donovan Hill
Brisbane, Australia Australien
Santos Place, Brisbane, Australia
Australien
Nomination 2010 *Nominierung 2010*

E

Ellerbe Becket
Minneapolis MN, USA
Kingdom Centre, Riyadh, Saudi Arabia
Riad, Saudi-Arabien
Submission 2004 *Einreichung 2004*

EMBA Estudi Massip-Bosch Arquitectes
Barcelona, Spain Spanien
Torre Telefónica, Barcelona, Spain
Spanien
Nomination 2012 *Nominierung 2012*

Estudio de Arquitectura Alonso Balaguer SLP
Barcelona, Spain Spanien
Bacatá Tower, Bogotá, Colombia
Kolumbien
Nomination 2020 *Nominierung 2020*

F

Fender Katsalidis Architects
Melbourne, Australia Australien
Eureka Tower, Melbourne, Australia
Australien
Nomination 2008 *Nominierung 2008*

Foster + Partners
London, UK Großbritannien

30 St Mary Axe, London, UK
Großbritannien
Finalist 2004

Deutsche Bank Place, Sydney, Australia
Australien
Nomination 2006 *Nominierung 2006*

Hearst Headquarters, New York NY, USA
Prize Winner 2008 *Preisträger 2008*

Regent Place, Sydney, Australia
Australien
Nomination 2008 *Nominierung 2008*

The Willis Building, London, UK
Großbritannien
Nomination 2008 *Nominierung 2008*

Jameson House, Vancouver, Canada
Kanada
Nomination 2012 *Nominierung 2012*

The Index, Dubai, UAE VAE
Nomination 2012 *Nominierung 2012*

The Troika, Kuala Lumpur, Malaysia
Finalist 2012

The Bow, Calgary, Canada Kanada
Nomination 2014 *Nominierung 2014*

Burj Mohammed Bin Rashid + World Trade Center, Abu Dhabi, UAE VAE
Nomination 2016 *Nominierung 2016*

South Beach, Singapore Singapur
Nomination 2016 *Nominierung 2016*

UN Plaza, New York NY, USA
Nomination 2016 *Nominierung 2016*

The Bund Finance Center, Shanghai, China
Nomination 2018 *Nominierung 2018*

Comcast Technology Center, Philadelphia PA, USA
Nomination 2020 *Nominierung 2020*

National Bank of Kuwait (NBK Tower), Kuwait City, Kuwait
Kuwait-Stadt, Kuwait
Nomination 2020 *Nominierung 2020*

425 Park Avenue, New York NY, USA
Nomination 2022 *Nominierung 2022*

DJI Headquarters, Shenzhen, China
Nomination 2022 *Nominierung 2022*

Samba Bank HQ Tower, Riyadh, Saudi Arabia Riad, Saudi-Arabien
Nomination 2022 *Nominierung 2022*

Varso Tower, Warsaw, Poland
Warschau, Polen
Nomination 2024 *Nominierung 2024*

Francis-Jones Morehen Thorp
Sydney, Australia Australien
EY Centre, Sydney, Australia Australien
Nomination 2018 *Nominierung 2018*

Frank Williams & Associates
New York NY, USA
Mercury City Tower, Moscow, Russia
Moskau, Russland
Nomination 2014 *Nominierung 2014*

G

Gatermann + Schossig
Cologne, Germany
Köln, Deutschland
KölnTriangle, Cologne, Germany
Köln, Deutschland
Nomination 2006 *Nominierung 2006*

Gehry Partners
Los Angeles CA, USA

Eight Spruce Street, New York NY, USA
Finalist 2012

Gensler
San Francisco CA, USA

Shanghai Tower, Shanghai, China
Nomination 2016 *Nominierung 2016*

555 Collins Street, Melbourne, Australia
Australien
Nomination 2024 *Nominierung 2024*

Gerber Architekten
Dortmund, Germany Deutschland
RWE Tower, Dortmund, Germany
Deutschland
Nomination 2006 *Nominierung 2006*

Gigon/Guyer Architekten
Zurich, Switzerland
Zürich, Schweiz
Prime Tower, Zurich, Switzerland
Zürich, Schweiz
Nomination 2012 *Nominierung 2012*

GKK+Architekten
Berlin, Germany Deutschland
Hauptverwaltung Süddeutscher Verlag, Munich, Germany
München, Deutschland
Nomination 2010 *Nominierung 2010*

gmp Architekten von Gerkan, Marg und Partner
Hamburg, Germany Deutschland

Guangzhou Development Central Building, Guangzhou, China
Nomination 2006 *Nominierung 2006*

Wanda Plaza, Beijing, China
Peking, China
Nomination 2008 *Nominierung 2008*

Neue Deutsche Bank Towers (revitalization), Frankfurt am Main, Germany Deutschland
Special Recognition 2012
Besondere Anerkennung 2012

Bund SOHO, Shanghai, China
Nomination 2016 *Nominierung 2016*

Greenland Central Plaza, Zhengzhou, China
Nomination 2018 *Nominierung 2018*

Nanjing Financial City, Nanjing, China
Nomination 2018 *Nominierung 2018*

Poly Greenland Plaza, Shanghai, China
Nomination 2020 *Nominierung 2020*

Shandong Port Tower, Qingdao, China
Nomination 2022 *Nominierung 2022*

Vipshop Headquarters, Guangzhou, China
Nomination 2022 *Nominierung 2022*

Goettsch Partners
Chicago IL, USA
150 North Riverside, Chicago IL, USA
Nomination 2018 *Nominierung 2018*

GRAFT
Berlin, Germany Deutschland
Luxe Lake Towers, Chengdu, China
Nomination 2020 *Nominierung 2020*

Gruber + Kleine-Kraneburg Architekten
Frankfurt am Main, Germany
Deutschland
TaunusTurm, Frankfurt am Main, Germany Deutschland
Nomination 2014 *Nominierung 2014*

H

Harry Gugger Studio
Basel, Switzerland Schweiz
The Exchange, Vancouver, Canada
Kanada
Nomination 2018 *Nominierung 2018*

Harry Seidler and Associates
Sydney, Australia Australien

The Cove, Sydney, Australia Australien
Finalist 2004

Riparian Plaza, Brisbane, Australia
Australien
Nomination 2006 *Nominierung 2006*

Meriton Tower, Sydney, Australia
Australien
Nomination 2008 *Nominierung 2008*

Heatherwick Studio
London, UK Großbritannien

The Bund Finance Center, Shanghai, China
Nomination 2018 *Nominierung 2018*

EDEN, Singapore Singapur
Finalist 2020

Heller Manus Architects
San Francisco CA, USA
181 Fremont, San Francisco CA, USA
Nomination 2018 *Nominierung 2018*

Henke Schreieck Architekten
Vienna, Austria
Wien, Österreich

TrIllple Towers, Vienna, Austria
Wien, Österreich
Finalist 2022

Herzog & de Meuron
Basel, Switzerland Schweiz

56 Leonard Street, New York NY, USA
Nomination 2018 *Nominierung 2018*

Beirut Terraces, Beirut, Lebanon Libanon
Finalist 2018

HOK
Houston TX, USA
PIF Tower, Riyadh, Saudi Arabia
Riad, Saudi-Arabien
Nomination 2022 *Nominierung 2022*

I

Ian Moore Architects
Manchester, UK Großbritannien
Air Apartments, Broadbeach, Australia
Australien
Nomination 2008 *Nominierung 2008*

Ian Simpson Architects
Manchester, UK Großbritannien

Beetham Hilton Tower, Manchester, UK
Großbritannien
Nomination 2008 *Nominierung 2008*

Holloway Circus, Birmingham, UK
Großbritannien
Nomination 2008 *Nominierung 2008*

ingenhoven architects
Düsseldorf, Germany Deutschland

Uptown München, Munich, Germany
München, Deutschland
Nomination 2006 *Nominierung 2006*

Breezé Tower, Osaka, Japan
Nomination 2010 *Nominierung 2010*

1 Bligh Street, Sydney, Australia
Australien
Prize Winner 2012 *Preisträger 2012*

Marina One, Singapore Singapur
Nomination 2018 *Nominierung 2018*

Toranomon Hills Towers, Tokyo, Japan
Tokio, Japan
Nomination 2022 *Nominierung 2022*

J

Jahn/, FGP Atelier
Chicago IL, USA

Cosmopolitan Twarda 2/4, Warsaw, Poland
Warschau, Polen
Nomination 2016 *Nominierung 2016*

50 West, New York NY, USA
Nomination 2018 *Nominierung 2018*

Shanghai Financial Exchange Plaza, Shanghai, China
Nomination 2022 *Nominierung 2022*

John Lee/Michael Timchula Architects
New York NY, USA
Shenzhen World Trade Center, Shenzhen, China
Submission 2004 *Einreichung 2004*

Johnson Fain
Los Angeles CA, USA
Constellation Palace, Los Angeles CA, USA
Submission 2004 *Einreichung 2004*

J.S.K. International Architekten und Ingenieure
Frankfurt am Main, Germany
Deutschland
Tornado Tower, Doha, Qatar Katar
Nomination 2010 *Nominierung 2010*

K

Kallmann McKinnell & Wood Architects
Boston MA, USA
Carl B. Stokes Federal Courthouse, Cleveland OH, USA
Submission 2004 *Einreichung 2004*

KCAP Architects & Planners
Rotterdam, Netherlands Niederlande
The Red Apple, Rotterdam, Netherlands
Niederlande
Nomination 2010 *Nominierung 2010*

Kengo Kuma & Associates
Tokyo, Japan Tokio, Japan
Alberni, Vancouver, Canada Kanada
Nomination 2024 *Nominierung 2024*

Kohn Pedersen Fox Associates
New York NY, USA

De Hoftoren, The Hague, Netherlands
Den Haag, Niederlande
Prize Winner 2004 *Preisträger 2004*

Roppongi Hills Mori Tower, Tokyo, Japan
Tokio, Japan
Submission 2004 *Einreichung 2004*

Adia Headquarters, Abu Dhabi, UAE VAE
Nomination 2008 *Nominierung 2008*

International Commerce Center, Hong Kong, China Hongkong, China
Nomination 2010 *Nominierung 2010*

Shanghai World Financial Center, Shanghai, China
Finalist 2010

Ventura Corporate Tower, Rio de Janeiro, Brazil Brasilien
Nomination 2012 *Nominierung 2012*

Lotte World Tower, Seoul, South Korea
Südkorea
Nomination 2018 *Nominierung 2018*

Ping An Finance Centre, Shenzhen, China
Nomination 2018 *Nominierung 2018*

China Resources Tower, Shenzhen, China
Nomination 2020 *Nominierung 2020*

MGM Cotai, Macau, China
Nomination 2020 *Nominierung 2020*

Robinson Tower, Singapore Singapur
Nomination 2020 *Nominierung 2020*

Bundang Doosan Centre, Seoul, South Korea Südkorea
Nomination 2022 *Nominierung 2022*

One Crown Place, London, UK
Großbritannien
Nomination 2022 *Nominierung 2022*

One Vanderbilt, New York NY, USA
Nomination 2022 *Nominierung 2022*

320 Granville, Vancouver, Canada Kanada
Nomination 2024 *Nominierung 2024*

Atlantis The Royal Resort, Dubai, UAE
VAE
Nomination 2024 *Nominierung 2024*

Citymark Tower, Shenzhen, China
Nomination 2024 *Nominierung 2024*

KSP Engel
Frankfurt am Main, Germany
Deutschland

WestendDuo, Frankfurt am Main, Germany Deutschland
Special Recognition 2008
Besondere Anerkennung 2008

Palais Quartier Office Tower, Frankfurt am Main, Germany Deutschland
Nomination 2010 *Nominierung 2010*

Great Mosque of Algiers Tower, Algiers, Algeria Algier, Algerien
Nomination 2022 *Nominierung 2022*

Kuwabara Payne McKenna Blumberg Architects
Toronto, Canada Kanada
Manitoba Hydro Place, Winnipeg, Canada
Kanada
Nomination 2010 *Nominierung 2010*

L

L. Benjamín Romano
Mexico City, Mexico
Mexiko-Stadt, Mexiko

Torre Reforma, Mexico City, Mexico
Mexiko-Stadt, Mexiko
Prize Winner 2018 *Preisträger 2018*

Legorreta
Mexico City, Mexico
Mexiko-Stadt, Mexiko

Torre BBVA Bancomer, Mexico City, Mexico
Mexiko-Stadt, Mexiko
Nomination 2016 *Nominierung 2016*

Miyana, Torre Chapulín, Mexico City, Mexico
Mexiko-Stadt, Mexiko
Nomination 2020 *Nominierung 2020*

Louis Karlsberger & Associates
Columbus OH, USA
Carl B. Stokes Federal Courthouse, Cleveland OH, USA
Submission 2004 *Einreichung 2004*

M

M. M. Posokhin
Moscow, Russia
Moskau, Russland
Mercury City Tower, Moscow, Russia
Moskau, Russland
Nomination 2012 *Nominierung 2012*

MAD Architects
Beijing, China
Peking, China

Absolute World Towers, Mississauga, Canada Kanada
Finalist 2012

Sheraton Huzhou Hot Spring Resort, Huzhou, China
Nomination 2014 *Nominierung 2014*

Fake Hills (Part 1), Beihai, China
Nomination 2016 *Nominierung 2016*

Chaoyang Park Plaza, Beijing, China
Peking, China
Finalist 2018

Nanjing Zendai Himalayas Center, Nanjing, China
Nomination 2022 *Nominierung 2022*

Maki & Associates
Tokyo, Japan
Tokio, Japan

4 World Trade Center, New York NY, USA
Finalist 2016

Mario Bellini Architects
Milan, Italy
Mailand, Italien

Neue Deutsche Bank Towers, Frankfurt am Main, Germany Deutschland
Special Recognition 2012
Besondere Anerkennung 2012

Mario Botta Architetto
Mendrisio, Switzerland Schweiz

Kyobo Gangnam Tower, Seoul, South Korea Südkorea
Finalist 2004

Mass Studies
Seoul, South Korea Südkorea

Missing Matrix Building, Seoul, South Korea Südkorea
Finalist 2008

S-Trenue: Bundle Matrix, Seoul, South Korea Südkorea
Nomination 2010 *Nominierung 2010*

Mecanoo Architecten
Rotterdam, Netherlands Niederlande

Montevideo, Rotterdam, Netherlands Niederlande
Finalist 2006

Meixner Schlüter Wendt
Frankfurt am Main, Germany Deutschland
Neuer Henninger Turm, Frankfurt am Main, Germany Deutschland
Nomination 2018 *Nominierung 2018*

Meurer Architektur + Stadtplanung
Frankfurt am Main, Germany Deutschland
One, Frankfurt am Main, Germany Deutschland
Nomination 2022 *Nominierung 2022*

Mitsubishi Jisho Sekkei Inc.
Tokyo, Japan Tokio, Japan
Breezé Tower, Osaka, Japan
Nomination 2010 *Nominierung 2010*

Morger & Degelo, Marques
Basel, Switzerland Schweiz
Basler Messeturm, Basel, Switzerland Schweiz
Submission 2004 *Einreichung 2004*

Morphosis Architects
Culver City CA, USA

Casablanca Finance City Tower, Casablanca, Morocco Marokko
Nomination 2020 *Nominierung 2020*

Hanking Center, Shenzhen, China
Nomination 2022 *Nominierung 2022*

Multiply Architects
Singapore Singapur

Singapore State Courts, Singapore Singapur
Finalist 2022

Murphy/Jahn Architects
Chicago IL, USA

Deutsche Post Tower, Bonn, Germany Deutschland
Submission 2004 *Einreichung 2004*

Highlight Towers, Munich, Germany München, Deutschland
Nomination 2006 *Nominierung 2006*

Veer Towers, Las Vegas NV, USA
Nomination 2012 *Nominierung 2012*

MVRDV
Rotterdam, Netherlands Niederlande

Shenzhen Women & Children's Center, Shenzhen, China
Finalist 2024

Valley, Amsterdam, Netherlands Niederlande
Finalist 2024

MVSA – Meyer en Van Schooten Architecten
Amsterdam, Netherlands Niederlande
New Babylon, The Hague, Netherlands Den Haag, Niederlande
Nomination 2012 *Nominierung 2012*

N

NBBJ
Seattle WA, USA
Tencent Seafront Headquarters, Shenzhen, China
Nomination 2018 *Nominierung 2018*

Nikken Sekkei
Tokyo, Japan Tokio, Japan

Museum Tower Kyobashi, Tokyo, Japan Tokio, Japan
Nomination 2022 *Nominierung 2022*

One Za'abeel Tower, Dubai, UAE VAE
Nomination 2024 *Nominierung 2024*

Novotny Mähner Assoziierte
Offenbach am Main, Germany Deutschland
Gallileo, Frankfurt am Main, Germany Deutschland
Submission 2004 *Einreichung 2004*

nps tchoban voss
Hamburg, Germany Deutschland
Federation Towers, Moscow, Russia Moskau, Russland
Nomination 2016 *Nominierung 2016*

O

OMA Office for Metropolitan Architecture
Rotterdam, Netherlands/Beijing, China Rotterdam, Niederlande/Peking, China

TVCC – Television Cultural Center, Beijing, China Peking, China
Finalist 2008

Shenzhen Stock Exchange, Shenzhen, China
Nomination 2010 *Nominierung 2010*

CCTV Headquarters, Beijing, China Peking, China
Nomination 2014 *Nominierung 2014*

De Rotterdam, Rotterdam, Netherlands Niederlande
Finalist 2014

MahaNakhon, Bangkok, Thailand
Finalist 2018

Norra Tornen – Innovationen, Stockholm, Sweden Schweden
Prize Winner 2020 *Preisträger 2020*

Eagle + West, New York NY, USA
Nomination 2024 *Nominierung 2024*

Hangzhou Prism, Hangzhou, China
Nomination 2024 *Nominierung 2024*

Omrania & Associates
Riyadh, Saudi Arabia Riad, Saudi-Arabien
PIF Tower, Riyadh, Saudi Arabia Riad, Saudi-Arabien
Nomination 2022 *Nominierung 2022*

P

Paul Davis & Partners
London, UK Großbritannien
Grosvenor Place, Hong Kong, China Hongkong, China
Submission 2004 *Einreichung 2004*

Pei Cobb Freed & Partners Architects
New York NY, USA
Torre Espacio, Madrid, Spain Spanien
Nomination 2008 *Nominierung 2008*

Pelli Clarke Pelli Architects
New Haven CT, USA

Two International Finance Center, Hong Kong, China Hongkong, China
Nomination 2006 *Nominierung 2006*

Torre Costanera, Santiago, Chile
Nomination 2014 *Nominierung 2014*

Salesforce Tower, San Francisco CA, USA
Nomination 2018 *Nominierung 2018*

Pelli Clarke & Partners
New Haven CT, USA
Mori JP Tower, Tokyo, Japan Tokio, Japan
Nomination 2024 *Nominierung 2024*

Perkins + Will
Chicago IL, USA
235 West Van Buren, Chicago IL, USA
Nomination 2010 *Nominierung 2010*

Powerhouse Company
Rotterdam, Netherlands Niederlande

Bunker Tower, Eindhoven, Netherlands Niederlande
Finalist 2024

Prof. Christoph Mäckler Architekten
Frankfurt am Main, Germany Deutschland

OpernTurm, Frankfurt am Main, Germany Deutschland
Nomination 2010 *Nominierung 2010*

Zoofenster – Waldorf Astoria Berlin, Berlin, Germany Deutschland
Nomination 2014 *Nominierung 2014*

Q

querkraft architekten
Vienna, Austria Wien, Österreich
Citygate Tower & Leopold Tower, Vienna, Austria Wien, Österreich
Nomination 2016 *Nominierung 2016*

R

R&AS Rubio & Álvarez-Sala
Madrid, Spain Spanien
Torre SyV, Madrid, Spain Spanien
Nomination 2008 *Nominierung 2008*

Rafael de La-Hoz Arquitectos
Madrid, Spain Spanien
Las Torres de Hércules, Los Barrios, Spain Spanien
Nomination 2010 *Nominierung 2010*

Rafael Viñoly Architects
New York NY, USA

432 Park Avenue, New York NY, USA
Finalist 2016

NEMA Chicago, Chicago IL, USA
Nomination 2018 *Nominierung 2018*

Rapp & Rapp
Amsterdam, Netherlands Niederlande
De Kroon, The Hague, Netherlands Den Haag, Niederlande
Nomination 2018 *Nominierung 2018*

Reiser + Umemoto, RUR Architecture PC
New York NY, USA
O-14, Dubai, UAE VAE
Nomination 2010 *Nominierung 2010*

Renzo Piano Building Workshop
Genoa, Italy Genua, Italien

New York Times Building, New York NY, USA
Finalist 2008

The Shard London Bridge Tower, London, UK Großbritannien
Nomination 2014 *Nominierung 2014*

Tribunal de Paris, Paris, France Frankreich
Nomination 2018 *Nominierung 2018*

Research Architecture Design Ltd.
Hong Kong, China Hongkong, China
SK Telecom Headquarters, Seoul, South Korea Südkorea
Nomination 2006 *Nominierung 2006*

Richard Meier & Partners Architects
New York NY, USA

Rothschild Tower, Tel Aviv, Israel
Nomination 2016 *Nominierung 2016*

Torres Cuarzo, Mexico City, Mexico Mexiko-Stadt, Mexiko
Nomination 2020 *Nominierung 2020*

Richard Rogers Partnership
London, UK Großbritannien
Hesperia Hotel and Conference Center, L'Hospitalet/Barcelona, Spain Spanien
Nomination 2008 *Nominierung 2008*

Riken Yamamoto & Field Shop
Yokohama, Japan

Jian Wai Soho, Beijing, China
Peking, China
Finalist 2006

Robert A. M. Stern Architects LLP
New York NY, USA
Comcast Center, Philadelphia PA, USA
Nomination 2010 *Nominierung 2010*

Roberto Perez-Guerras Architects
Madrid, Spain Spanien
Neguri Gane, Benidorm, Spain Spanien
Submission 2004 *Einreichung 2004*

Rocco Design Architects Ltd.
Hong Kong, China Hongkong, China
One Beijing Road, Hong Kong, China
Hongkong, China
Submission 2004 *Einreichung 2004*

Rogers Stirk Harbour & Partners
London, UK Großbritannien

8 Chifley Square, Sydney, Australia
Australien
Nomination 2014 *Nominierung 2014*

The Leadenhall, London, UK
Großbritannien
Nomination 2014 *Nominierung 2014*

Torre BBVA Bancomer, Mexico City, Mexico Mexiko-Stadt, Mexiko
Nomination 2016 *Nominierung 2016*

3 World Trade Center, New York NY, USA
Nomination 2020 *Nominierung 2020*

S

SAA Schweger Associated Architects
Hamburg, Germany Deutschland
Federation Towers, Moscow, Russia
Moskau, Russland
Nomination 2016 *Nominierung 2016*

Safdie Architects
Somerville MA, USA

SkyHabitat, Singapore Singapur
Finalist 2016

Golden Dream Bay, Qinhuangdao, China
Nomination 2020 *Nominierung 2020*

Altair, Colombo, Sri Lanka
Nomination 2022 *Nominierung 2022*

Raffles City Chongqing, Chongqing, China
Nomination 2022 *Nominierung 2022*

Santiago Calatrava LLC
Zurich, Switzerland
Zürich, Schweiz

HSB Turning Torso, Malmö, Sweden
Schweden
Finalist 2006

SCDA Architects
Singapore Singapur

SkyTerrace@Dawson, Singapore
Singapur
Nomination 2016 *Nominierung 2016*

Echelon, Singapore Singapur
Nomination 2018 *Nominierung 2018*

schneider + schumacher
Frankfurt am Main, Germany
Deutschland

Westhafen Tower, Frankfurt am Main, Germany Deutschland
Submission 2004 *Einreichung 2004*

Silver Tower (revitalization), Frankfurt am Main, Germany Deutschland
Nomination 2010 *Nominierung 2010*

Qianhai Telecommunication Center, Shenzhen, China
Nomination 2024 *Nominierung 2024*

Serie Architects
London, UK Großbritannien

Singapore State Courts, Singapore
Singapur
Finalist 2022

SHoP Architects
New York NY, USA

461 Dean Street, New York NY, USA
Nomination 2018 *Nominierung 2018*

American Copper Buildings, New York NY, USA
Nomination 2018 *Nominierung 2018*

111 West 57th Street, New York NY, USA
Nomination 2022 *Nominierung 2022*

Collins Arch, Melbourne, Australia
Australien
Nomination 2022 *Nominierung 2022*

SimpsonHaugh
London, UK Großbritannien
Dollay Bay, London, UK Großbritannien
Nomination 2018 *Nominierung 2018*

Skidmore, Owings & Merrill
Chicago IL, USA

Tower Palace III, Seoul, South Korea
Südkorea
Nomination 2006 *Nominierung 2006*

7 World Trade Center, New York NY, USA
Nomination 2008 *Nominierung 2008*

Burj Khalifa, Dubai, UAE VAE
Finalist / Special Recognition 2010
Finalist / Besondere Anerkennung 2010

The Broadgate Tower, London, UK
Großbritannien
Nomination 2010 *Nominierung 2010*

Trump International Hotel & Tower, Chicago IL, USA
Nomination 2010 *Nominierung 2010*

Tianjin Global Financial Center, Tianjin, China
Nomination 2012 *Nominierung 2012*

Cayan Tower, Dubai, UAE VAE
Nomination 2014 *Nominierung 2014*

Pearl River Tower, Guangzhou, China
Nomination 2014 *Nominierung 2014*

1 World Trade Center, New York NY, USA
Nomination 2016 *Nominierung 2016*

Baccarat Hotel & Residences, New York NY, USA
Nomination 2016 *Nominierung 2016*

Jiangxi Nanchang Greenland Central Plaza, Nanchang, China
Nomination 2016 *Nominierung 2016*

Poly International Plaza, Beijing, China
Peking, China
Nomination 2018 *Nominierung 2018*

The Lexicon, London, UK Großbritannien
Nomination 2018 *Nominierung 2018*

The Stratford, London, UK Großbritannien
Finalist 2020

Tianjin CTF Finance Centre, Tianjin, China
Nomination 2020 *Nominierung 2020*

Shenzhen Rural Commercial Bank Headquarters, Shenzhen, China
Nomination 2022 *Nominierung 2022*

Hangzhou Wangchao Center, Hangzhou, China
Nomination 2024 *Nominierung 2024*

Karlatornet, Gothenburg, Sweden
Göteborg, Schweden
Nomination 2024 *Nominierung 2024*

One and Two Manhattan West, New York NY, USA
Nomination 2024 *Nominierung 2024*

Snøhetta
Oslo, Norway Norwegen
Airside, Hong Kong, China Hongkong, China
Nomination 2024 *Nominierung 2024*

Somdoon Architects
Bangkok, Thailand
Ideo Morph 38, Bangkok, Thailand
Nomination 2014 *Nominierung 2014*

Steidle + Partner
Munich, Germany
München, Deutschland
Chaowei Men, Beijing, China
Peking, China
Nomination 2008 *Nominierung 2008*

Stefano Boeri Architetti
Milan, Italy Mailand, Italien
Nanjing Vertical Forest, Nanjing, China
Nomination 2024 *Nominierung 2024*

Steven Holl Architects
New York NY, USA

Sliced Porosity Block – Raffles City Chengdu, Chengdu, China
Finalist 2014

Studio Daniel Libeskind
New York NY, USA
Reflections at Keppel Bay, Singapore
Singapur
Nomination 2012 *Nominierung 2012*

Studio Gang
Chicago IL, USA

Aqua Tower, Chicago IL, USA
Finalist 2010

MIRA, San Francisco CA, USA
Nomination 2020 *Nominierung 2020*

One Hundred, St. Louis MO, USA
Nomination 2022 *Nominierung 2022*

St. Regis Chicago, Chicago IL, USA
Nomination 2022 *Nominierung 2022*

11 Hoyt, New York NY, USA
Nomination 2024 *Nominierung 2024*

StudioVlayStreeruwitz
Vienna, Austria Wien, Österreich
The One, Vienna, Austria Wien, Österreich
Nomination 2024 *Nominierung 2024*

T

T. R. Hamzah & Yeang Sdn. Bhd.
Ampang Selanger, Malaysia
Singapore National Library, Singapore
Singapur
Nomination 2006 *Nominierung 2006*

Tabanliogu Architects
Istanbul, Turkey Türkei
Sapphire, Istanbul, Turkey Türkei
Nomination 2012 *Nominierung 2012*

Tago Architects
Istanbul, Turkey Türkei
Dumankaya Ikon, Istanbul, Turkey Türkei
Nomination 2014 *Nominierung 2014*

Takenaka Corporation
Osaka, Japan
Abeno Harukas, Osaka, Japan
Nomination 2016 *Nominierung 2016*

Tange Associates
Tokyo, Japan
Tokio, Japan

Mode Gakuen Cocoon Tower, Tokyo, Japan
Tokio, Japan
Finalist 2010

One Raffles Place Tower 2, Singapore
Singapur
Nomination 2012 *Nominierung 2012*

Tectum Architects
Riga, Latvia Lettland
Hansabanka Central Office, Riga, Latvia
Lettland
Nomination 2006 *Nominierung 2006*

TEN Arquitectos
New York NY, USA
Mercedes House, New York NY, USA
Nomination 2014 *Nominierung 2014*

TFP Farrells
London, UK Großbritannien
KK 100, Shenzhen, China
Nomination 2012 *Nominierung 2012*

Toyo Ito & Associates
Tokyo, Japan
Tokio, Japan
CapitaGreen, Singapore Singapur
Nomination 2016 *Nominierung 2016*

U

UNStudio
Amsterdam, Netherlands Niederlande

Ardmore Residence, Singapore Singapur
Nomination 2014 *Nominierung 2014*

Raffles City, Hangzhou, China
Nomination 2018 *Nominierung 2018*

The Scotts Tower, Singapore Singapur
Nomination 2018 *Nominierung 2018*

V

Valode & Pistre Architects
Paris, France Frankreich
T1 Tower, Paris, France Frankreich
Nomination 2010 *Nominierung 2010*

W

WilkinsonEyre
London, UK Großbritannien

Guangzhou International Finance Center, Guangzhou, China
Nomination 2012 *Nominierung 2012*

One Barangaroo, Sydney, Australia Australien
Nomination 2022 *Nominierung 2022*

Wingårdh Arkitektenkontor AB
Gothenburg, Sweden Göteborg, Schweden
Victoria Tower, Stockholm, Sweden Schweden
Nomination 2012 *Nominierung 2012*

WOHA
Singapore Singapur

Newton Suites, Singapore Singapur
Finalist 2008

The Met, Bangkok, Thailand
Prize Winner 2010 *Preisträger 2010*

SkyVille @ Dawson, Singapore Singapur
Finalist 2016

Huaku Sky Garden, Taipei, Taiwan
Nomination 2018 *Nominierung 2018*

Oasia Hotel Downtown, Singapore Singapur
Finalist 2018

Sky Green, Taichung, Taiwan
Nomination 2020 *Nominierung 2020*

Hills and Valleys Skyscraper, Shenzhen, China
Nomination 2022 *Nominierung 2022*

Pan Pacific Orchard, Singapore Singapur
Nomination 2024 *Nominierung 2024*

Woods Bagot
Melbourne, Australia Australien

Collins Arch, Melbourne, Australia Australien
Nomination 2022 *Nominierung 2022*

Heritage Lanes, 80 Ann Street, Brisbane, Australia Australien
Nomination 2024 *Nominierung 2024*

Y

Yuko Nagayama & Associates
Tokyo, Japan Tokio, Japan
Tokyu Kabukicho Tower, Tokyo, Japan Tokio, Japan
Nomination 2024 *Nominierung 2024*

Z

Zaha Hadid Architects
London, UK Großbritannien

CMA CGM Head Office Tower, Marseille, France Frankreich
Nomination 2012 *Nominierung 2012*

D'Leedon, Singapore Singapur
Nomination 2016 *Nominierung 2016*

Wangjing SOHO, Beijing, China Peking, China
Nomination 2016 *Nominierung 2016*

Generali Tower, Milan, Italy Mailand, Italien
Nomination 2018 *Nominierung 2018*

Nanjing International Cultural Centre, Nanjing, China
Nomination 2018 *Nominierung 2018*

Leeza SOHO, Beijing, China Peking, China
Finalist 2020

Morpheus Hotel & Resorts at City of Dreams, Macau, China
Nomination 2020 *Nominierung 2020*

The Henderson, Hong Kong, China Hongkong, China
Nomination 2024 *Nominierung 2024*

Picture Credits

Abbildungsnachweise

Cover
Umschlag

CapitaSpring, Singapore Singapur
Photo Foto **Finbarr Fallon**
Singapore Singapur

Preface
Vorwort

4/1 Uli Maier, BFF; 4/2+3, 5/1+2, 7/1, 8/1–4 Kirsten Bucher

Prize Winner
Preisträger

All photos Alle Fotos **Finbarr Fallon; All plans** Alle Pläne **BIG – Bjarke Ingels Group; except** außer **38/1 Peter Körner; 38/2+3 Peter Cachola Schmal; 38/4, 39/1 Peter Körner; 39/2, 57/1 Peter Cachola Schmal**

Finalists
Finalisten

67/1 BICUBIK; 68/1+2, 69/1+2 Pablo Casals Aguirre; 70/1–3 BIG – Bjarke Ingels Group; 71/1+2 Pablo Casals Aguirre; 72/1 MVRDV; 73/1, Xia Zhi/courtesy of MVRDV; 75/1 MVRDV; 75/2+3 Xia Zhi/courtesy of MVRDV; 75/4 MVRDV; 76/1–3 Xia Zhi/courtesy of MVRDV; 77/1 MVRDV; 77/2 Xia Zhi/courtesy of MVRDV; 78/1 Ossip van Duivenbode/courtesy of MVRDV; 80/1+2 MVRDV; 81/1 Ossip van Duivenbode/courtesy of MVRDV; 81/2 MVRDV; 82/1+2 Ossip van Duivenbode/courtesy of MVRDV; 82/3 Daria Scagliola/courtesy of MVRDV; 83/1 Ossip van Duivenbode/courtesy of MVRDV; 83/2 MVRDV; 84/1 Christian van der Kooy; 85/1 Anna Odulinska 86/1–4 Sebastian van Damme; 88/1 Powerhouse Company; 88/2 Anna Odulinska; 88/3+4 Powerhouse Company; 88/4, 89/1 Sebastian van Damme

Nominations
Nominierungen

92/1 Adam Mork; 93/1 3XN; 93/2–4 Adam Mork; 94/1+95/1, 94/2–3 AS+GG; 95/2 AS+GG/Michael Young; 95/3+4 As+GG/Evan Joseph; 95/5 As+GG/Paul Clemence; 96/1–3, 97/1 Nuno Grande; 97/2 Álvaro Siza; 98/1–3 Ateliers Jean Nouvel; 98/4 Roland Halbe; 99/1 Frédéric Betsch; 99/2 Roland Halbe; 100/1+2, 101/1 Laurian Ghinitoiu; 101/2 BIG – Bjarke Ingels Group; 101/3 Laurian Ghinitoiu; 101/4+5 BIG – Bjarke Ingels Group; 102/1 Trevor Mein; 103/1–3 COX Architecture & Gensler; 103/4–6 Trevor Mein; 103/7 COX Architecture & Gensler; 103/8 Trevor Mein; 104/1 Aaron Hargreaves/Foster + Partners; 104/2+3, 105/1 Foster + Partners; 105/2-4 Aaron Hargreaves/Foster + Partners; 106/1 Graham Handford; 106/2 Kengo Kuma & Associates; 106/3+4 Ema Peter; 106/5, 107/1+2 Kengo Kuma & Associates; 107/3, 108/1–4, 109/1 Ema Peter;109/2+3 Kohn Pedersen Fox Associates; 110/1, 111/1–3 HG Esch; 111/4+5 Kohn Pedersen Fox Associates; 112/1 Justin Szeremeta; 112/2 Kohn Pedersen Fox Associates; 113/1–3 Justin Szeremeta; 113/4+5 Kohn Pedersen Fox Associates; 114/1, 115/1 Hufton + Crow; 115/2+3 Nikken Sekkei; 115/4 Hufton + Crow; 115/5+6 Nikken Sekkei; 116/1 Jason O'Rear; 116/2+3 OMA Office for Metropolitan Architecture; 116/4, 117/1+2 Jason O'Rear; 117/3 OMA Office for Metropolitan Architecture; 117/4 Ossip van Duivenbode; 118/1 Xia Zhi/courtesy of OMA; 119/1+2 OMA Office for Metropolitan Architecture; 119/3–5 Xia Zhi/courtesy of OMA; 120/1-4, 121/1 Jason O'Rear; 121/2–4 Pelli Clarke & Partners; 122/1+2, 123/1+2 Kang Yu courtesy of schneider + schumacher; 123/3 schneider + schumacher; 123/4 Kang Yu courtesy of schneider + schumacher; 123/5 schneider + schumacher; 124/1, 125/1+2 Qingyan Zhu; 125/3+4 SOM; 125/5 Qingyan Zhu; 125/6 SOM; 126/1+2 Kasper Dudzik; 127/1 SOM; 127/2 Kasper Dudzik; 127/3 SOM; 128/1 SOM; 128/2–4, 129/1–3 Dave Burk/courtesy of SOM; 129/4 SOM; 130/1–3, 131/1 Kevin Mak; 131/2–4 Snøhetta; 132/1–3, 133/1 Qian Xirui/courtesy of Stefano Boeri Architetti; 133/2+3 Stefano Boeri Architetti; 134/1+2 Tom Harris; 135/1+2 Studio Gang; 135/3+4 Tom Harris; 136/1–3 Bruno Klomfar; 137/1–3 StudioVlayStreeruwitz; 137/4+5 Bruno Klomfar; 138/1+2 Darren Soh for WOHA; 138/3 Eurthe; 139/1 Darren Soh for WOHA; 139/2+3 WOHA; 140/1+2, 141/1 Trevor Mein; 141/2+3 Woods Bagot; 141/4–6 Trevor Mein; 141/7+8 Woods Bagot; 142/1, 143/1+2 Daici Ano; 143/3 Yuko Nagayama & Associates; 143/4 Daici Ano; 144/1+2 Virgile Simon Bertrand; 144/3–5 Zaha Hadid Architects; 145/1 Virgile Simon Bertrand

The International High-Rise Award 2004–2024
Internationaler Hochhaus Preis 2004–2024

#
Ethan Rohloff

A
David Phan; HG Esch; Wikimedia Commons, Martaalvarezarana; Simon Wood; Roland Halbe

B
Kirsten Bucher; Nils Koenning; Ema Peter; Finbarr Fallon; BICUBIK; Kirsten Bucher; Iwan Baan

C
Finbarr Fallon; Finbarr Fallon

D
Simon Menges; Hertha Hurnaus

F
Nigel Young/Foster + Partners; Chuck Choi; Aaron Pocock

G
DBOX; Thomas Wolf

H
Eric Sierins; Hufton + Crow; Christian Pichlkastner; Iwan Baan

I
HG Esch

K
Young-Chea Park; Shinkenchiku; Jean-Luc Valentin

L
Moritz Bernoully

M
Tom Arban; Hufton + Crow; TECTONIC; Thomas Wolf; Young-Chea Park; Yong-Kwan Kim; Ky-Man Cheng; Finbarr Fallon; Xia Zhi/courtesy of MVRDV; Ossip van Duivenbode/courtesy of MVRDV

O
Frank P. Palmer; Wikimeda Commons, Martin Falbisoner; Iwan Baan; Anders Bobert

P
Anna Odulinska

R
DBOX; Michel Denance; SOHO China

S
Edward Hendricks; HSB Malmö/Pierre Mens; Finbarr Fallon; Nick Merrick; Hufton + Crow; Iwan Baan; Steve Hall/Hedrich Blessing

T
Horiuchi/Shin Shashin Kobo

W
Albert Lim; Kirsten Bucher; Patrick Bingham; K. Kopter

Z
Hufton + Crow

Imprint
Impressum

Imprint Project Coordination
Impressum Projektkoordination

City of Frankfurt am Main
Stadt Frankfurt am Main

DAM Deutsches Architekturmuseum
Peter Cachola Schmal / Director Direktor
Peter Körner / Coordination Koordination
Moritz König / Coordination Koordination
Brita Köhler, Anna Wegmann /
Public Relations Öffentlichkeitsarbeit
Jacqueline Brauer, Inka Plechaty /
Administration Verwaltung

Department of Culture and Science
Dezernat Kultur und Wissenschaft
Jana Kremin /
Press Officer and Head of Public Relations Pressesprecherin und Leiterin der Öffentlichkeitsarbeit

DekaBank
Silke Schuster-Müller /
Head of Corporate Social Responsibility
Leiterin Gesellschaftliches Engagement
Valery Trosdorf /
Corporate Social Responsibility
Gesellschaftliches Engagement
Björn Korschinowski /
Head of Corporate Communications
Leiter Unternehmenskommunikation
Dr. Daniela Gniss /
Press Officer Pressesprecherin

Event organization
Veranstaltungsorganisation
Stefan Generalov, Lars Augustin, Jazzunique GmbH, Frankfurt am Main

Members of the jury 2024
Mitglieder der Jury 2024

Yasmin Al-Ani Spence /
Architect, Director Architektin, Direktorin,
WilkinsonEyre, London

Roland Bechmann /
Architect, Partner Architekt, Partner,
Werner Sobek, Stuttgart

Dr. Ina Hartwig /
Head of the Department of Culture of the City of Frankfurt am Main Kulturdezernentin der Stadt Frankfurt am Main

Jürgen Heinzel /
Architect, Associate Design Director
Architekt, Assoziierter Design-Direktor,
UNStudio, Amsterdam

Christopher Lee /
Architect, Co-founder and Principal
Architekt, Geschäftsführender Gründungspartner,
Serie Architects, London

Kim Herforth Nielsen /
Chair of the jury Juryvorsitzender
Architect, Co-founder
Architekt, Gründungspartner,
3XN, Copenhagen Kopenhagen

Mari Randsborg /
Architect, CEO Architektin, Geschäftsführerin, **Cobe, Copenhagen** Kopenhagen

Peter Cachola Schmal /
Director Direktor, **DAM Deutsches Architekturmuseum, Frankfurt am Main**

Victor Stoltenburg /
Managing Director, Head of Acquisitions and Sales Geschäftsführer, Leiter Globale Akquisition, **Deka Immobilien GmbH, Frankfurt am Main**

Deputy members of the jury 2024
Stellvertretende Mitglieder der Jury 2024

Andrea Jürges /
Deputy Director Stellvertretende Direktorin, **DAM Deutsches Architekturmuseum, Frankfurt am Main**

Horst R. Muth /
Head of Real Estate Management
Leiter Projektmanagement Immobilien,
Deka Immobilien GmbH, Frankfurt am Main

Imprint Catalog
Impressum Katalog

This catalog has been published in conjunction with the exhibition "Best High-Rises 2024/25," organized by Deutsches Architekturmuseum, Department of Culture and Science, Frankfurt am Main, Germany, taking place from 14 November 2024 until 12 January 2025 at Museum Angewandte Kunst, Frankfurt am Main. Dieser Katalog erscheint anlässlich der Ausstellung „Best High-Rises 2024/25" des Deutschen Architekturmuseums, Dezernat Kultur und Wissenschaft, Stadt Frankfurt am Main, vom 14. November 2024 bis 12. Januar 2025 im Museum Angewandte Kunst, Frankfurt am Main.

An imprint of Walter de Gruyter GmbH, Berlin/Boston
Ein Verlag der Walter de Gruyter GmbH, Berlin/Boston

Cover image
Umschlagmotiv
Finbarr Fallon

Editors
Herausgeber
Peter Körner, Peter Cachola Schmal

Editing
Redaktion
Peter Körner, Moritz König

Texts (unless otherwise stated)
Texte (wenn nicht anders angegeben):
Peter Körner, Rebekka Rass

Copyediting (German texts)
Lektorat (deutsche Texte)
Jutta Ziegler

Copyediting (English texts)
Lektorat (englische Texte)
Bianca Murphy

Translation (from German)
Übersetzung (aus dem Deutschen)
Bianca Murphy

Translation (from English)
Übersetzung (aus dem Englischen)
Jutta Ziegler

Graphic Design
Gestaltung
blila. GbR, Studio für Gestaltung

Coordination publishing house
Koordination im Verlag
Theresa Hartherz

Production
Herstellung
Susanne Rösler

Lithography
Lithografie
ORT Studios Frankfurt GmbH

Printing and binding
Druck und Bindung
GRASPO CZ, a.s., Zlín

Paper
Papier
Content Inhalt **GardaPat 13 Bianka**
Cover material Bezug **Century Cotton Wove, Premium White**

Bibliographic information published by the Deutsche Nationalbibliothek: The Deutsche Nationalbibliothek lists this publication in the Deutsche Nationalbibliografie; detailed bibliographic data are available on the Internet at http://dnb.d-nb.de.
Bibliografische Information der Deutschen Nationalbibliothek: Die Deutsche Nationalbibliothek verzeichnet diese Publikation in der Deutschen Nationalbibliografie; detaillierte bibliografische Daten sind im Internet über http://dnb.d-nb.de abrufbar.

jovis Verlag
Genthiner Straße 13
10785 Berlin

www.jovis.de

jovis books are available worldwide in select bookstores. Please contact your nearest bookseller or visit www.jovis.de for information concerning your local distribution.
jovis-Bücher sind weltweit im ausgewählten Buchhandel erhältlich. Informationen zu unserem internationalen Vertrieb erhalten Sie in Ihrer Buchhandlung oder unter www.jovis.de.

jovis

ISBN 978-3-98612-143-3

Imprint Exhibition
Impressum Ausstellung

Director Direktor **DAM**
Peter Cachola Schmal
Curator Kurator
Peter Körner
Curatorial Assistant Kuratorische Assistenz
Moritz König

Exhibition design
Ausstellungsgestaltung
Deserve Gbr Raum und Medien Design, Wiesbaden / Berlin, Mario Lorenz

Exhibition production
Ausstellungsproduktion
inditec GmbH, Bad Camberg

Head of exhibition setup
Leitung Ausstellungsaufbau
Christian Walter

Exhibition setup
Ausstellungsaufbau
Hans Brückner, Ömer Simsek, and others und weitere

Registrar
Wolfgang Welker

Models
Modelle
BIG – Bjarke Ingels Group,
MVRDV,
Powerhouse Company

Model restoration
Modellrestaurierung
Christian Walter

Public relations
Öffentlichkeitsarbeit
Brita Köhler, Anna Wegmann, Rebekka Rass

Architectural mediation
Architekturvermittlung
Rebekka Kremershof

Guided tours
Führungen
Yorck Förster

Administrative staff
Sekretariat und Verwaltung
Inka Plechaty, Jacqueline Brauer

Graphic design print media
Gestaltung Printmedien
blila. GbR, Studio für Gestaltung

Graphic design logo
The International High-Rise Award
Gestaltung Logo
Internationaler Hochhaus Preis
blila. GbR, Studio für Gestaltung

For its generous funding, DAM would like to thank its partner DekaBank, sponsor of The International High-Rise Award and exhibition.
Das DAM dankt seinem Partner DekaBank, Sponsor des Internationalen Hochhaus Preises und der Ausstellung, für die großzügige finanzielle Unterstützung.

Corporate footprint
Measuring CO_2
PBN-CFMCP-059235
www.preferredbynature.org

FSC
www.fsc.org
MIX
Paper | Supporting responsible forestry
FSC® C010798